FISHING FOR BUFFALO

Dr. Spencer F. Baird: the man who brought carp to America.

Fishing for Buffalo

*A guide to the pursuit, lore and cuisine
of buffalo, carp, mooneye, gar
and other 'rough' fish*

ROB BUFFLER   TOM DICKSON

Culpepper Press ● Minneapolis

Fishing for Buffalo
*A guide to the pursuit, lore and cuisine of buffalo, carp,
mooneye, gar and other 'rough' fish*

Copyright ©1990 J. Robert Buffler and Thomas J. Dickson

All photographs and illustrations by the authors except the following used by permission of:
p. 3, Minnesota Historical Society; p. 16, Walker (Minnesota) Pilot/Independent; p. 17, Walker
(Minnesota) Pilot/Independent; p. 20, Michigan Department of Natural Resources/David Kenyon;
p. 24, Michigan Department of Natural Resources/Dr. Ned Fogle; p. 32, Mary Gibbs Logan photo,
Minnesota Historical Society; p. 39, lip illustration, James Underhill, University of Minnesota; p. 56,
Nebraska Game and Parks Commission; p. 70, Minnesota Historical Society; p. 73, Michigan
Department of Natural Resources/David Kenyon; p. 75, Minnesota Historical Society; p. 77, Michigan
Department of Natural Resources/David Kenyon; p. 98, Minnesota Historical Society; p. 100,
Minnesota Department of Natural Resources; p. 102, Minnesota Historical Society; p. 104, Minnesota
Department of Natural Resources; p. 107, Michigan Department of Natural Resources/Bob
Harrington; p. 109, Muscatine (Illinois) Journal; p. 110, Minnesota Department of Natural Resources;
p.122, Nebraska Game and Parks Commission; p. 129, top and bottom: Lake Region Life, Waterville,
Minnesota; p. 138, Carl Linde photo, Minnesota Historical Society; p. 140, University of Wisconsin
Sea Grant Institute; p. 142, Minnesota Department of Natural Resources; p. 145, Minnesota
Department of Natural Resources; p. 147, Gallagher Studio photo, Minnesota Historical Society;
p. 152, Seth Eastman watercolor, Minnesota Historical Society; p. 154, Henry Lewis lithograph,
Minnesota Historical Society; p. 158, Keith Sutton; p. 162, Keith Sutton; p. 166, Keith Sutton; p. 171,
Keith Sutton; p. 172, Keith Sutton; p. 174, Wilderness Inquiry; p. 184, Minnesota Department of
Natural Resources; p. 186, Minnesota Department of Natural Resources; p. 187, Minnesota
Department of Natural Resources; p. 188, Minnesota Department of Natural Resources; p. 194,
Minnesota Department of Natural Resources; p. 195, University of Minnesota Sea Grant Institute.

Front cover photograph by J. Robert Buffler; hand-colored by Craig Thiesen.

For more information on roughfish angling write:

North American Roughfish Institute
PO Box 14891
Minneapolis, Minnesota 55414

To roughfish and roughfish anglers everywhere.

Contents

Preface

WHAT'S THE BEST WAY to approach roughfish?

That's the question we had to answer before writing *Fishing for Buffalo*. We didn't have much to go on. Fish like carp, buffalo, suckers, redhorse, gar, mooneye, burbot, drum, and bowfin aren't on the lips of too many sport anglers—as conversation or as dinner. They're not discussed much in scientific or conservation circles, either. These species inspire few reports, and even fewer articles in fishing and conservation magazines.

But just because roughfish information isn't on the news each night doesn't mean it's not out there. It is, and we found it. After countless (we tried but couldn't keep track) hours of field study, library research, and interviews with fisheries biologists and roughfishing experts, we came up with the answer, which is the book you now hold in your hands.

Most folks approach roughfish with fear, loathing, and ignorance. They've been taught that carp are inedible, suckers are dirty, and freshwater drum are not to be trusted. That's too bad, because what they've been taught is wrong. Their approach blinds them to a lot of good fishing and eating. We, on the other hand, don't like to miss any fishing opportunities that come our way, so we take a totally different approach to these fish with lips, large scales, and mysterious origins. We've learned that the best approach to roughfish is simple: quietly, from downstream. Besides a desire to catch fish, it helps to have a sense of humor, love of good food, and some concern for the environment, too.

Fishing for Buffalo is a bunch of things, all of which help anglers approach roughfish from this different angle. First of all, it is a *fishing* book written by two anglers who weren't the first to discover the only difference between having a 5-pound carp and a 5-pound walleye on the end of your line is the carp fights harder.

It's also a *fish* book that reveals where the fish live, what they eat, and how they behave. As any good angler learns, the more you know about the fish themselves, the more fish you hook. Life can be richer knowing about the flora and fauna that exist along with us wherever we live. Since roughfish are the chief inhabitants of most inland waters, it's in our best interest to learn more about them.

It's also a book on conservation. Fish thrive or die based on the health of their aquatic environment, the watery world they swim in. Carp are the most common big fish on this continent—not because they pollute water and drive out other species, but because they can tolerate the many waters humans have polluted. It wasn't until 1874 that carp first swam in North America. Today, this husky fish is found in almost every watershed in the country, an indication of how badly we've fouled many waters where native species like the greater redhorse, walleye, and lake sturgeon once lived in abundance.

Finally, this book is just plain interesting, not because we wrote it that way, but because roughfish are sometimes so bizarre and have such topsy-turvy relations with humans. You'll read about the American eel, the only fish you can catch by casting towards land away from the water; about people who fish for 60-pound flathead catfish by reaching under riverbanks and sticking an arm through the mouth of the fish and out the gills; and about how carp were once so prized they were carefully handed out only to the nation's most prominent citizens to be stocked in their private ponds. Roughfish are a lot of things, but one thing they are not is boring.

Just as many roughfish are odd, so is *Fishing for Buffalo*. We don't deny the absurdity of a book about catching carp on a fly made to imitate a mulberry, eating reamed dogfish on toast, and advocating the catch-and-release of redhorse. Though we're serious about roughfishing, we can't take it too seriously. It's pretty hard not to laugh as you watch the faces of incredulous anglers when you kneel for a photograph before releasing the carp you just took on a 7-weight fly rod. Sometimes, the whole idea of roughfishing cracks us up. But while we're laughing, we're catching fish and having a blast on the water.

We're sure after reading this, you will too.

—TD & RB

FISHING FOR BUFFALO

Anyone who has battled and then released a 6-pound river redhorse while standing waist deep in a clear northern Wisconsin wilderness river knows the joys of roughfishing.

I

Roughfishing in America

IT WAS A NICE DAY to be outside, but not if you wanted to catch roughfish. The weather was sunny and warm, but the sun was too bright on the water for the fish to be anything but cautious. To make matters worse, a wind blew in hard gusts, yanking our lines across the water surface so much we had no feel for the activity below.

We were fishing the Namekagon River in northern Wisconsin on a stretch we hoped held trophy redhorse. Driving from bridge to bridge, we worked our way upstream from where the river merges with the St. Croix, looking for water with redhorse written on it: stretches of riffles interspersed with deep, shaded pools.

The Namekagon is a beautiful coldwater river fed by icy springs that rise from the bedrock below Wisconsin's Bayfield and Sawyer counties. It is a nationally known brown trout stream. Being clear and clean, it also holds a good number of redhorse, a sucker species so intolerant of silt, pesticides, and other pollutants it lives only in clean, riffly streams. We'd been catching loads of carpsuckers, freshwater drum, and mooneye all summer, so we were eager to try a new species and explore water we'd never fished before. Besides, the beautiful coloration, decent size (up to 11 pounds), and fine flavor of the redhorse make it a great sport fish. We couldn't wait to catch some.

Our main problem, besides the bright sun and wind, was our unfamiliarity with the water. We had been on the Namekagon years before, farther upstream near the headwaters, fishing for trout and had hooked several small redhorse with spinners. We figured bigger fish were downstream, where the water was deeper and slower.

We were hoping to find a dam each time we stopped the car and explored upstream from a bridge. Redhorse stack up in the pools and riffles below dams. We would probe the water with a piece of nightcrawler on a small hook, a visitor usually irresistible to a bottom-hugging redhorse. But the water we found had no major obstructions to concentrate fish, forcing us to look harder for more subtle indicators of where they might lie.

Below the one bridge we caught and released a few small fish, redhorse of 12 inches or so that we had spotted by their red fins waving in the clear water. We drove along the highway that roughly parallels the river until we reached the next place the road crossed the river. Here, the water looked promising: It twisted more than it did downstream, creating deep runs.

The wind died down, and the sun dropped lower in the sky, sending long shadows of birch trees out across the water. We began to fish in earnest.

Sport fishing for roughfish is nothing new. In Britain, the practice dates back to before 1486, when Dame Juliana Bernes wrote about roughfishing techniques in A Treatyse of Fysshynge With an Angle.

Presenting a bit of nightcrawler to a fish takes some knack. Too much weight creates the false feeling of continual bites. Too little and the morsel never gets near the fish, which hug tight to the bottom. The trick is to keep changing the weight until you get the lead to lightly tick-tick-tick across the bottom.

We must have found the right weight just as we reached a wide bend in the river that created a deep run, because we began catching redhorse. Each drift was snatched by a hungry fish, and after an hour we had lost track of the number of 3- and 4-pounders we'd hooked, fought, and released. It wasn't until our stomachs started growling that it dawned on us we'd better keep a few and head home if we were to have any dinner. The next 2 eating-sized redhorse we put on a stringer, then waded back downstream to the car.

Back in St. Paul, we filleted the fish and scored the fillets. We poached the meat in a mixture of wine, shallots, onions, parsley, and thyme, and served it with wild rice and freshly steamed asparagus—a scrumptious meal!

Who Are You Calling Rough?

We have found that many roughfish swim in clean water, put up a strong fight, and provide delicious meat. Yet, call a fish a "roughfish" and most anglers won't consider fishing for it, much less eating it. To be a roughfish is to be dirty, bony, sluggish, odd-looking, lipped, a destroyer of game fish, or some combination of these features. Many people won't even talk about them. "We don't fish for roughfish around here," they say. "They're not fit for decent folks."

And yet, these fish Americans call roughfish are highly valued in other countries. Carp are considered a symbol of nobility in Asia and deemed the pinnacle of angling achievement by millions of Europeans. Throughout the world, more people eat carp than they do any other

freshwater fish. Here in the United States, about 120 million pounds are poached, grilled, baked, and broiled each year. Obviously, someone knows how to get around those bones. The freshwater drum, another fish disparaged by sport anglers, tastes exactly like its saltwater relative the red drum, one of the stars of New Orleans cuisine. And the burbot, despised by many anglers for its eel-like tail, is so prized in Europe and in some northern areas of the United States that it is in danger of being overfished in certain lakes.

Where did this name roughfish come from, and why do anglers feel such vehemence about it? The name itself doesn't sound so terrible. Any animal that's rough isn't despised for its rugged character. If a fish is to be sneered at because of its name, it should be the weakfish, but this ocean species is the apple of any saltwater fly rodder's eye. The name can't refer to texture, either, since many roughfish are smooth skinned, and no fish is as raspy feeling as the walleye, considered the dream catch of anglers in many states.

The term "roughfish" was coined in the mid-1800s to describe fish that weren't minnows and weren't commonly caught for sport. The name probably came from the term "coarse fish," used by anglers in Europe and England to describe freshwater species other than trout and salmon. There, coarse fish were pursued by anglers for sport. When anglers first arrived in North America, they discovered endless waters filled with bass, crappies, trout, and walleye. Drum, buffalos, suckers, and other species similar to coarse fish back in the old country didn't seem sporty enough to pursue, or were too bony to fillet and eat quickly. After all, the pioneers had a continent to conquer. Who had time to be picking out Y-bones?

Over the years the name "roughfish" stuck, and today it is used by most anglers to mean fish they don't want to catch.

People reading the term "roughfish" for the first time wouldn't know the term designates fish scorned by most anglers. But after hearing the word used, they would know a roughfish wasn't something to bring home for Sunday dinner. When talking about the sport of fishing, fisheries managers commonly distinguish "fish that people want to catch" from "roughfish." And the way the word is spoken—*rough*fish—leaves no doubt in a beginning angler's mind that these are fish to be avoided at any cost. "Hey, kid. What are you keeping those for? Those are *rough*fish." No wonder people don't want to eat them.

Big, Tasty Fish

Contrary to what your uncle told you, roughfish are well worth catching. In fact, there are so many great things about carp, drum, gar, whitefish, suckers, and bullheads we had to write a book about them.

Open your fishing repertoire to include these outcasts of the angling community, and you can double, even triple, the number of hard-fighting fish you catch each trip out. And not just more fish, but bigger fish. Catching carp averaging 5, 7, or even 10 pounds until your arm cramps up is not uncommon.

There's no denying most walleye and bass anglers look down on roughfish. But for what reasons, we haven't a clue.

Most suckers, like this greater redhorse, can only survive in clean, silt-free water.

You say you want to catch predators? Check out the longnose gar, a muscular cylinder of teeth and armor that can tip the scales at over 60 pounds. If it's sheer power you're looking for, set your hook into a lake sturgeon or flathead catfish and hold onto the nearest tree. Flatheads weighing over 60 pounds have been taken probably no farther than 100 miles from where you sit reading this right now. And lake sturgeon bigger than the humans who hooked them have been caught in the central United States.

If it's food fish you're after, start heating the oil. It's a plain fact that roughfish are the most widely eaten fish in the world, whether served as a carp stirfry in Bejing, as burbot pâté on toast in Brussels, or as smoked sucker with a cold bottle of beer in St. Louis, Missouri. Fried and served with hush puppies, poached in sherry and garnished with truffles, or baked in a cheese sauce with stewed tomatoes, roughfish are in recipes of the finest cookbooks of Asia, Europe, and the United States. For the dining pleasure of our readers, we have found what we think are the best, dishes such as Burbot à la Provençale, Sucker Casserole au Vin, Iowan Pickled Bullhead, Chinese Poached Catfish, Bayou Bill's Barbequed Gar, and Creamed Bowfin on Toast, and included recipes at the end of each chapter.

Fishing without Doodads

If big and good tasting fish aren't enough, roughfishing also offers anglers a chance to return to the basics of fishing. By wading rivers for carp, suckers, and drum, you can walk away from the philosophy of electronic gadgetry that permeates the fishing information anglers receive from TV and magazines. The way most sportfishing is portrayed these days is anything but fun, relaxation, and adventure. It has turned into a materialistic free-for-all to see who can buy the most graphite and neoprene. If nothing else, roughfishing lets you reexamine your sport from another angle, one that doesn't depend on boats, motors, digital reels, and color-coded lures for catching fish and having a good time, but instead makes use of your common sense and appreciation for the outdoors.

Twenty years ago, anglers caught walleyes without depthfinders, snuck up on bass without electric motors, and hooked salmon without downriggers. Today, anglers get the impression from TV shows and magazine ads that a person can't catch fish or even have fun fishing without this year's newest potion, pattern, or product. The more fishing stuff you own, the ads tell us, the happier you'll be.

But it doesn't work that way. Eventually more gear means more things to worry about, more repairs, more maintenance, and more things to lose. Here at roughfishing headquarters U.S.A., we believe what makes fishing fun is exploring new waters—puttering around in a little boat up a new stream or wading the shallows in tennis shoes, shorts, and a T-shirt.

We don't deny that the new developments in boats, fishfinders, line, and rods over the past few decades have increased the number of fish caught. In fact, many fishing lakes today are shadows of their former selves because anglers have so refined their equipment and ability to locate fish underwater that the fish can't

Roughfishing can make your wrist ache with fatigue. Drum top out at 55 pounds, bigmouth buffalo go over 70, and a flathead catfish can be bigger than the angler who catches it.

reproduce as fast as they're being fished out.

What we decry is the ethic that gadgetry erodes. The *sport* of fishing is the contest, the creation of a balance that favors the fish as much as it favors the angler. If the balance tips too much in favor of humans, the sport turns into commercial fishing, into a harvest.

We're not purists. Like anyone, our resolve weakens when we read about how better craftsmanship, engineering, and innovation can help us catch more fish. Sometimes we use depthfinders to locate structure or neoprene waders to fish icy streams. We'll be the first to admit that a $150 graphite spinning rod actually *feels* like it will catch more carp, and that

This "small" bigmouth buffalo went 17 pounds. Unlike crowded walleye and bass waters, buffalo rivers and lakes are lightly fished.

a reel outfitted with dials, levers, and knobs gives us a sense that we've got the equipment necessary to handle a big buffalo heading downstream to the Gulf of Mexico. But usually we put that stuff down and head to the water with our simple gear, knowing we won't ever have a big fish on in the first place if we don't know much about fish. Ultimately, that's what *Fishing for Buffalo* is about: learning about fish while having fun catching fish.

Probably the most selfish reason to start looking at roughfishing in a new light is to give yourself more fishing opportunities. Let's face it: For a sport that is supposed to be about solitude and relaxation, fishing's gotten to be busier than a post office in mid-December. Boat ramps are full to overflowing, trout streams hold an angler at every good pool, and even the secret spots you thought only you knew about are showing up as feature-length where-to-go articles in fishing magazines.

In the United States, 60 million people buy fishing licenses each year, and the sport is expected to grow faster than any other during the next 20 years. All these anglers are pouring into the same old spots, fishing for the same old species. Learn a thing or two about roughfish, and you can leave the crowd and be off on your own, working the quiet waters for species most anglers don't know exist.

The Great Chain of Being Uninformed

"Dad? What did I catch?"

"It's a carp. Throw it up on shore."

"I thought carp had whiskers."

"Well, errr . . . uhh . . . then it's a sucker. Don't touch it."

"Can't I put it back in the water?"

"No. Roughfish pollute the water. Now throw it up on the bank like I told you."

No wonder most anglers dislike roughfish. They probably picked up that attitude from their parents early in life. As with sex, either they've been told things about roughfish that aren't true—roughfish are dirty and unpalatable—or they've been told nothing. A dad who can tell his kids ways to distinguish a tiger muskie from a pure strain muskie probably doesn't know a white sucker from a golden redhorse. A mom who can find largemouth bass on a river no matter what the season probably doesn't know shovelnose sturgeon swim in that same river. Ice anglers will spend an entire day to catch puny crappies for a few business-card-sized fillets, but will throw a 6-pound burbot out of the ice house in disgust, unaware the fish holds as much white, bone-free meat as a similar-sized walleye. Ignorance might be bliss when you're eating a hotdog, but not if you want to enjoy fishing more.

People don't like roughfish because they never read about them, never see them caught on TV, never hear about them from relatives, and never see other anglers bring a few in to the boat launch. Roughfish are the great mystery of North American waters. We've met experienced anglers who think bullheads have stinging whiskers, suckers are unfit for human consumption, and burbot are some sort of lizard.

No roughfish is the perfect sport fish. But neither is any sport fish. Like walleyes, some roughfish don't fight too hard. Like northern pike, some have bones that need a few extra minutes of work to remove. Like any fish, roughfish don't taste good when taken from muddy water. And it's no secret that some roughfish look weird, what with their large scales, lips, barbels, or long beaks. Yet they only look odd compared to fish like sunfish and bass. Compared to some of the curiosities commonly caught and eaten by saltwater anglers, such as rockfish, pompano, and flounder, a freshwater roughfish looks downright ordinary.

Interestingly, the disdain held for certain fish species in the United States varies by region and state, and even within a county. Many anglers in northern Wisconsin and Michigan wouldn't be caught dead fishing for catfish, but call that fish a roughfish in Iowa, Missouri, or Arkansas and you'll be laughed out of the bait shop. In Minnesota, the walleye has for decades been prized above all other species. But to Gopher State bass anglers looking for a scrappy fight, a walleye is the last thing they want at the end of the line. A muskie angler catches a 10-pound northern pike and curses. An hour later, on the same lake, a fly rodder's day is made catching that same pike on a Dahlberg Diver.

Another reason roughfish remain such a mystery to anglers is that some of these fish have a dozen or more different common names. A freshwater drum is a gaspergou in Louisiana, but in other states it's known as a sheepshead, croaker, or thunder pumper. The bigmouth buffalo is a member of the sucker family. However, it's often mistaken for the carp, a member of the minnow family. People also call the bigmouth buffalo a baldpate, roundhead, bullmouth, pug, redmouth, and stubnose. The names of the burbot are just as varied and confusing. Ling, cusk, grinnel, dogfish, eelpout, lechy, and Maria loch are just some of the nicknames given to this slick-skinned freshwater member of the cod family.

Compared to some saltwater species, roughfish don't look too bad.

The only name consistent for burbot from coast to coast over the past 100 years has been lawyer.

In *Fishing for Buffalo*, we've made it easy for you to identify the roughfish you catch. Our descriptions aren't perfect, however. Even fisheries biologists have a tough time telling some suckers apart, and salmonid experts continue to argue late into the night whether there's a difference between a cisco and a tullibee. But at least after reading this book, you'll be able to tell a carp from a buffalo, a channel catfish from a flathead, a burbot from a bowfin, and which of the 3 types of bullheads you just stepped on.

What roughfish need is a little illumination to let anglers see them for what they are: plain old fish like any other. This book is just a start. To win respect, roughfish need national recognition, appreciation from the media, and a new breed of devoted roughfish anglers. It's already happening in Britain and Europe, where carp fishing and research organizations have tens of thousands of members, some of whom devote their lives to learning about the habits of carp.

Such devotion to roughfish is spreading across the Atlantic. "Carp Man" Dan Geigerich, of St. Louis, Missouri, tells us he's just been named secretary of the Missouri Chapter of the London-based Carp Anglers Association, the fourth chapter in the United States: "I have no doubt in my mind that the carp is going to be very big in this country within 5 years."

Catfish have been making inroads even faster than carp. Until the past few years they were pretty much ignored in the northern states, even though southern anglers have been enjoying the sport, taste, and accessibility of these fish for decades. Lately, catfish stories have been appearing more and more in national fishing publications. The public's taste for catfishing has been eclipsed only by a taste for

Another good thing about roughfishing: You don't need a boat. In fact, you can catch more fish in a week from shore than most anglers do in a year equipped with the newest motors, tri-hulls, and electronic gadgets.

the catfish themselves. Annual sales of commercially raised catfish are around 300 million pounds, making it one of the most widely eaten fish in the country.

While these roughfish species are slowly swimming upstream into the headwaters of American sport angling, many remain mired in the muck of myth and ignorance. The sucker, a fish that lives primarily in clean streams, is still regarded by many anglers as an unclean creature. Some anglers even think suckers pollute the water, as though the *fish* were manufacturing the raw sewage, PCBs, lead, pesticides, mercury, topsoil and other effluents that humans send into lakes and rivers. While it is true that suckers feed off the bottom, that doesn't make them any more tainted by the dirty water than other fish are. Suckers eat primarily nymphs and crustaceans, the same food of trout and sunfish. Pike and walleyes eat suckers, so any toxins in the flesh of the bottom feeders are multiplied in the predators.

Many roughfish are actually cleaner than fish commonly caught by anglers. The greater redhorse, for example, can't tolerate pollution much better than a brook trout can. Both need clean, silt-free water to survive. In many areas, the sturgeon has died out in part because of its intolerance of pollution. Like many species of sucker and redhorse, sturgeon have disappeared in waters where largemouth bass, northern pike, and even walleyes can survive.

It's true some roughfish are fatty and hold in their fat higher concentrations of toxins. Carp and buffalo are rich, oily fish, but no more so than lake trout or big brown trout. Some roughfish, like burbot and drum, are leaner than most game fish.

Taken from unpolluted water, a carp is one of the cleanest fish that swims, because, unlike many native species, it has few parasites. However, carp tend not to live in pristine northern waters, but in warm, stagnant lakes and rivers choked with pollutants. That's because carp

Quillback carpsuckers, like this one about to be released by Sarah Vest, can't tolerate silt or pollution. The disappearance of native fish like this one from rivers is an environmental barometer of our own health.

can tolerate extremely low levels of dissolved oxygen and high amounts of chemicals and human waste that most fish species can't take.

It's a fact that carp uproot plants and stir up sediment as they root around a lake bottom looking for food, sometimes to the point that other fish can't see to feed and ducks have no plants to eat. In some shallow midwestern lakes, carp have actually taken over, displacing bass and panfish. But the damage to water by carp is relatively minor compared to that done by humans. Carp usually don't harm fisheries that haven't already been degraded by agricultural runoff, erosion, or industrial discharge. Carp exist in almost every watershed in the contiguous United States, yet relatively few fisheries have been dramatically harmed by their presence.

Who Made the Cut?

None of the species in *Fishing for Buffalo* is considered by all American anglers as undesirable. Every species weighing over a pound that swims has at least a few angling fans. There are anglers who fish for nothing but gar. Others fish for nothing but bullheads. How about burbot, isn't that a roughfish? The angler who catches the largest one at the annual International Eelpout Festival in Walker, Minnesota wouldn't even be able to answer that question, he would be so busy trying to tie the 7½-foot first place trophy onto his snowmobile.

Can everyone at least agree that a carp is a roughfish? Bill Richar won't. Richar, of St. Louis, Missouri, says he has more respect for the whiskered exotic than he has for some of his lesser friends. And Richard Dawson, a British angler who spent 2 summers in Michigan fishing exclusively for carp, would probably say the claim that carp are undesirable is "bloody ridiculous."

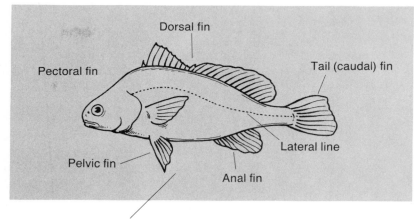

Although no fish is a roughfish everywhere, many fish are considered roughfish in most states in the central part of the nation. The fish we've included in *Fishing for Buffalo* are generally considered roughfish, less so in the South and more so in the North. We picked fish for the book by selecting those that: 1. weigh at least a pound, can be caught with hook and line, but are ignored or disparaged by most sport anglers (such as carp and suckers); 2. provide good sport and food, but are known to few anglers (like drum and goldeye); or 3. are for the most part valued, but in the past were regarded as roughfish or are still seen as undesirable in some regions (like catfish and sturgeon).

We didn't include chubs, which are too small; paddlefish, which can only be caught by the barbaric practice of snagging; or species out of our region, such as Florida gar.

The Sermon

Years ago, miners carried canaries down into the mines—not as pets, but as a way to tell if gas was leaking into the shaft. If the canary died, the miners scrambled to get above ground, before they breathed the poisoned air.

Fisheries biologists can use delicate native species, often designated as roughfish, in the

This book lists 41 different roughfish, all from the central United States. To identify them, you might want to get familiar with the basic features of your average roughfish.

Freshwater drum are so plentiful and delicious even a walleye diehard like Dave Greer has started pursuing them. "I didn't know what I was missing," he said.

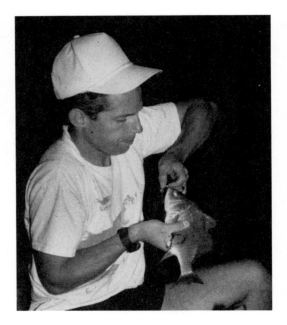

same way. When a fish that's intolerant of pollution or siltation, like the blue sucker, stops showing up in test nets and anglers' creels, it's a sign water quality is going down.

Two hundred years ago, the lakes and rivers in North America were clean. The Mississippi River, for example, was wild and riffly, with massive rapids, pools, bends, channels and other fish-producing features. The water was clean enough to drink and clear enough to support a rich, diverse aquatic ecosystem. The roughfishing in those days must have been incredible. But as dams slowed and warmed waters, erosion silted in insect-producing gravel and spawning areas, and pollution outright killed fish or caused oxygen levels to drop, the Mississippi and other rivers became ghosts of what they were.

Anglers have not demanded that factories stop dumping chemicals, that farmers stop draining wetlands, that the Army Corps of Engineers stop damming rivers and streams, nor have they stopped keeping so many big fish. Instead they have been content to pay their state agency a few dollars each year to raise and stock fish, all the while keeping their eyes closed to the real reasons fishing has gone downhill.

The more anglers get curious about what is still being dumped into their favorite lakes or rivers, the better are the chances that something can be done about the continual abuse of water in this country. What those anglers will find if they start looking is that their own lifestyles do much of the damage. The 240 million gallons of used motor oil that do-it-yourselfers dump into the sewer each year ends up in the lakes and rivers we all fish. The corn we buy and townhouses we live in are often raised and built on land that once was wetlands, which filtered pollution and eroded soil from water flowing into lakes and rivers.

What does this environmental discourse have to do with roughfish? Only that roughfish are often seen as abnormalities when in fact most are as natural to this region as white-tailed deer and mallard ducks. They are also viewed as trash, even though they're as much fun at the end of a line as a bass and as tasty fried in butter as a crappie. Anglers' minds should be open to the importance of roughfish and to the understanding of how humans live their lives, how that lifestyle affects land and water, and how the quality of land and water determines the quality of life—for everyone.

We hope this book at least helps people to overcome their mistrust of roughfish and to see them for what they are: creatures that, like humans, are products of their environment.

Sometimes, when we are standing waist-deep in a cool river, our reels screaming from the demands of ornery carp, we look around and wonder, Where are all the other roughfish anglers? Why isn't anyone else doing this? Roughfishing is such a blast we'd like to see more anglers involved. We wouldn't mind the company. It gets lonely when you're the only ones catching fish day after day.

—TD & RB

A Short Glossary

This is not a technical book. It's written for the average angler. However, to save you time, we use some technical terms some anglers might not know.

Adipose fin—A small, fleshy fin located between the dorsal fin and the tail fin.

Anal fin—The single fin located on the bottom of the fish behind the vent.

Barbels—Long sensory tendrils, usually located on the head of fish. Also called "whiskers."

Caudal fin—The big fin at the end of the body, also known as the tail.

Crankbait—A fishing lure that usually resembles a minnow and is designed to dive upon retrieve.

Dorsal fin—The single fin located on the top or back of the fish.

Lateral line—An organ used to detect vibrations, made up of a series of pores along the side of the body.

Leader—A short piece of line or wire, attached to the end of the fishing line and tied to the hook, fly, or lure.

Live bait—Living minnows, worms, frogs, salamanders, and other animals used to catch fish.

Pectoral fins—The upper, or forward, pair of fins, located directly behind the gills.

Pelvic fins—The pair of fins below or behind the pectoral fins.

Pharyngeal teeth—Bony toothlike or comblike plates in the throat of some fish.

Plankton—Tiny floating plants and animals eaten by certain fish.

Split shot—Small balls of lead with a slit in them, through which fishing line is passed. Used to provide weight to cast and sink a lure or bait.

Subterminal mouth—A mouth below the snout of the fish.

Vent—The opening at the end of the digestive tract through which waste passes.

Winterkill—The death of fish in a lake or river during the winter. Caused when deep snow blocks sunlight from reaching a lake's plants, which die, decompose, and use up oxygen needed by fish.

2

Burbot

They didn't long for rainbow trout,
Or sunnies in the pan;
They wanted Ernie Eelpout,
Each ruddy, rugged man.
They dragged their shacks onto the ice,
With trusty four-wheel drive,
Across the heaves at any pace,
It made them feel alive.
Their chainsaws ripped, their augers tore
Great holes into the lake.
Who knew what treasures lay in store
To smoke, to fry, to bake?
—FROM "THEY CAME FOR ERNIE,"
AUTHOR UNKNOWN

ON A BITTERLY COLD NIGHT in midwinter 1936, a Wisconsin fisheries scientist stood near a hole on a frozen lake and witnessed a sight few people ever see. "On the night of February 12 the interesting phenomenon of breeding was observed," wrote A. R. Cahn. "At first, a dark shadow was noted at the edge of the ice, something which appeared to be a large ball. Eventually this moved out into view and it was seen to be indeed a ball—a tangled, nearly globular mass of moving, writhing lawyers. The fish were all intertwined, slithering over one another constantly, slowly, weaving in and out of the living ball."

Cahn was observing the mating ritual of the burbot, a freshwater cousin of the saltwater cod. A reclusive, deepwater fish, the burbot is a mystery to biologists, and such sightings are so rare this evocative report is still used in fisheries textbooks more than a half century later.

As intriguing as the mating ritual he describes is Cahn's use of the nickname "lawyer." The burbot has almost two dozen nicknames. In the Midwest, it is also called 'pout and dogfish, and in Maine burbot are cusk. Wyoming anglers call the fish ling or ling cod, and in Kansas, where it is rarely found, it goes by the name mother of eels. Maria or maria

Rob drills a hole on a burbot lake near Canada. Top ice-fishing baits include dead smelt fished just off the bottom, Swedish Pimples, and jigs dabbed with luminescent paint.

Nowhere else are burbot, also called "eelpout" and "pout," celebrated like at the annual International Eelpout Festival in Walker, Minnesota.

loch are what Canadians in Saskatchewan, Manitoba and northern Ontario call burbot. Alaskans know them as lush, and in northern Canada the species is called wethy. Other names are loche, barbot, mud shark, skin ling, spineless catfish, gudgeon, and mud blower. But in all regions, from Alaska to Maine, from Wyoming to Ontario, the name lawyer is used consistently.

It's not a new coinage. In his book, *North American Game Fishes*, written in 1936, David Andrews identifies the burbot as, among other names, lawyer. The name was common even before the turn of the century. Ulysses O. Cox, in his book *Fishes of Minnesota* (1897), notes that the common names for eelpout were "burbot, ling and lawyer." The name is also accepted by the Freshwater Fishing Hall of Fame, which lists burbot in its record books as "Burbot (eelpout/lawyer)."

Why is the burbot commonly named after one of the oldest and most highly regarded professions? Some speculate its name comes from the burbot's slimy, eel-like tail, which wraps around your arm when you pick it up.

Others guess it refers to the burbot's high intelligence, or aggressive behavior. Determined to get to the bottom of this nomenclature puzzle, I called my uncle, Gary Pashby, who is president of the South Dakota Bar Association, and asked him if he had any idea why the burbot would be commonly called lawyer. "My guess," he replied, "would be that the name comes from the fact that, like lawyers, the burbot works extremely hard and is often undervalued by society." I asked about the theory that the name could stem from the burbot's eel-like appearance. "I can't imagine there would be any connection," he answered. With that settled, I am now able to call burbot, "lawyers," without fear of insulting those in the legal profession.

Although the name lawyer does not appear to stem from its physical characteristics, another name certainly does. The name eelpout, used by anglers in the Upper Midwest, comes from the burbot's long, slippery body and a tail that extends almost half its body length.

Whether people think the fish is ugly or not, those who've eaten burbot say it is one of the best-tasting fishes in North America. The bone-free meat is firm, white, and dense, like cod's. One of the most common—although fattening—ways to eat burbot is to boil chunks in saltwater and then dip them in drawn butter. In Maine, this dish is called Poor Man's Lobster.

The commercial market for burbot is primarily in the large cities on the East Coast, where it is served in European ethnic neighborhoods. In Europe, especially in Scandinavia, the fish is eaten smoked, fried, or canned and is sold for up to $10 a pound in fish markets. Finlanders set nets through holes in the ice and pull in burbot to serve as a holiday treat in fish soup and *kukka*, a fish pie. Burbot roe is another European delicacy. Called *maate* in Finland, it is whipped, seasoned, and served on fresh bread.

It is no surprise burbot tastes so good. The fish is the only freshwater member of the tasty cod family (Latin name *Gadidae*) and is closely related to Atlantic cod, haddock, pollock, and hake. Burbot liver, like cod liver, is rich in vitamins A and D. Currently, tests are being conducted to see if burbot liver oil can be used in ointments as is cod liver oil. In France, connoisseurs prize *foie de lotte de rivière* (liver of the river cod), either poached in white wine or made into pâté or canapés.

In the mid-1930s, Canada began a program to promote the abundant burbot as a food fish. Dressed burbot were sent to hotels and restaurants in Toronto, and chefs were asked to prepare the fish and report on what they thought of its taste and texture. "Excellent," judged one chef. Another exclaimed, "Burbot compares very favorably with any fish which I have obtained from the wholesalers!" The program failed, however, because of the public's reluctance to accept the fish.

Why did burbot never catch on in Canada's finest restaurants, even though it tastes like lobster and costs a fraction of the price? And why isn't the species eagerly sought by anglers throughout its wide range in North America?

"I think it's the tail," ventured Al Maas, a fishing guide on Leech Lake in northern Minnesota. "Most guys don't like it wrapping around their arm, so they either cut the line or ask me to take it off the hook." The revulsion is so great that some anglers will not touch the fish, even knowing it lives in clean water, eats the same foods as walleyes and lake trout, and tastes delicious when cooked.

In areas where the citizens have overcome their fear of burbot, the fish are sought as eagerly as are trout and walleyes. "I think ling is the best-tasting fish there is," said John Baufman, a fisheries biologist in Wyoming. "People out here will trade you a walleye for a ling any-day." Some of the nation's most ardent burbot sport anglers live in central and western Wyo-

ming, where burbot ice fishing is a major winter sport.

Burbot angling has become so popular at some lakes in Maine that Scott Roy, state fisheries biologist, envisions setting regulations to maintain the burbot populations: "There's no doubt that in some lakes the cream of the crop has been removed. I wouldn't be surprised to see the state impose an 18- or 20-inch minimum size limit on cusk." In Maine, burbot are second only to lake trout in popularity during the winter, and ice anglers catch about 23,000 of the fish during the cold months. "Twenty years ago, a lot of people out here didn't want cusk," said Roy. "Today, you go out on a lake and you couldn't buy one off a fisherman."

A big burbot means big hardware at the Walker Eelpout Festival, held at Leech Lake, one of America's premiere burbot waters.

Anglers looking to catch burbot should begin at lakes and rivers in their state that consistently produce catches of these fish. Here is a list of state hotspots:

Indiana: Whitewater River and fishing ponds

Michigan: Upper Peninsula bays such as Saginaw, Green Bay, Little Bay du Noc, Noe, Munuscong

Minnesota: Upper Mississippi River, Leech Lake, and Lake of the Woods

Nebraska: Gavins Point Dam

North Dakota: Knife River, Lake Sakakawea

South Dakota: Lake Sharpe, Lake Oahe

Wisconsin: Lake Winnebago, Green Bay, and the Nemadji, Middle, Amnicon (Black) rivers, and at the mouth of the Duluth and Superior harbor.

Frank Van Hooley, director of fisheries for the Alaska Department of Game and Fish, said over 30,000 burbot are taken in Alaska each year. "It's a real easy species to fish out, so in some places we've had to reduce the bag limit to 2 a day, 2 in possession."

Natural History

Burbot

Lota lota

Lota lota, from *la lotte*, French for "codfish."

The burbot looks like a cross between a catfish and an eel. It is similar to a saltwater cod in appearance, but smaller and more slender. The burbot has tiny scales set in a heavy, slick skin that feels like a trout's. Its white belly, which is often distended, gives the burbot a permanently pregnant look. Small eyes sit on top of its broad, flat head, similar to that of a catfish. Its medium-sized mouth is filled with fine teeth. A light-colored lateral line runs from the pectoral fins to the base of the tail.

The burbot, which averages 2 pounds and reaches 20 or more, has extremely long dorsal and anal fins that stretch almost one-half the length of its long body. A small barbel, or whisker, extends from each nostril, and a large one sticks down from the fish's chin. The fish is superbly colored for hiding on a lake bottom in wait for prey. Its sleek skin is marked with a lively camouflage pattern of dark brown or black splotches on an olive, yellow, or dark brown background. The skin color varies from yellowish in the south of its range to dark gray, brown, and even black in the northernmost parts.

Like the lake trout, the burbot's range is primarily in the northern states, reaching only as far south as Kansas and occasionally Missouri. In North America, the burbot lives in deep cold lakes, large rivers, and coldwater streams from Alaska, the Yukon, and the Northwest Territories down to the Columbia River watershed in Oregon and Washington, and then east through Montana, northern Wyoming, the Dakotas, and the Great Lake states and provinces to New England. Burbot are one of the deepest-dwelling freshwater fish in North America, having been found at 1,000 feet in Lake Superior, a depth at which scientists once thought no fish could live.

In the Upper Midwest, burbot are found throughout northern Minnesota, Wisconsin, Michigan, North Dakota, and in the Missouri and Mississippi rivers. Like lake trout, burbot were seriously hurt by the lamprey invasion of the Great Lakes in the 1940s, but they have rebounded since the mid-1960s, when lamprey controls were carried out by the U.S. Fish and Wildlife Service and the Great Lake states. Burbot were once common in Lake Pepin, a natural impoundment of the Mississippi River, but commercial anglers today report rarely seeing the species in their nets, probably because siltation and pollution of the big river have eliminated the habitat of the fish.

Burbot is the only fish that spawns in the winter under ice, usually from December to March, depending on the latitude. In Minnesota and Wisconsin, for example, the peak period is late January through early February. When it's reproduction time, burbot move from the depths into the shallows of lakes, usually in 1 to 10 feet of water over mud flats or sandy shoals, reefs, and bays. Burbot will also run up rivers to spawn.

Spawning takes place in the dark. The males are the first to arrive at the spawning areas and the females follow. Rather than pair off as most fish species do, burbot breed in a massive group of dozens of fish, moving in and out of the mass, randomly releasing sperm and eggs. Because the spawning is so haphazard, a single female must produce up to 1.5 million eggs at a time to ensure enough get fertilized.

When they hatch, the young burbot often move from lakes into the weedy shallows of clean, coolwater streams. When the fish get a bit older, they move into gravelly riffles where they feed on nymphs. In streams, adult burbot stay near deep undercut banks or move downstream to bigger water. Contrary to what people think of a roughfish, burbot need clean, rocky-bottomed water to survive. Baufman said one reason burbot can't reproduce well in older reservoirs is that siltation from a lack of current fills in the riprap that acts as nurseries for the young. "The juvenile fish need those

rocky areas," he explained. "We've found they actually get right in there and live in the rubble."

Burbot are a large fish, similar in size to the walleye. The world record, shared by Tom Courtemanche of Pinconning, Michigan and a Minnesota angler named Robert T. Wilmes, is 18 pounds, 4 ounces. Larger fish have been netted in the Mississippi River, Missouri River, and the Great Lakes, however, and a 19-pounder was caught on a set line through the ice in Wyoming, but was not substantiated as a world record.

No matter what its size, the burbot is a vo-

The burbot looks like a cross between an eel and a catfish. Actually, it is the only freshwater member of the cod family, which includes the tasty haddock and hake.

racious eater that will devour anything that comes its way. "If it swims, a cusk will eat it," declared Roy. Scientists and anglers examining the stomach contents of burbot have found so many different kinds of fish, animals, and items usually thought inedible that it is hard to say what the species will not eat. Frogs, crayfish, Q-tips, cigarettes, suckers, carp, mollusks, mice, burbot, crappies, rock bass, smallmouth bass, sculpin, smelt, crustaceans, minnows, shrews, perch, cisco, sunfish, insects, invertebrates, fish eggs, rocks, wood chips, and plastic pieces have all been found inside burbot. A fisheries biologist in Wisconsin netted a 22-inch burbot from Lake Winnebago that had swallowed all of a 16-inch walleye except the tail. Two burbot caught by James E. Morrow, professor emeritus at the University of Alaska, had adult bank swallows in their stomachs.

According to a study conducted by the Maine Department of Inland Fisheries and Wildlife, burbot feed primarily at night. Scientists examined the stomach contents of burbot during different times of the year, and found that during the summer, burbot sulk on the bottom of a lake's deepest holes and stop feeding. When the temperature cools in the fall, feeding activity picks up, and peaks in the late winter and early spring. Burbot feed heavily after they spawn, sometimes moving into river inlets to find food.

Its voracity makes the burbot an important predator in the food chain. If it has a choice, a burbot will seek out small panfish. One biologist netted a burbot, cut it open, and found 135 young sunfish in the fish's bloated stomach. When introduced to lakes with too many stunted sunnies, for example, burbot cull out the small fish and increase the average size of sunnies there. In Wisconsin, some fisheries managers are looking to the burbot, gar, and bowfin as possible natural biological controls to panfish.

Finlanders serve burbot in a fish pie called *kukka*. In Sweden, the fish is a delicacy, purchased canned or smoked. Maine anglers boil chunks of burbot in salted water and dip them in butter.

Fishing Made Incredibly Easy

Fishing is a lot like working a computer. If you've never done it before, it seems impossible. There are so many magazines, books, instruction guides, and videos on fishing that it seems like you need a Ph.D. in *something* just to walk into a bait shop without feeling like an idiot. And if you are already an angler, you can't help feeling a little out of it when you read ads that make it sound like buying the latest NASA development is the only way to even put a few sunnies in your boat.

Well, let us put some myths to bed and the minds of both beginner and experienced anglers at ease. There's no more to fishing than finding where fish live, figuring out what they will eat, and getting that food—with a hook hidden inside—to the fish.

First, forget about what other fishing books say about practicing casting in the backyard. No one does it. Instead, head to the closest water you can find and start casting there. Don't use a practice plug; tie on a Mepps spinner. Keep moving up and down shore as you cast into the water. You probably won't catch anything at first, but at least you'll be fishing while you practice casting.

What type of water should you go to? Any water. Don't worry if it doesn't have a reputation as a good fishing hole. If it's water, there are fish of some kind swimming in it, and there are bound to be a few anglers around you can watch.

If there's not much going on to watch (and there usually isn't), you'll want to screw up the courage to ask other anglers what they've seen that day or know about the fishing in this spot. Here are some practice phrases commonly used by anglers all over the United States to start a conversation. We use at least one almost every time we go fishing:

"How're they biting?"

"Doin' much of anything?"

"How's it going?"

"Any luck?"

These are fishing passwords that open a door to an incredible body of knowledge: the experience of your fellow angler. Except for some muskie, steelhead, and sturgeon anglers who guard their fishing secrets with their lives, most anglers like to talk about fishing. However, sometimes they are embarrassed that they aren't catching anything and don't like to admit they've been standing in the same spot for 6 hours without a nibble. In this case, try the opener, "See anyone catch anything?" This takes the pressure off the angler you've approached and lets him or her talk about what's been happening on the water that day.

Don't worry about appearing to be prying for information. All anglers know what you're after. What are they biting on? What's been caught? When did they stop hitting? These and other questions and their answers make up the dialogue of the angling community.

Another key to catching fish is to keep moving and experimenting. If one spot doesn't produce after 15 minutes, try another. If one lure isn't getting hit, tie on something else. Usually, fish don't cruise around much; they stay put and wait for food to come to them. Don't sit and wait for fish because you waste time that could be spent finding fish. Also, fish are fickle. What they hit yesterday they may let pass with nary a glance today. That's why you have to keep changing your presentation until you hit upon the combination of depth, speed of retrieve, and bait or lure that says "Eat me" to the fish below.

In a nutshell, that's most of what you need to start fishing. Ask around, keep moving, and experiment. Follow that advice and whatever else you can find hidden in this book and you'll catch more fish than any sonar-producing nuclear-powered crankbait could ever hope to.

Fishing for Burbot

The key element to all burbot angling, advises Baufman, is to fish at night: "Ling are primarily night feeders. They don't move much because they aren't good swimmers. I think they survive because they are well camouflaged and feed at night." To catch a burbot in a river, he recommends fishing with a minnow in deep holes in still water that is close to cover—the classic catfish hole. Because eelpout feed in big schools, catching one usually means catching several.

As in night fishing for most species, no moon produces more burbot than does a full moon. Burbot, like other fish, are affected by changes in barometric pressure. Nights of storm and wind with a falling barometer are better than calm and clear nights with a rising barometer.

Fishing guide Maas reveals that his best burbot fishing through the ice of Minnesota's Leech Lake is with a jig: "We fish a hook and a minnow sometimes, but the people who consistently catch them jig a Swedish Pimple, Kastmaster, Jig-a-Whopper, or any other jigging spoon tipped with a minnow tail." Recently, Minnesota's top burbot anglers have been using fluorescent-colored barracuda saltwater jigs, shaving off the hair from the back

end of the lure. "Another killer for 'pout has been luminescent paint," said Maas. "After painting the jig, we hold it to a light for 30 seconds, and it glows for up to half an hour. The fish really go after that." He continued, "Eelpout are fun to catch. They fight harder than a walleye, and if you get an 8- to 12-pounder, you've got your hands full."

Anglers on Leech Lake fish the rocky reefs in February over 10 to 12 feet of water. Those who get into a group of feeding fish can take 30 or 40 fish in a night.

Maas admitted that not all the burbot he catches are through the ice. He also runs into some in May when walleye season opens: "They are up on the flats then, scarfing up crayfish." As the water warms up in Leech Lake, the burbot go deep, and Maas doesn't pick up any again until late fall.

In Maine, where 89 burbot lakes are open to ice fishing, winter anglers usually fish a dead minnow right on the bottom, said Bill Woodward, assistant regional fisheries supervisor for the Maine Department of Inland Fisheries and Wildlife. Although most of the fishing is at night and with tip-ups, Woodward says some anglers jig and catches are made when the sun is up, too.

One of the most accessible burbot fisheries in the Midwest is the burbot run up the

Nemadji River, located in Superior, Wisconsin in December. According to Dennis Pratt, western Lake Superior fisheries manager for the Wisconsin Department of Natural Resources, burbot make late fall spawning runs from Lake Superior into the streams on the big lake's south shore. Toward the end of November, burbot begin congregating along the shore near river mouths, and by the time the rivers are frozen enough to walk on, usually by early December, the fish are swimming underneath on their way upstream.

"They're not too hard to catch; just drill a hole in the river ice over a spot where you think the main channel is and start fishing," said Pratt, who fishes aggressively for burbot to satisfy his wife's hunger for seafood. "She likes lobster best, but I can't afford it. This is second best." Pratt fishes with a weighted jig tipped

He came, he saw, he conquered . . . burbot. Tom Courtemanche, of Pinconning, Michigan, holds the 18-pound, 4-ounce monster burbot he caught in 1980 that broke the world record. "My friend said, 'Tom, that's the biggest lawyer I've ever seen.' "

One of the World's Biggest Sport-Caught Burbot

January 31, 1980 was cold and windy on Lake Michigan. That morning on a blustery, frozen bay, Tom Courtemanche of Pinconning, Michigan set his hook into what is officially one of the two largest recorded burbot ever caught on hook and line. At about 9 a.m. the fish hit the orange Cleo that Courtemanche had been jigging in 6 feet of water. Hooked firmly, the fish fixed itself on the bottom of the bay directly beneath where Courtemanche and his fishing partner stood.

"I tried to move it, but nothing happened," said the world record-holder. Knowing a big fish was on, he quickly unwrapped his 14-pound-test line from the jigging stick and wound it around his left mitten, "so I could quickly play out line in case the fish took off." For the next quarter of an hour, Courtemanche played the massive burbot by walking slowly away from the hole, pulling the fish up from the bottom, and then moving slowly back towards the hole when the fish began to run.

"After I landed it, I didn't know I had a record," he admitted. "I took it to a friend who liked ling, and he looked down on it and said, 'Tom, that's about the biggest lawyer I've ever seen. I'll bet it's some kind of state record.'" Two days later, the fish was weighed in the Lansing DNR office, where it was verified as a state record. Later it was certified as the world record by the International Game Fish Association and the Freshwater Fishing Hall of Fame. (The number one spot was tied by Robert T. Wilmes in 1988.)

"I'll never forget the day I caught it," said Courtemanche. "It was my wife's and my tenth wedding anniversary."

with a smelt through a hole in the ice. "We make sure to fish where there is current," he said. In November, anglers can catch burbot by fishing from boats in Superior harbor, or by fishing off the shore and fishing piers at the harbor entry or at the mouth of the St. Louis River in Minnesota.

Although burbot are voracious and aggressive feeders, they swim relatively slowly, so they can't tear after crankbaits and spinners like faster fish can. They do hit spinning gear such as small metal spinners and large spoons in the spring. Most burbot in Michigan are caught by anglers trolling plugs in the Great Lakes for salmon. Biologists there have seen a recent increase in the number of burbot in streams and on anglers' stringers, possibly because many streams are cleaner than they were 20 years ago.

Burbot can also be caught with flies, although the fishing has to be early in the season or late in the fall when the fish are in shallow water. Nymphs and streamers work best. We've never heard of burbot rising to dry flies, but we can imagine it has happened.

A subspecies of burbot weighing up to 60 pounds and stretching 5 feet long lives in Siberia. While a dream trip to the Soviet Union for these monsters is beyond the reach of most anglers, plenty of trophy fishing spots exist in North America. Burbot up to 75 pounds were reported caught in Alaska and Canada at the turn of the century. Although no fish that big have been verified in North America, possibly 30-pound-plus fish lurk in the depths of the continent's prime burbot waters. Alaska's sport record, caught in Lake Louise, is slightly over 24 pounds, 12 ounces (state records often exceed world records because the qualification criteria is different or because the angler doesn't enter the fish as a world record). Bob Lafferty, a fisheries biologist with the Alaska Department of Game and Fish, says the top water for big burbot in Alaska is the Tanana

River: "Many of the ice anglers there are looking specifically for the large burbot. They fish herring or whitefish on a single hook, just off the current in the same water you'd expect to find a catfish."

No single water can claim to have the best burbot fishing in the world; however, Leech Lake in northern Minnesota is certainly home to the largest concentration of burbot anglers each year. Every February since 1979, the town of Walker on the lake's southwestern end has held the Walker International Eelpout Festival. The celebration, which draws up to

Featured in Sports Illustrated and on "ABC Sunday World News," the Walker Eelpout Festival draws anglers from as far away as Cuba.

8,000 spectators and 2,000 anglers, runs in mid-February from Friday noon to Sunday noon.

Besides a fishing tournament, the festival offers a 5-kilometer race across the lake (the Eelpout Peel-out), volleyball games, softball, frisbee, bowling, and billiards—all on the frozen surface of the famous muskellunge lake at temperatures that reach as low as minus 30 Fahrenheit. On Saturday night a formal black-tie dinner graces the ice. The entire town celebrates this freshwater cod by serving eelpout chowder in local restaurants, electing an eelpout festival mayor, and using the interest in eelpout to sell goods and services throughout the town. "Strain yourself pulling in the big one?" begins an ad from the local chiropractic center in the weekly paper.

Featured in *Sports Illustrated* and on "ABC Sunday World News," the Walker International Eelpout Festival draws anglers who vie for a 7½-foot trophy that goes to the largest eelpout caught. Throughout the 48-hour tournament, anglers fish furiously, and cries of "Pout on!" echo out from the dark lake on Friday and Saturday night. Most of the fish caught in the tournament are filleted, dipped in beer batter, and fried at the annual Pine River Sportsman's Club Aftermath Eelpout Dinner the following weekend.

Having Your Cusk and Eating It, Too

A meal of burbot is always delicious because the flesh is so tasty and because it is usually served fresh. When frozen, an enzymatic reaction causes the flesh to toughen. Although this gives the fish a pleasant texture if frozen only for a few days, after a few months in the freezer the meat gets rubbery. One tip for preserving burbot is to cook the fish before freezing. Cooking destroys the enzymes that cause toughening. Poach or steam the fillets, and

wrap them in plastic and freeze.

Burbot is a low-fat fish that is good steamed, poached, boiled, fried, deep-fried, smoked, or canned. The meat has more protein than bluegill, less fat than walleye, and fewer calories than almost any fish in fresh- or saltwater. Because the burbot, like other cod, lacks the enzyme thyaminose, it has a large liver rich in vitamins A and D.

RECIPES

There's no better way to describe burbot than to compare it to lobster. These recipes, 3 for the fillet and 1 for the liver, will allow you to taste this fine food fish at its best.

Burbot Pâté

Preheat oven to 325°.
Substitute burbot livers for those of geese or chicken and use this easy pâté recipe:
Divide 1½ pounds burbot liver into 3 parts.
Blend one part liver with 2 eggs.
Blend the second part liver briefly with ¼ cup whipping cream
Blend the third part liver with 4 slices chopped bacon, 1 egg, 3 tablespoons cognac, 2 tablespoons port wine, ¼ cup flour.
Mix the three blends together very lightly with 1 teaspoon ginger, 2 teaspoons salt, ½ teaspoon black pepper, 1 teaspoon nutmeg.
Line a loaf pan with dough.*
Put the mixture in the loaf pan. Top with thin-sliced salt pork. Cover tightly with foil and bake the pâté in a pan of hot water for 1½ to 2 hours.
Cool. Refrigerate for 2 hours. Unmold.
It should yield about 24 ½-inch slices.

*Work together with your fingers until you have achieved the consistency of coarse corn meal: 6 cups sifted all-purpose flour, 2 teaspoons salt, 1½ cups lard or shortening. Make a well in these ingredients and break into the center, one at a time, 2 eggs, working them into the flour mixture from the inside and adding gradually about 3 cups water. Work the dough into a smooth mass and roll into a ball.

Burbot Boulangère

Preheat oven to 350°.

Parboil in separate pans 16 small peeled potatoes, 12 small white onions.

Place a large fillet of burbot in a shallow buttered heatproof dish. Arrange the onions and potatoes around it. Sprinkle with a pinch of thyme and brush with melted butter.

Bake for about 30 minutes, basting frequently with melted butter. Serve in the same dish, garnished with chopped parsley and slices of lemon.

Fresh Burbot à la Provençale

Take a pound of burbot fillet, boil in salted water for 10 minutes, drain and cut into 2-inch cubes.

In a large saucepan, fry gently until golden 3 tablespoons olive oil, 1 minced glove garlic, 3 large chopped onions, 1 large sliced leek, white part only.

Add and simmer gently for about 15 minutes 1 quart hot water, ¼ cup tomato paste, ¼ tea-spoon each dried sage, thyme, rosemary, 1 bay leaf, 1 small hot Spanish pepper, 1 chopped green pepper, seeds and ribs removed.

Add to the sauce and simmer until tender 2 cups peeled potatoes cut Parisienne (like french fries).

Add burbot to the hot sauce, and set the pan over very low heat until the burbot is heated through. Garnish with triangles of fried French bread and chopped parsley.

Poor Man's Lobster

Cut fillets into thumb-sized chunks. Drop into boiling salted water and let boil for 10 minutes. Drain and serve hot with drawn butter for dipping.

Drawn butter is simply melted butter without the milk solids. To make, melt butter over a low heat. When liquid, let it stand for a few minutes to let the sediment settle to the bottom. Skim the butter fat from the top and place in a small bowl for dipping.

—TD

3

Suckers

The bigmouth buffalo is the muskie of the Southern Wisconsin streams; the wariest, most mysterious, and most sought-after native fish that swims."
— A WISCONSIN ANGLER

IT WASN'T ACTUALLY AN ARGUMENT, but it did get down to one of us giving in. The problem? We had too many places to go sucker fishing. Rob wanted to return to the Cannon River, in southern Minnesota, where we'd caught dozens of quillback carpsuckers the weekend before. I wanted to try the Rush River, in southwestern Wisconsin, which I'd heard had a run of river redhorse from the Mississippi River in the early spring. And we both wanted to also fish tributaries of Lake Superior for the longnose sucker run.

So many suckers, so little time.

"Listen," Rob said. "If we go to Wisconsin we'll have to buy out-of-state licenses."

"But last week you said you wanted to catch redhorse," I countered. "Besides, we'll have to buy Wisconsin licenses anyway to fish the Brule in the fall."

"But if we're going to take a trip, why not go north for longnose?"

"I can't afford the gas."

"And I can't afford an out-of-state license yet. So let's go to the Cannon."

So we did. And we caught so many quillback carpsuckers I forgot about the Rush and Lake Superior. For a week, anyway.

That's the problem with sucker fishing. Sometimes there are more places to fish than there is time to do it. Suckers are so widespread throughout the United States, so common in lakes, rivers, reservoirs, and streams, and during the spawning season so concentrated in certain areas that an angler can become paralyzed by the sheer number of fishing opportunities.

You'll never get a clearer picture of just how many suckers there are until you fish the spawning run. It's almost too much for a roughfish angler to handle. One early spring, before trees had even begun to bud, I hiked up the Black River in Wisconsin and saw suckers everywhere I looked. In riffles they were packed side by side like piano keys. In pools they milled around in groups of 10, 40, even 100 fish. Crossing the stream at one point, I couldn't take a step without suckers exploding under my feet, rushing ahead by the dozens in water so shallow their fins stuck out.

I didn't know what to do, there were so many fish. Winter had locked me in the house for months, and I had hoped to catch no more than one or two fish this first time out for the fishing season. With hundreds of suckers at my

The only thing we don't like about sucker fishing is having to decide which species we want to catch first. Here Rob decided on quillback carpsuckers.

feet, I was ready to blow a circuit. I decided it must be like going through the buffet line at the Jolly Troll Smorgasbord. You can't get overwhelmed by the sheer volume of food, but must focus on individual items one at a time. So that's what I did on the suckers.

Breathing deeply, I tried to pick out an individual fish from the countless shadows darting about in the clean, cold water. Finally I saw one off to the side. A big white sucker, maybe 3 pounds, was finning quietly in an eddy, oblivious to my careful approach. I reached into the carton I carried in my vest, pinched off a piece of nightcrawler, and stuck it on my hook. This I tossed upstream of the fish and watched it slowly tumble along the small rocks and get swept by the current into the eddy, where it dropped to the bottom.

The sucker waited a few moments, and then, in one motion, turned sideways and sucked up the bait. I set the hook lightly, and the fish leaped out of the still water into the rapids, plunging downstream with the hard current. I raced after it, holding my rod high and backreeling to give the fish slack. After 50 yards, I pulled it off the current into a pool, where it allowed itself to be slid onto shore so I could remove the hook and return it unharmed into the stream.

A Fish by Any Other Name

The sucker gets its name from a toothless, lipped mouth it uses to suck up food. In its throat (pharynx), are pharyngeal teeth. In some suckers, these teeth are like molars and can crush clams and snails. In others, the teeth are more like combs that filter plankton and algae from the water.

What bothers people most about suckers? Too much lip. Perhaps it is because a sucker's lips look so humanlike that many anglers have a hard time touching them. But unlike our lips, which have evolved to help us kiss and articulate speech, a sucker's lips are there only to find and vacuum up the bottom-dwelling food they eat. From a biological point of view, there's nothing odd about a sucker's mouth; it's simply a practical tool.

For years, anglers hated suckers for eating walleye eggs. Suckers move into rivers about a week or so after walleyes spawn. Anglers observed the bottom feeders sucking up walleye eggs and blamed them for harming walleye populations. However, studies in Iowa and Wisconsin showed that suckers only take in walleye eggs randomly along with other bottom matter.

Suckers are mistakenly thought of as "dirty," a misconception that comes from their habit of feeding on the bottoms of lakes and streams. However, where a fish feeds has little to do with its cleanliness. Trout, for example, also eat much of their food off the bottom. The sucker prefers clean water, and so contrary to popular belief, if you catch a sucker you are probably fishing in the *least* polluted water around.

This misconception could also come from the fact that many sucker species look like carp, which can tolerate water thick with mud, chemicals, and garbage. However, like trout and walleyes, most suckers can survive only in the cleanest waters. The longnose sucker, for example, lives primarily in the pristine waters of Lake Superior, Canada, and the Rockies, and other suckers are so repulsed by pollution that some fisheries biologists use them as living barometers for water quality: Where these species swim, the water is still relatively clean. The range of these pollution-shy suckers, such as the greater redhorse and the spotted sucker, have been so reduced by siltation and industrial discharge they have disappeared from waters where only 50 years ago they commonly swam.

Another reason many anglers look down on suckers is they don't really know what is and

isn't a sucker. Of the 65 different sucker species in North America, 17 live in the Upper Midwest. Some are buffalos, others are redhorses, others are carpsuckers, and the rest are called suckers of one type or another. All these fish are in the *Catastomidae* family and are collectively known as suckers, but many look completely different from the fish anglers commonly refer to as the sucker.

What makes suckers even more baffling is some of them look a lot like carp. But the carp is in a completely different family, and is no more related to suckers than a bass is. Besides that, the carp is a foreigner, imported to this continent less than 150 years ago. Suckers are native to North America. In fact, they are found nowhere else in the world, except in northeastern Russia, the results of a few defections across the Bering Strait.

The diversity of common names used for fish also confuses people. Documents from the 1700s and 1800s refer to anglers catching "sand bass," "river trout," "lunkheads," and "bull fish." Could any of these have been what are now known as suckers? As early as 1893, Ulysses O. Cox wrote in *Fishes of Minnesota* that northern hog suckers had 5 different names. Today, the names given to suckers can make it hard for anglers to tell what species they are catching. Hogmolly, plain sucker,

Contrary to popular myth, most suckers live in the cleanest, clearest waters of North America.

Suckers—which include buffalos, carpsuckers, and redhorses—are only native to North America. When settlers first came to the Midwest, they found these good-tasting fish plentiful and easy to catch.

mud sucker, corncob sucker, whistling pike, reefer, pugamoo, pighead, sweet sucker, schooner, mullet, blue rooter, blue pancake, gourdhead, and buoy-tender are a few of the evocative nicknames used.

Despite variances in names, size, color, habitat, and shape, all suckers have in common these features: soft-rayed fins, a toothless jaw, a scaleless head, smooth-edged scales, a forked tail, and a single fleshy dorsal fin. Another common feature of all suckers is they are extremely adaptable. Most can tolerate a wide range of water types and temperatures. However, as mentioned earlier, one thing most suckers can't tolerate is pollution and siltation.

Suckers are also a fairly good-sized fish. Compared to panfish, which are also abundant in the spring, suckers are giants. White suckers, the most common sucker species, reach 5 pounds. To catch a dozen or more 2-pounders in a day's fishing is common.

It is their adaptability and ability to eat bottom matter that has made the sucker one of the most productive fish on the continent. They don't have to work too hard to find food, because they consume mostly bottom matter that

many fish ignore, and they can find food by their senses of sight, touch (through their lips), and smell. As a result, suckers can develop into massive populations without affecting other fish populations.

Suckers are astonishingly productive. Each mating season, a single female will produce about 100,000 eggs. Suckers like to spawn in fast water over gravel—hence their numbers in shallow streams in the spring—but they'll spawn about anywhere, adapting quickly to the environment. During the mating season, to make sure mating is a success, male suckers actually develop stickers that hold them to the females. Called "pearl organs," these tiny spikes grow out of the male's fins in the spring and disappear after spawning.

In addition to their abundance and size, suckers are delicious when cooked. Smoked sucker is a delicacy throughout the United States. In Missouri, anglers can't wait for the spring to bring the annual white sucker fish fries. From just the Mississippi River alone, over 30 tons of bigmouth buffalo are netted and shipped to fish markets in the southern and eastern states.

Sucker Identification and Natural History

Before you rush out and start looking for sucker waters, you might want to know how to tell one species of sucker from another. In some cases this is as easy as distinguishing a grayling from a brown trout; in others it's like trying to tell a hen mallard from a hen black duck 200 yards away.

Why learn to tell suckers apart? Primarily to know what you're catching. And to explain to others what you're catching. Imagine returning to work after a weekend of fishing and telling your colleagues you caught "a bunch of suckers." Will that impress anyone? Not like if you'd told them you caught "a smallmouth

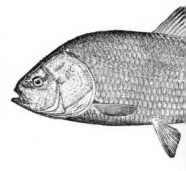

buffalo, two quillback carpsuckers, a northern hog sucker and half a dozen golden redhorse."

To tell suckers apart, first figure out if you've got a member of the sucker family or if you've got a carp. A lot of first-time roughfish anglers think a carp is a sucker, or the other way around, because both have a suckerlike mouth and because some suckers have a body shape and large, clearly outlined scales like a carp's.

Here's a rough guide to figuring out what the fish is.

1. Does it have a suckerlike mouth? If not, you are holding an eel or a walleye or a tuna or something else that is not a sucker. (There is one exception to this rule. See Bigmouth Buffalo.) If it does have a sucker mouth, then you have to:

2. Look to see if it has barbels, or whiskers. If it does, then you have caught a carp or a sturgeon.

3. If it has a sucker mouth and no barbels, then you are holding a sucker of some kind.

To really get to know your suckers you need to know their range, lip shape, average size, coloration, and the number of scales on the lateral lines of each species. You also will want to have at least a working understanding of the system used by biologists to classify fish and other life forms (see the sidebar "What's in a Name?").

These sucker species are grouped in 7 genera: 1. *Ictiobus* (the three buffalos: bigmouth, smallmouth, black), 2. *Carpiodes* (the three carpsuckers: highfin, river and quillback), 3. *Moxostoma* (the six redhorses: river, silver, black, greater, shorthead, golden), 4. *Cycleptus* (blue sucker), 5. *Minysteama* (spotted sucker), 6. *Hypentelium* (northern hog sucker), and 7. *Catostomus* (white sucker and long-nosed sucker). For our discussion, we have simplified those seven into four convenient categories: buffalos, carpsuckers, redhorses, and other suckers.

Buffalos

Why are these big, stocky fish called buffalos? No one knows. One theory is their name comes from the fact that they are big and stocky, like buffalos (American bison).

When pioneers first settled this country, they found waters filled with these huge fish. Lewis and Clark dined on buffalo, writing in their journal in 1804 that they "Cought a Buffalow fish." An 1873 addition of the *Peck Gazette* in Illinois mentioned that "Peoria Lake . . . abounds with various kinds of fish, such as . . . buffalo." J. B. Walton, an Iowan from the town of Muscatine, wrote in 1893 that in the middle part of the 19th century massive numbers of buffalo schooled around Muscatine Island, on the Mississippi River. He calculated if all the buffalo in that part of the river were placed on land, they would cover 100 acres of land at 10 tons to the acre.

All three buffalo species look like carp, with big scales and wide bodies. The difference is that carp have barbels and buffalo don't.

The bigmouth buffalo is the easiest sucker to identify because it is the only one *without* a suckerlike mouth. Unlike all other suckers, which have subterminal (below the head) mouths, the mouth of the bigmouth buffalo is in the front of its head, like a trout's. Bigmouth buffalo are big fish that can weigh over 70 pounds.

Smallmouth buffalo are also widebodied, but they have a suckerlike mouth. This is the fish most often mistaken for carp by anglers who don't know their suckers. The last buffalo species is the rarest. The black buffalo runs over 70 pounds, but they are so uncommon that few anglers ever catch one.

Bigmouth Buffalo
Ictiobus cyprinellus
Ictiobus is the Greek word for "bull fish," and *cyprinellus* is Latin for "small carp."

I caught this "small" bigmouth buffalo on a nymph. Had I hooked a good-sized bigmouth, which run 50 pounds or more, I'd still be trying to land it.

The bigmouth buffalo has more nicknames than any freshwater fish. Depending on the region, it is called baldpate, stubnose, pug, redmouth, trumpet buffalo, carp, white buffalo, bullhead buffalo, bullmouth, lake buffalo, slough buffalo, blue buffalo, common buffalo, gourd head, redmouth buffalo, roundhead, bull-nosed buffalo, mud buffalo, chub-nosed buffalo, brown buffalo, common buffalofish, and pug-nosed buffalo.

The bigmouth is one of the largest freshwater fish to swim in North America. The largest on record was an 80-pounder, taken from Spirit Lake in northern Iowa. Unlike most other suckers, the bigmouth travels in schools, roaming around lakes in search of food. Often in midsummer, groups of these buffalo rest quietly near the surface in the middle of dense algae blooms.

This sucker—distinguished from all others by its mouth, which is at the front of its head instead of below—prefers large rivers, lakes, and swamps. It is found all over the United States, from the upper Missouri River to the Appalachian Mountains, south along the Ohio River and in the Mississippi River to the Gulf of Mexico.

Bigmouth buffalo prefer shallow, slow-moving water over rich silt or mud bottoms. They can withstand some turbidity, but would rather swim in clear waters filled with suspended zooplankton. Bigmouth buffalo have comblike filters in their throat, which they use to filter zooplankton and algae from the water. They are heavily harvested commercially by the millions of pounds each year in the St. Croix and Mississippi rivers for their tasty, rich meat, which is sold in eastern and southern states. Of all the suckers, this is the one most commonly eaten. Although this fish eats primarily microscopic organisms, it has been caught by sport anglers with doughballs, corn, worms and even small jigs.

One reason the bigmouth buffalo is so abundant is that it can stand water temperatures up to 90 degrees Fahrenheit and water that has practically no dissolved oxygen. Even a stagnant pool of warm water would be a suitable home for these fish. Shallow lakes, swamps, and marshes rarely support fish any larger than bullheads except for the bigmouth buffalo.

The bigmouth buffalo has a strange way of spawning. A female gets in the middle of three or four males in shallow water, then sinks to the bottom and deposits her eggs. The males follow, crowding around and under her, and

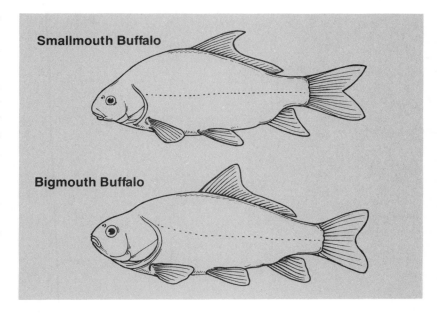

Smallmouth Buffalo

Bigmouth Buffalo

then push her up to the surface until their fins break out of the water. All at once, the fish rush forward 15 to 20 feet, churning the water into foam with their tails. This behavior, called "tumbling," helps mix the eggs and milt.

Smallmouth Buffalo
Ictiobus bubalus
Ictiobus is Greek for "bull fish," and *bubalus* is Latin for "buffalo."

This is the smallest buffalo. Although it can reach 40 pounds, it averages only about 5 pounds and 15 inches. Unlike the bigmouth buffalo, the smallmouth buffalo eats mostly aquatic insects and other plant and animal food on a stream bottom.

Also called roachback, razorback buffalo, highback buffalo, channel buffalo, humpback buffalo, thick-lipped buffalo, liner buffalo, brown buffalo, blue pancake, quillback buffalo, river buffalo, black carp, baitnet buffalo, and southern buffalo, the smallmouth is mostly found in the southern part of the United States, in the Mississippi, Missouri, and Ohio rivers and their tributaries.

Range of the bigmouth buffalo

Smallmouth buffalo—
another large sucker
species—look a lot like
carp. This 10-pound
smallmouth took a night-
crawler on the Mississippi
River at Lake Pepin.

Once rarer than the black and the bigmouth, the smallmouth buffalo has lately been
staging a comeback as the pollution in some
midwestern rivers like the upper Mississippi
has decreased over the past 20 years. The
smallmouth likes moderate-to-swift river currents in clear, deep stretches over sand, gravel,
or silt. It seeks out sunken riprap and scour
holes behind wingdams, but is sometimes
found schooling in open water with bigmouth
buffalo.

Black Buffalo
Ictiobus niger
Ictiobus is Greek for "bull fish," and *niger* is
Latin for "black."

The black buffalo looks like a darkened cross
between its two buffalo cousins. It has the
round body of the bigmouth, but the subterminal mouth of the smallmouth and the other
suckers.

Also called mongrel buffalo, round buffalo,
current buffalo, rooter, chopper, reefer, bu-
gler, blue rooter, bastard buffalo, deepwater
buffalo, chucklehead buffalo, round buffalo,
prairie buffalo, kicker, bastard buffalo, mongrel buffalo, and buoy-tender, this species is

rare north of Iowa in the Mississippi River, but
common in the Missouri River drainage.
Blacks like swift currents over gravel, sand, or
rock, which is why their numbers have
declined in the dammed and channelized Mississippi and Missouri rivers. They also are
found near the main channels of large rivers,
which is where the name bouy-tender comes
from.

This is one of the largest suckers, weighing
up to 70 pounds. It eats mollusks, insect larvae, and crustaceans.

Carpsuckers

Carpsuckers have been confusing anglers for
hundreds of years. When Europeans first came
to North America, they speared and netted
these large-scaled, tall-bodied fish, which they
called carp because they looked like the carp
back home. But then someone noticed the fish
had no barbels and figured they were probably
a type of sucker like the other suckers they
found in the rivers and lakes. So people started
calling the fish carpsuckers. At least that's one
theory.

Range of the quillback carpsucker

However the name came about, anglers should know that the 3 carpsucker species—river, quillback, and highfin—are in no way related to carp except that they are all fish. And despite long-lived confusion, the 3 carpsuckers are fairly easy to identify. You can tell the river, highfin and quillback carpsuckers from the somewhat similar-looking carp and smallmouth buffalo by the carpsuckers' tall dorsal fin, a feature that has earned them the name "grain belt grayling." If you catch a fish with lips, no barbels, and a tall dorsal fin, you've got a carpsucker.

Of the three, the highfin has the tallest dorsal fin. When flat, it extends way past the back of the fin's base. The quillback carpsucker's dorsal fin extends to the back of the base. The river carpsucker has the smallest dorsal fin, going back only about halfway to the base when flat (see illustration).

Quillback Carpsucker
Carpiodes cyprinus
Carpiodes is Latin for "carplike," and *cyprinus* comes from the island of Cyprus, from which the carp was supposedly first introduced to Europe.

This species weighs from 9 pounds and reaches about 3 feet in length. It feeds on the bottom, eating mostly bottom matter, plant material, and aquatic insect larvae.

Depending on where you live, you call the quillback a white carp, grain belt grayling, silver carp, plains carpsucker, lake quillback, coldwater carp, mullet, breme, drum, broad mullet, or long-finned sucker. Quillbacks swim in clear large streams and rivers with large, deep, quiet pools near gravel or rubble bottoms. They are found throughout the central United States; however, they are less tolerant of pollution and silt than other carpsuckers. Unlike the river and highfin carpsuckers, the quillback has no fleshy knob on its lower lip.

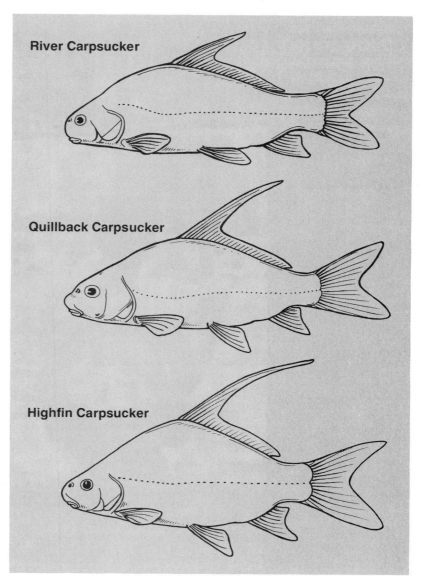

River Carpsucker

Quillback Carpsucker

Highfin Carpsucker

River Carpsucker
Carpiodes carpio
Carpiodes is Latin for "carplike," and *carpio* is Latin for "carp."

Also called silvery carp, white carp, and northern carpsucker, the river carpsucker looks a lot like a quillback, but its dorsal fin is not quite as long. It reaches 10 pounds, and has a fleshy knob on its lower lip.

The river carpsucker: note the clean water, beautiful scale pattern, and relatively short dorsal fin.

This is the least common carpsucker. Its range is restricted primarily to the Mississippi River and tributaries from St. Anthony Falls to the Gulf of Mexico.

Highfin Carpsucker
Carpiodes velifer
Carpiodes is Latin for "carplike," and *velifer* is Latin for "sail bearer."

Also called long quill, hump-backed carp, river carp, blunt-nosed river carp, spearfish, sailfish, silver carp, skimback, and skimfish, the highfin is found throughout the central United States; however, not in huge numbers. This is the smallest carpsucker, rarely growing to weigh over a pound. The largest ever recorded strained the scales at 3.8 pounds.

Although the highfin carpsucker mostly feeds on the bottom, it occasionally cruises near the surface, with its tall fin cutting through the water like a shark's. It, too, has a fleshy knob on its lower lip.

Redhorses
The redhorses and the other suckers are somewhat harder to identify. In the north-central United States, there are 6 kinds of redhorses: shorthead, silver, river, golden, greater, and black; and 5 other suckers: blue, spotted, northern hog, white, and longnose. At a glance, most of these suckers and redhorses look similar. The big difference between the redhorse and the other suckers is the redhorse has reddish fins, especially the tail. Also, the dorsal fin on the redhorse is sickle shaped, while the other suckers have straight dorsal fins.

If you want to know exactly what type of redhorse, buffalo, carpsucker, or other sucker you've caught, refer to the Redhorse Lip Chart and the individual species descriptions.

Getting your suckers mixed up is nothing to feel ashamed about. Thomas Jefferson did it back in 1784 when he wrote in his "Notes on Virginia" about the importance of the Mississippi River as a reservoir of economic opportunity for the expanding nation: "The Mississippi River will be one of the principal channels of future commerce for the country westward of the Allegheny. . . . This river yields turtle of a peculiar kind, perch, trout, gar, pike, mullets, herrings, *carp*, [italics ours] spatula fish of fifty pound weight, catfish of one hundred pounds weight, buffalo fish and sturgeon." Since carp weren't introduced to the fledgling nation for another 100 years, Jefferson must have meant "carpsucker."

Greater Redhorse

Moxostoma Valenciennesi

Moxostoma is Greek for "mouth to suck," and *Valenciennesi* derives from Achille Valenciennes, the 19th century French naturalist who first described this species from a specimen taken from Lake Ontario.

Also called redhorse and common redhorse, the greater is the largest and one of the rarest of the redhorses, sometimes reaching 13 pounds. The dorsal fin of the greater redhorse is gray, but all other fins are red.

It ranges from North Dakota to the St. Lawrence River along the Great Lakes, although it is not known in the Lake Superior drainage. Recently, these fish have been discovered in the upper Missisippi River above St. Anthony Falls in Minneapolis and in the Red River drainage, where they had not been known to live. Because they are so sensitive to pollution, greater redhorse have become increasingly rare in the past 50 years. The species lives in clear lakes and streams and has no tolerance for pollution and silt.

Black Redhorse

Moxostoma Duguesne

Moxostoma is Greek meaning "sucking mouth," and *Duguesne* is named for Fort Duguesne (now Pittsburgh), Pennsylvania, where the first species was identified.

The black redhorse is a beautiful fish. Its slen-

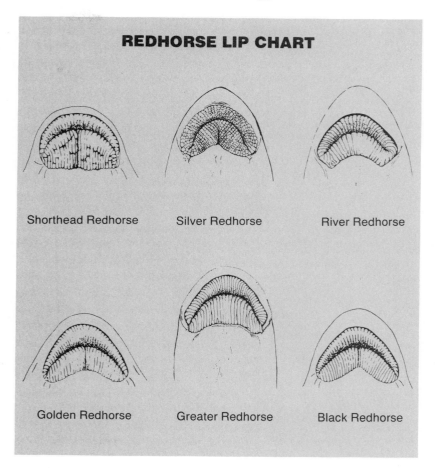

REDHORSE LIP CHART

Shorthead Redhorse   Silver Redhorse   River Redhorse

Golden Redhorse   Greater Redhorse   Black Redhorse

der body is a silver and dark green iridescent color, with light orange fins. This is one of the smallest redhorse, rarely growing to be over a pound. As several of its nicknames imply, the black has extremely small scales, almost like a trout's.

Also called black horse, black mullet, fine-scaled mullet, fine-scaled redhorse, white sucker, and blue sucker, the black redhorse is another species that has become rare because of pollution. In Minnesota it is found in the shallow, clean branches of the Root and Zumbro rivers. In Iowa and Nebraska it is found only in a few clearwater streams. Sadly, the species probably no longer swims in Wisconsin; the last time it was seen there was in the early part of the century.

Rob releases a 7-pound river redhorse into a stream clean enough to drink.

Golden Redhorse
Moxostoma erythrurum
Moxostoma is Greek for "sucking mouth," and *erythrurum* is Latin for "red tail."

The golden can reach 2 feet and up to 5 pounds in southern states, but rarely gets over 2 pounds in the North. It is olive on top, gold on the sides, and despite its scientific name, has a slate-colored tail.

Also called golden mullet, golden sucker, white sucker, small-headed mullet, and yellow sucker, the golden redhorse is caught throughout the upper Mississippi River and Ohio River watersheds, but it is rare in the Missouri River drainage.

Silver Redhorse
Moxostoma anisurum
Moxostoma is Greek for "sucking mouth," and *anisurum* is Latin for "unequal tail."

The silver looks just like a golden redhorse, except that its dorsal fin has 15 rays, while all other redhorse have 12 or 13. The silver gets its name from its silvery sides. Like a shark, the silver's tail is longer on top than on the bottom.

It is also known as silver mullet, silver sucker, white sucker, white-nosed redhorse, bay mullet, redfin mullet, long-tailed sucker, and red-finned sucker. This is a northern range sucker. It is not found south of Missouri and ranges up into middle Canada. It reaches 8 pounds in the Mississippi River and up to 10 in the Ohio River.

River Redhorse
Moxostoma carinatum
Moxostoma is Greek for "sucking mouth," and *carinatum* is Latin for "keeled."

Also called pavement-toothed sucker, big-jawed sucker, and river mullet, the river is one of the largest redhorse, reaching 11 pounds and 3 feet long.

This is an extremely rare redhorse species, found only in clean, riffly rivers with many mollusks. Unlike other redhorses, which have comblike teeth that filter tiny aquatic insects and plant material from the water, the river redhorse has molars in its throat that it uses to crush the clams that make up most of its diet. Because clams are easily killed by pollution, the river redhorse has been wiped out from much of its original range. Today it is found only in the upper Mississippi River below St. Anthony Falls and in the St. Croix River.

Shorthead Redhorse
Moxostoma macrolepidotum
Moxostoma is Greek for "sucking mouth," and *macrolepidotum* is Latin for "large-scaled."

This fish is also called large-scaled redhorse, red sucker, redhorse mullet, Des Moines plunger, big-scaled sucker, and redfin sucker.

Range of the shorthead redhorse

Like most redhorse, it has an olive green back and sides and red fins.

Usually the shorthead redhorse is a small fish, but in some rivers it can reach 4 or 5 pounds. The shorthead, which can be distinguished from other species in the genus *Moxostoma* by its short head and large scales, has a strange feeding method. It flicks its fins rapidly and pokes its head between gravel and stones to find larvae, worms, and crayfish.

Other Suckers

Blue Sucker
Cycleptus elongatus
Cycleptus is Greek for "small round mouth" and *elongatus* is Latin for "elongate."

The blue sucker is one of the most handsome fish in the sucker family. As its Latin name implies, the blue is slender, its small head tapering to a pointed snout like a trout's. Most striking is its dark blue color.

The blue is also called Missouri sucker, razor back, slender head sucker, gourdseed sucker, blackhorse, blue fish, suckerel, schooner,

and muskellunge (only in the lower Wabash River in Indiana). It is one of the best-tasting of the suckers, which is why some people call it the "sweet sucker."

Rare in the Upper Midwest, the blue is found mostly in states along the latitude of Missouri and south, except in the Missouri River, where it lives all the way north to Montana. In the Mississippi River, blues are found in Iowa, Illinois, Minnesota, and Wisconsin, but only occasionally. At one time blue suckers, big fish weighing up to 20 pounds, were common in the Mississippi River and its major tributaries, and made up a large part of the commercial harvest in the spring, when they congregated in swift, riffly water. The construction of dams on the Mississippi has stopped many of their upstream migrations and flooded riffles and rapids where they spawn.

What type of redhorse? A quick glance back to the handy redhorse lip chart shows it's a greater.

Spotted Sucker
Minytrema melanops

Minytrema, Greek for "reduced aperture," refers to the imperfection in the fish's lateral line, and *melanops* is Latin for "black appearance."

Also called corncob sucker, striped sucker, speckled sucker, black sucker, winter sucker, pighead, and spotted redhorse, this sucker is distinguished from the others by a dark spot on each scale, which appears as rows of stripes along the fish's sides. The spotted sucker is a dark fish with a dark green-brown back, gray belly, and large scales. Like the blue, it cannot tolerate pollution and siltation. In the upper midwest, its range has been reduced to only the Mississippi and St. Croix rivers. The blue sucker still swims in the South and in the eastern Great Lakes states, from Lake Erie to Florida and the Carolinas and west to Kansas and Texas.

An adult spotted sucker runs 10 to 20 inches long, and weighs up to 3 pounds. It likes clear, warm water with not much current and a soft bottom with plenty of decayed vegetation to eat.

Spotted suckers spawn by 2 males positioning themselves on either side of a female and pressing against her. While rising up in the water, the 3 fish vibrate, which stimulates the release of eggs and milt. Vibrations also stir up sediment, which covers the eggs as it settles. The eggs drift among rocks and gravel and hatch unattended.

Northern Hog Sucker
Hypentelium nigricans

Hypentelium is Greek for "below 5 lobes," which refers to the lobes on the lower lip, and *nigricans* is Latin for blackish.

This species is also called black horse, blue sucker, hogmolley, hognose sucker, black sucker, stoneroller, spotted sucker, riffle sucker, hammerhead sucker, hog mullet, crawl-a-bottom, stone lugger, stone toter, pugamoo, boxhead. Just looking at the nicknames, you know this is one weird-looking fish. Its large head is caved in between huge eyes. Thick lips are covered with bumps. And although they can occasionally reach 20 inches long, most northern hogsuckers don't grow to be over a pound. The hogsucker is brown-green above and mottled with six dark bars down its sides, making the fish hard to see against the bottom.

The northern hogsucker is common in Minnesota, Iowa, Missouri, Wisconsin, and Illinois. It's not found in the Missouri River drainage, but it does swim in the clear small tributaries of the Minnesota, Mississippi, and St. Croix rivers. To the east, it is found in the tributaries of all the Great Lakes and south to northern Alabama and Georgia.

Rare in big rivers, the hog sucker likes rocky, riffly areas in gravelly streams, where it feeds by turning stones over and eating sediment and larvae below. Because of its heavy head, slender tapering body, and big pectoral fins, it can hold itself in swift water on the bottoms of swift rocky riffles. This fish is important to a stream's ecosystem because it overturns rocks, exposing food to minnows and other small fish.

White sucker
Catastomus Commersoni

Catastomus is Greek for "subterminal mouth," and *Commersoni* is named after Philibert Commerson, a 19th century French naturalist who first identified this species.

This is the most common sucker in the United States. Although uncommon in big rivers, the white sucker is extremely adaptable to different habitats. Compared to the more sensitive suckers, it can withstand somewhat-polluted water. Whites reach up to 5 pounds. They are greenish on the back and sides and, like the longnose sucker, have small scales near the front of the body and larger ones at the back.

Also called common sucker, coarse-scaled sucker, eastern sucker, brook sucker, gray sucker, mud sucker, sucker, mullet, black mullet, slender sucker, June sucker, and whitehorse, the white sucker likes small rivers and streams and natural and manmade lakes.

Longnose sucker
Catstomus catastomus
Catstomus is Greek meaning "subterminal mouth."

Another fine-looking sucker, the longnose looks like the blue sucker, only lighter in color. It reaches 2 feet and 8 pounds, has a long tapering snout, and is black on its sides and back. Like the spotted sucker, it spawns in teams of three.

Also known as sturgeon sucker, red sucker, redside sucker, finescale sucker, black sucker, mullet, and northern sucker, the longnose is the only sucker found outside North America. Recently it has been found in the eastern part of the Soviet Union swimming in several rivers flowing into the Bering Strait.

A small-scaled sucker, the longnose lives in the Arctic and in the Lake Superior river drainages. This sucker likes deep water and has been found in Lake Superior as far down as 600 feet.

Fishing for Suckers

As Jeff Duis watched the line peel off his cracked spincast reel, he knew it was no bullhead on the other end. Fishing the spillway at East Okoboji Lake in northern Iowa one April morning in 1986, Duis and a couple of friends had been pulling bullheads from a deep hole in the fast current. That was when a huge fish sucked in his nightcrawler and took off downstream. Twenty minutes later, Duis pulled out

Range of the white sucker

of the water the largest fish ever taken by rod and reel in Iowa, stretching just shy of 4 feet long. The fish was entered in the Iowa state record books as a 51-pound bigmouth buffalo.

"To tell you the truth, it might have weighed more than that," Duis said afterwards. "We took it to a bait shop, but the scale was too small, so we ended up weighing it on some rusty old platform scales."

A wallhanger buffalo like this is a possibility for any angler fishing the backwaters of big, warmwater rivers. Each year, some of the largest fish caught in many states are bigmouth buffalo and smallmouth buffalo. Although these fish don't make spectacular runs or leap from the water, their sheer power is enough to weaken the knees of any angler.

Besides being big, many suckers put up heroic fights. We've had redhorse smack a worm and then rocket out of the water more than once, and a big white sucker hooked with a nymph can take a fly reel into its backing.

On September 29, 1983, Glen Dittman caught what could be an unbeatable roughfish record for the state of Iowa: a 15-pound, 1-ounce blue sucker. After fighting the fish for 20

minutes, Dittman had to wade in after the fish and haul it onto shore. Not knowing what it was, he almost released the record sucker back into the water before it could be weighed and verified.

Fortunately, Dittman put the sucker into the back of his pickup and took it to a nearby Iowa Department of Natural Resources office the next day. Once weighed and verified, the state's largest blue sucker was mounted and displayed at the Lake Rathbun Fish Hatchery, where it will remain until someone breaks Dittman's record. Considering the scarcity of blue suckers and the fact that it broke the old record by 3 pounds, Dittman's sucker might be there for a long time.

Like Dittman, anglers can often catch big suckers in the fall. However, the best time to fish is in the spring, because that's when the fish are concentrated in streams to spawn. The early sucker run is a good warmup for anglers rusty after a winter of no fishing. These first fish of the season are often jammed into riffles so tight you could walk across their backs if they'd let you, and they are eager to bite any morsel drifted past their mouth.

Generally, suckers are found in most freshwater streams and rivers. To find good sucker water, look at a map, find a squiggly blue line, and drive to it. If the water is relatively clean with a moderate current and gravelly riffles, then start fishing. A sucker should be on the end of your line in no time. That's an oversimplification, of course. It is easy to get blanked, especially if you are not fishing the spring run. The point is, however, that very few rivers don't have suckers.

The lower parts of trout streams usually have good sucker populations because the water is clean and in their lower stretches have often warmed to a temperature suckers prefer. Many trout anglers have mistaken a 2-pound sucker finning in the riffles for a large, nymph-feeding brown.

To improve our odds of catching suckers, we try to find a dam, especially the first ones up on the tributaries of the Great Lakes or big rivers. Like other migratory fish, suckers stack up below dams in the spring on their journey upstream to spawn. In the summer, they stay near dam discharges to feed on the organisms attracted to the well-oxygenated water. As the weather warms, we fish deep holes downstream of riffles and dams, where suckers sit waiting for food to wash down.

We had one of our best days sucker fishing at a dam on the Cannon River, in southern Minnesota. It was early April, a few weeks after the last of the snow melt. The river had only

Fishing Stony Brook in northern Minnesota, Rob landed several ornery white suckers on 4-pound-test tippet. His fly? A Woolly Bugger.

Thusi Van Rensburg reaches for a tackle-busting white sucker on the St. Croix River.

recently stopped overflowing its banks, but had cleared enough for us to see several large fish below the bridge at the town of Welch. The dam there stops suckers and other fish moving upstream to spawn from the Mississippi River 8 miles to the east.

Rob and I waded out to an island just below the dam, while our friend Dave Greer walked across the bridge to fish the fast water flowing over the dam near the far bank. As we sloshed through the warm shallows, 2- and 3-pound northern pike darted between our legs. They were moving upstream to spawn, and seemed insulted that the dam was stopping their progress. Occasionally one would try, unsuccessfully, to leap the 6-foot falls like a steelhead.

The only other anglers were several families who had already filled two 5-gallon buckets with white suckers and highfin carpsuckers. Mothers, fathers, kids, and grandpas had lined up along the end of the island facing the dam and were casting jigs and worms methodically into the fast current.

After about an hour of fishing, Rob and I had both caught and released several medium-sized quillback carpsuckers, and Dave had hooked but lost a few big fish none of us ever saw. The fish seemed to be moving around in pods in the calm pockets within the fast flow below the dam. One slot would present a strike with each drift and then suddenly go dead, forcing us to probe around the bottom with our weights until another fish latched on.

Then the fish stopped biting altogether. After half an hour without a strike, I added a few split shot and flipped my worm directly into the base of the falls. With my right arm straight out, I held the rod horizontal, feeling the lead move across the small stones below the foamy water. Nothing. I added more weight and tried again.

This time, my rod shot forward. I was too

What's in a Name?

Razorback, blackhorse, gordseed, bluefish, suckerel, Missouri sucker, and blue sucker are all regional or common names for the same species of fish—*Cycleptus elongatus*. As you can imagine, with anglers in one region calling a fish a completely different name from what anglers in another region call it, it's hard for anyone to know who is catching what. In order for anglers to talk about, study, and appreciate a particular roughfish, they first have to agree on one name to call it. But which one? Fortunately, scientists have already solved the problem by creating a simple naming system for all living organisms discovered on earth.

Scientific names of species consist of two parts. For example, the scientific name for the bigmouth buffalo is *Ictiobus cyprinellus*, and for the smallmouth buffalo it's *Ictiobus bubalus*. The second half is the species name. Species are a group of similar fish that look alike and can breed together. The first half is the genus name. A genus is a group of related species that look similar, but don't breed together naturally. The bigmouth buffalo and the smallmouth buffalo look similar and therefore are in the same genus *Ictiobus* ("bull fish"). Still, they have a few differences and don't breed together, so they are classified as different species: *cyprinellus* ("small carp") and *bubalus* ("buffalo").

Where do scientific names come from? Usually they are Greek and Latin adjectives that describe the species, but they are also derived from the names of people, geographic places, and mythological figures. Each of the 1½ million species that have been discovered living on earth has a unique scientific name.

In *Fishing for Buffalo*, we list the scientific names of the roughfish we discuss for several reasons. One, to ensure the reader knows exactly what fish we are talking about. Many people can't tell one from another. The bigmouth buffalo (pictured on the cover), which is a native sucker, is often called a carp, but a true carp is an exotic minnow. Scientific names clear up this confusion. Two, the names help tell the story of the fish. *Lepisosteus platastomus* — Greek for "bony-scale broad-mouth" — is the scientific name for the shortnose gar, an apt description of this fish. Three, if you want to learn more about roughfish, you'll need to know their scientific names to find information in fisheries libraries.

Although scientific names are useful and interesting, we recommend the common names while fishing, You'll get strange looks if you yell to your partner, "Hey, I got a nice *Coregonus clupeaformis* on the line."

Because we don't want to sound like Latin professors, but still want to be as vernacularly exact as possible, we use the most widely accepted common names for each fish in the various chapters. In addition, we offer a brief, formal introduction, using each species' scientific name.

late setting the hook, and the weight settled back to the bottom. Fortunately, the fish made another grab. I pulled back. It pulled again. I pulled back harder and felt the fish fight the hook and swim straight at the dam.

"Sucker on!" I yelled above the roar of the falls. Dave stopped fishing along the far bank long enough to wave his hat, and I waved back and waded into the current. My line ran straight out into the fast water, the fish undaunted by the resistance of the curved rod. I moved my left hand up the rod 2 feet from the reel to give myself more leverage, and began applying side pressure, pulling the fish across the current as much as I dared hope the 6-pound line would stand. The fish rose to the surface and rolled. "It must be a carp," I thought, certain by the sight of the round side and huge gold scales, but puzzled there would be carp at the dam so early in the year.

After 10 minutes of sitting still, the fish decided to head downstream. Not wanting to follow it to the Mississippi River, where it seemed destined, I walked slowly up the bank away from the water to see if I could take some force from its run. Fortunately, it didn't take long. The fish rounded a bend, made one last run deep into the fast current, and then allowed itself to be slid up onto shore.

I was surprised to see I'd caught about a 15-pound bigmouth buffalo, a fish that usually eats zooplankton. Instead of teeth, the buffalo has slender gill rakers in its neck to comb out microscopic organisms in the water, feeding much as the blue whale does. As a result, buffalos are few and far between on a fishing line.

A carp is certainly a catch worth bragging about, but a bigmouth buffalo . . . well, you just don't catch one everyday. And what makes it even more valuable is its meat, considered by many anglers the most delicious of all suckers.

I was excited and held the fish up for Rob to see. It was so big, I couldn't get my hands firmly around the body and it slid through my arms into the shallows. Stunned, the fish just

"Nice blue pancake, partner," Rob called to me when he saw I'd landed this jumbo smallmouth buffalo on the Mississippi River. I quickly released the powerful fish so someone else would have a chance at it.

sat there. Stunned, I just stood there. We both recovered at the same time, but the fish swam away just out of reach as I waded desperately into the river after it.

Rob went back to his fishing.

A person who is a "sucker" is easily duped. While that is sometimes true for the fish of the same name, it's not always the case. Suckers are fairly intelligent, as far as fish go. At times they can feed as selectively as trout, a species

some fly-fishermen award almost humanlike intelligence in their ability to distinguish a real insect from one made of thread and feathers. Suckers can also be indiscriminate when feeding, sucking up anything from rocks and wood to crayfish and clams. But they are no less selective than trout that have been caught on marshmallows, corn, doughballs and hotdogs.

Sucker bait can be about anything from live minnows to a piece of chewed gum. Most anglers use a worm or a 'crawler on a small hook and fish along the bottom, where the fish feed. When the water is cold—say below 50 degrees—try still fishing instead of drifting, because the sluggish fish won't chase after a moving worm. The problem with still fishing is that you can't cover much water. You're fishing in one spot, and a sucker holding 5 feet away might not want to swim over and suck up your worm. The trick is to wait 10 or 15 minutes, and if you don't get a pickup, reel in and cast to a different spot.

Suckers are also caught with small doughballs, grubs, tiny jigs fished below a bobber, grasshoppers, strips of meat, small bits of nightcrawler, corn, crayfish, cut bait, hellgrammites, live nymphs, fish eggs. Some species, like white suckers and shorthead redhorse, hit small spinners. During midsummer, when the streams have warmed up, suckers are more likely to hit the hardware than they are in the cooler months.

Arkansas angler Keith Sutton recommends baiting a buffalo hole with "livestock range cubes"—hard, high-protein chunks that dissolve quickly in water. He says the cubes should be dropped into a deep hole, which is fished later in the day with worms or doughballs after the odor has attracted the buffalo.

Once the water warms up to over 50 degrees, it's best to move your bait around the bottom by drift fishing. We use a drifting outfit for river roughfish: a graphite fly rod blank (8 or 9 weight) with spinning guides and a spin-

Rob, deftly lifts an eating-sized redhorse from a northern stream. Redhorse have a sweet, finely textured meat that's great broiled, baked, or fried.

Redhorse thrive in clean, silt-free rivers and streams, like Wisconsin's famed wild brown trout water, the Namekogan River.

take the bait, open the bail, count to 5, and yank.

Few anglers fly-fish for suckers, probably because when suckers are running the trout season has just opened and most fly-anglers are searching for trout. If you like fishing for trout and suckers, try fishing the lower stretches of a trout stream, where the water warms up a bit. Here, the sucker populations are greater because the fish prefer water warmer than what trout like. Often there are big brown trout in these stretches if a spring or cold feeder stream is nearby. The minnow life in the warm water gives the browns some heavy chow to feed on, so this is often where the biggest trout are caught. By fishing a nymph or streamer in the deep pools of these waters, you can have a chance at catching big trout or big suckers.

At midday on small streams, suckers will swim up into riffles and feed on nymphs, just as trout do. That's a good time to break out the fly rod and tie on a nymph imitation. Standard mid-sized stream fly-fishing gear will work: 4 or 5 weight rod, 7X leader and a size 16 to 10 gold-ribbed Hare's Ear, Pheasant Tail, scud imitation, Woolly Bugger, or stonefly nymph. Since suckers have a keen sense of smell, a drop or two of fish scent won't hurt, although fly-fishing purists may turn up their noses at the idea. It is important when nymphing to get the fly down to the bottom. Crimp on a split shot, and use a strike indicator about 8 feet up from the lead so you can see even the lightest strikes.

ning reel loaded with 6-pound-test line. To the end of the line, we tie on a size 10, 8, or, 6 bait-holder hook, stick on a nightcrawler, and then add a few split shot up the line 12 inches or so. When cast upstream to the head of a pool or into some fast water near an eddy, the weight carries the worm down to where the fish lie. Once the weight touches bottom, we use the rod tip to lead the bait along at the speed of the underwater current (which is slower than the surface current), lightly dancing the lead along the rocks to make sure the bait is always down deep where the suckers feed. This is a good way to cover the bottom of streams and medium-sized rivers and be directly connected to nibbling fish.

It is hard to know when to set the hook when fishing suckers. If you are practicing catch-and-release, wait no more that a second or two after feeling a tug and then set the hook. That way, you'll have a better chance of hooking the fish in the mouth rather than deep in the throat. If you are fishing for dinner, let the fish

Preparing Succulent Fish

Sucker meat is white, finely textured and delicately sweet-flavored. A misconception about suckers is they have firm flesh only in the spring, when the water is cold. After that, the flesh of the fish supposedly gets mushy. Although it's true that any fish taken from cold water tastes best, suckers caught even in mid-

Rob's Longnose

Forty-two miles southwest of the Canada–Minnesota border, the Arrowhead River empties into Lake Superior. About 200 yards upstream from the mouth of the river is a deep pool formed by the river plunging over a basalt ledge. The ledge slows fish migrating up from the big lake to spawn, making it a perfect place to fish.

It was late May, and a few steelhead remained in the river. The ones I saw as I walked up to the pool seemed out of place: The water was low, clear, and too warm for these migrating rainbows, which usually make their run earlier in the spring. Their time for spawning was over, and they should have been down in the lake.

Although tempted to try for the steelhead, I was more interested in catching a different, rarer fish species. Approaching the small waterfall, I saw though my polarized glasses a school of dark shapes finning along the bottom near the tail of the pool. Keeping low and away from the bank, I crimped a small split shot to the leader, 18 inches above a number 12 Pheasant Tail nymph, and attached a strike indicator—a small piece of fluorescent orange foam—8 feet above the lead. I moved quietly to the pool and flipped the fly into the water, waiting for it to sink deep before inching it back along the bottom. On the third drift, the indicator did a little dance on the water surface, and I set the hook.

A steelhead reacts to a hook in its mouth by leaping up and out of the water. This fish stayed in the river and shook its head back and forth, against the resistance of my deeply bowed rod. I let out line as the fish pulled deep into the pool and then slowly reeled in as it followed my line back into the shallows, where it met my net. I lifted its thrashing, gleaming form into the midday sun.

It was a longnose sucker, a species that spends most of its life in the depths of Lake Superior and other deep northern lakes but heads inland briefly each spring to spawn in feeder rivers and streams. To midwestern roughfish anglers, few species are more elusive than the longnose. Found primarily in Lake Superior, it represents the clean, unspoiled north woods. And because it swims up rivers only briefly to spawn, the longnose sucker is rarely caught by anglers.

I was lucky the fish were actively hitting nymphs that day. Suckers continued to hit the Pheasant Tail for the rest of the afternoon, biting more fiercely as the water warmed in the spring sun. Moving downstream, I found several suckers from 2 to 4 pounds in each pool. Only occasionally did a small pesky rainbow trout break the rhythm of drifting and then hooking, fighting, landing, and releasing suckers.

With a brace of 3-pounders for dinner filling the back of my vest, I walked up to the car and headed home. In a few days the suckers would head home, too, returning to the depths of Lake Superior.

August have fine meat if kept on ice. The way to get the best taste out of any fish — whether it is a sucker, gar, walleye, or bowfin — is to put it on ice the moment the fish is caught.

Probably the only thing that keeps suckers from being as popular as crappies for food is their bones. Suckers are bony, and there is no getting around that fact. The trick to bypassing the bones and getting to the sucker's white, sweet meat is to not fry suckers like you do walleyes or bass, but to use one of the following methods.

Rundi Myklebust and Tom Twohing spent a hot August afternoon hammering white suckers on the upper Mississippi River. Bait: nightcrawlers. Line: 6-pound-test. Location: riffles below pools.

Steaming. Clean the sucker, and cut off the head and tail. Put the body on a rack in a roasting pan that has an inch of water, 1 cup wine, some chopped celery, oregano, and a bay leaf on the bottom. Cover, bring liquid to a boil, and steam 10 minutes or so. Take the fish out. The meat will easily flake off the bones with a fork.

Microwaving. Cut off the head and tail. Put the fish in a shallow glass dish with ½ inch water and 1 tablespoon butter. Microwave 3 minutes. Turn the fish over and microwave another 3 minutes. The meat will flake off the bones easily with a fork.

Smoking. Brine the body of the fish in 1 cup salt, 1 cup sugar and enough water to cover the fish. Put in refrigerator overnight. Dry the fish. Smoke in a wood smoker 4 hours. The bones soften in the smoking process.

Pickling. This process also softens the bones enough to eat. Cut 3 pounds of sucker into bite-sized pieces. Add enough white vinegar to cover the fish, along with ¾ cup canning salt. Mix, and let stand in the refrigerator 5 days, stirring the mixture each day. Rinse well and cover with cold water. Let stand 8 hours in the 'fridge and drain. In a separate pot, mix and bring to a boil ¾ cup sugar, 1 tablespoon pickling spice, ¾ cup dry white wine, ¾ cup water. Add raw onion rings and 1⅓ cups white vinegar to mixture, and pour over the fish in a shallow casserole dish. Refrigerate 48 hours. Eat.

Grinding. Fillet the fish. Grind the fillets with celery, potatoes, onion, and bread crumbs. Form into patties. Fry or broil. The bones are all ground up so you won't feel them, and the calcium is good for you.

Scoring. Scale the sucker. Fillet as you would any other fish, leaving the skin on. Run a knife crossways through the fillet almost to the skin, making a cut about every ¼ inch. Fry the fish in oil. The hot grease will fry the cut bones, making them delicate and easy to eat.

Canning. This process makes the bones soft and easy to chew and digest. To keep the fish from spoiling, it is essential when canning to process in a pressure cooker for at least 100 minutes at a pressure of 10 pounds.

Cut fresh or smoked sucker fillets into strips, and pack tightly in pint canning jars, within an inch of the top. Add 1 teaspoon salt, ¼ cup vinegar, ¼ cup tomato cocktail sauce, 1 teaspoon brown sugar. Put cap on jar and screw band down tightly. Pressure cook the fish at 10 pounds for 100 minutes or 15 pounds for 80 minutes. Fish is ready to eat. Use as you would canned tuna.

RECIPES

Sucker Casserole au Vin

Preheat oven to 450°.

Cook 2 cups noodles until tender.

Drain 1 pint canned sucker.

Grease a medium-sized casserole dish. Alternate layers of noodles, fish, noodles, fish, and noodles. Pour 1 can condensed mushroom soup seasoned with Worcestershire sauce, good red wine, and curry powder over the top layer of noodles. Cover with buttered cornflakes or cracker crumbs.

Bake until crumbs are golden brown, approximately 30 minutes.

Sucker Pudding

Boil 6 medium potatoes, unpeeled, in salted water. While potatoes boil, slowly add 16 ounces canned sucker to a blender at medium speed.

Add ½ cup milk, 1 tablespoon at a time, and 3 tablespoons olive oil. Blend until smooth.

Peel cooked potatoes, mash and whip until fluffy with ¼ cup butter, ½ teaspoon dry mustard, salt, pepper, and sucker purée.

Turn mixture into a well-foiled, 5-cup fish mold. Chill 2 hours.

To serve, unmold and frost with mayonnaise. Garnish with cucumbers, shrimp, lettuce, hard-boiled eggs, and parsley.

Great Balls of Sucker

Grind 1 pound raw sucker fillets. Mix with ⅓ cup butter, ½ cup potato flour, and salt and pepper. Grind this mixture 8 times.

Add 2 cups milk slowly, beating all the time. Beat in 2 eggs.

Form mixture into small balls. Drop into boiling water, cooking slowly for 5 minutes. Drain. Serve warm or cold.

—TD

4

Freshwater Drum

"Is the sheepshead a better walleye? Yes, it is."
— A MINNESOTA ANGLER

IN THE SPRING OF THE YEAR, a low rumbling noise emanates from certain lakes and rivers of the Upper Midwest. An angler hearing this mysterious rumble and accompanying grunts cannot find the source at first, but after careful listening will realize they well up from under water.

It's the male drum, croaking away as part of its mating ritual. The sound comes from a male drum rubbing a unique set of tendons and muscles across its swim bladder, similar to an inflated balloon. Fisheries scientists believe that during the spring, female drum swim towards the males they hear calling from a distance.

Many of the drum's nicknames such as thunder pumper, croaker, grinder, and bubbler refer to this sound. On Lake Winnebago, Wisconsin, the noise produced by big drum in June resembles "a motorcycle gang racing in the distance," said one fisheries biologist there. James Gowanloch commented in *Fish and Fishing in Louisiana*, "The members of this family are peculiarly able to produce quite vigorous sounds, so vigorous indeed that a school of drum, swimming past an anchored boat can awaken a sound sleeper."

Just because the drum is the noisiest fish that swims doesn't mean it's not one of the tastiest. In 1758, the French historian Le Page Du Pratz wrote in *Histoire de la Louisiana*, "The casse-burgo is an excellent fish; it is usually 12 to 18 inches; its body is round with gilded scales; in its mouth it has two bones shaped like a file, with which it crushes the shells Burgo, a fact that has given rise to its name. Its flesh, though delicate, is very firm; it is best eaten with red wine."

It would come as no surprise to anyone who has eaten them that the fish Du Pratz was describing over 200 years ago is the drum. Its light-colored, bone-free meat, like that of a walleye, is delicious in casseroles, soups, with sauce, or simply broiled and served with butter and lemon.

Another peculiar characteristic of the sheepshead is its two otoliths. Although many animals, including humans, have otoliths, the drum's are particularly large. These white, circular calcareous stones located in the fish's inner ear look like half a thick clam shell. Grooved into the rounded surface is a shape that resembles the letter "L." The stonelike otoliths are located on either side of the fish's head in sacks lined with sensitive hairs. When the drum rolls onto its side, the stones move around, pushing on the hairs, which send signals to the brain. In this way, the drum can tell

"The drum is a better walleye," says Tom, shown here battling a stubborn 4-pounder from his float tube in the middle of the Mississippi River. "They fight harder, taste better, and are easier to catch."

Taken from Nebraska's Carter Lake, this big drum contains two otoliths over 1½ inches wide — big enough to make belt buckles.

small holes that presumably were strung together as necklaces or bracelets. Drum otoliths have even been found buried in the Southwest of the United States, where the species is not native. Cultural anthropologists suspect the stones were carried there by aboriginal natives and exchanged for items that were rare in the Midwest. At the beginning of this century, otoliths were used as a preventative and cure for colic. The stone was hung around the neck of the sick person until the ailment went away. One winter, Tom taped an otolith to his forehead to cure a mild hangover. He said it worked, because the next day he felt fine.

Natural History

Freshwater Drum
Aplodinotus grunniens
Aplodinotus means "simple back" in Greek and refers to the fish's long, joined dorsal fin, and *grunniens,* also Greek, means "grunting."

how its body is oriented, even in large expanses of muddy water where it can't see a thing.

Large specimens of drum have otoliths as large as 1½-inches wide. In *Fishes of Minnesota Region,* Samuel Eddy wrote that in the 1920s, any boy in the Upper Midwest "who had any prestige" carried a pair of otoliths in his pocket and called them "lucky stones." Tom and I each carry an otolith, marked with an "L" for "Lucky," in a pocket for good luck while fishing, driving, and filling out the Publisher's Clearinghouse Sweepstakes.

Eddy also reported that large numbers of otoliths have been collected by anthropologists from excavations of ancient encampments, indicating that Native Americans were eating drum thousands of years ago. Besides using the drum for food, Indians used otoliths as jewelry and money. Anthropologists in Wisconsin have excavated ancient otoliths pierced with

The old Louisiana French name for drum — *casse-burgo,* literally "to break a clam"— refers to the species' ability to crush the shells of mollusks. It evolved into the name commonly used today for drum in Lousiana, gaspergou. Drum are also called sheepshead, bluefish, and crocus, as well as white, silver, rock, or gray perch, and Canadian bass.

The freshwater drum is one of the most biologically sophisticated fish that swims in the United States. Its eggs float on the surface of the water until they hatch; its highly developed inner ear provides balance in muddy water; it can detect vibrations from a lateral line that extends from its head through the tail; it can call its mates; and it has the greatest north-to-south range of any freshwater fish in North America. The gar and the bowfin are sort-of living fossils; at the other end of the evolutionary chart for fish swims the freshwater drum.

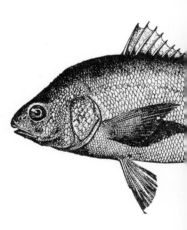

The freshwater drum is a remarkably adaptable creature. It has the greatest range from north to south of any North American freshwater fish. The Mississippi River watershed is the heart of the drum's range; from there it is found north to the Nelson River in Manitoba, south along the east coast of Mexico to the Rio Usumacinta in Guatamala, east in Lakes Erie and Ontario and Lake Champlain in Vermont, and as far west as the Missouri River in the Dakotas.

The drum is shaped like a largemouth bass, except for a high, sloping forehead and a compact tail. A blunt snout hangs slightly over the lipped mouth. Its scales are heavy to protect it from predators. This armor has helped drum withstand attacks from the sea lamprey, a parasitic fish that invaded the Great Lakes and killed most game fish there.

Another distinct feature of the drum is its lateral line, a thin dashed stripe running down the length of the fish's body from the gills to the back of the tail. No other North American spiny-rayed fish has a lateral line that runs across its tail. The lateral line is an organ, which the fish uses to detect vibrations of food and enemies. Having such a long line, the drum gains an advantage over other fish because it can live in muddy water and feed at night.

The sloping head, lips, and long lateral line make the drum easy to identify. However, not everyone pays close attention to the fish they catch. In 1964, an 11½ pound "smallmouth bass" won the Molson Export Big Fish Contest in Ontario. The fish stands as the record for the contest, but it is not recognized as the official provincial record smallmouth because some fisheries biologists believe the fish was a drum. Jerry Smitka, who keeps angling records for Ontario, said that after the fish was weighed a biologist asked to confirm it as a bass. The proud record holder refused to show the fish to anyone, leading many local anglers to conclude it was a drum, many of which also live in the lake where the fish was caught.

Drum are found in a variety of waters, especially those that are shallow and open. A hard bottom and calm to moderate current, in both lakes and rivers, are where drum are usually located. Found in the shallows of streams and lakes, sheepshead rarely enter water over 40 feet deep. They prefer clear water if given the choice, but can survive well in muddy water. They feed using their well-developed senses of taste, smell, and touch.

Drum have unique mouths, not located underneath like a sucker's or jutting forward like a walleye's, but in between these positions. This mouth position enables drum to feed on many different types of food. A young drum, like a smallmouth bass, feeds mostly on insect larvae such as mayflies and caddis flies. As the fish grows older, it switches to crayfish, snails, clams, and minnows. A drum often enters rocky areas where it uses its high snout and forehead to flip stones so it can capture dislodged insects, crayfish, and darters. Tough

Range of the drum

pharyngeal molars at the back of the drum's mouth crush the hard shells of snails and clams.

When a female drum spawns, she releases about 300,000 floating eggs. The eggs, unique among North American freshwater fish, often drift hundreds of miles with the currents until they hatch. The floating eggs have helped give the drum a wide geographic range.

Freshwater drum spawn when the water temperature reaches 65 to 70 degrees Fahrenheit in the spring. This can be from March to July, depending on where the fish is living. Drum gather on the surface in open water, their backs sticking out. At times, when groups of fish crowd together, some are actually squeezed completely out of the water.

Although the average drum is about 2

pounds, they can get much larger. Twenty-pounders are taken from the Mississippi River each year, and the world record is 54½ pounds, caught in Nickajack Reservoir, Tennessee; a 46-pound fish was caught in Spirit Lake, Iowa; and a 36-pound, 8-ounce fish was caught in South Dakota's Missouri River. A 10-year-old sheepshead from Lake Erie averages 17½ inches and weighs about 2 pounds. There is some evidence that fish from the Ohio River grow faster than those from Lake Erie. Nonetheless, a large sheepshead over 10 pounds has been around for many years and should be released with care.

Fishing for Drum

Is the drum a better walleye? Yes, when you consider that drum fight harder, taste as good, have as few bones as walleye, and are more abundant. Yet for some reason anglers look down on drum. Tom Boland, a fisheries biologist for the Iowa Department of Natural Resources, says "The freshwater drum is one of the most underrated sport fish. If the value or worth of a sport fish has anything to do with its fighting ability, catchability, and palatability, then the drum should rank much higher as a desirable fish." This doesn't mean that no one fishes for drum: They rank a high fourth in both commercial and sport catch in the upper Mississippi River, and in the southern United States the drum is a highly prized sport fish.

Although southern anglers pursue the drum for food and sport, most anglers in the Midwest have no idea the drum is so worthwhile. Once Tom and I watched a man fishing below a dam on the Minnesota River use his landing net to scoop fish trapped in a pool and throw them to a flock of white pelicans floating on the water. As we walked down to where he was fishing, we noticed he had caught and placed on a stringer several small white bass and bull-

Drum are beautiful fish that yield boneless, white, tasty fillets. We often take home a stringerful for a meal of Egyptian Gaspergou or Drum Rolls.

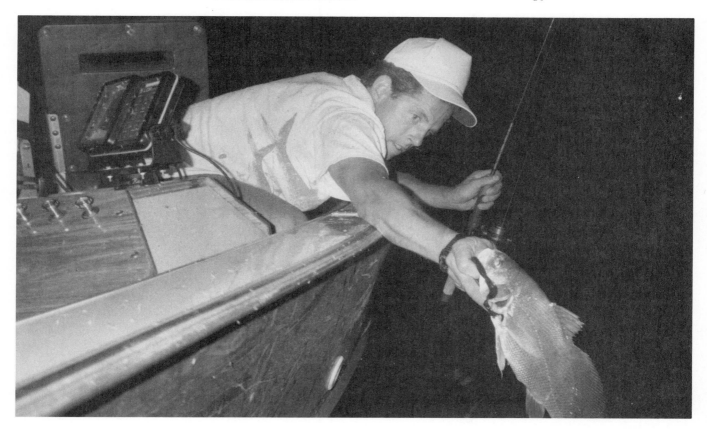

heads. The fish he was throwing to the birds were drum. I asked him if he'd ever kept the drum to eat, and he replied, "No, I didn't know you could." Had he known about the fine-fleshed drum, they most likely would have been on his stringer, too.

Until I caught my first drum, I didn't know a thing about them, either. I was fishing the St. Croix River upstream from Taylor's Falls, Minnesota, wading up to a dam about a mile from the bridge where I parked. From downstream, the dam did not look promising. Barely a trickle of water flowed over the face, and the streambed below was a jumble of dry boulders, between which only thin lines of water flowed. A dam blocks the upstream passage of migrating fish and, by the action of the falling water, often produces a deep plunge pool be-

low its face. This is what I hoped to find, if I could only make it through the slippery rocks leading to the dam.

The St. Croix, a tributary to the Mississippi, holds dozens of catchable fish species. As a new arrival to the Midwest from New Hampshire, I had never seen many of these fish, let alone caught them. I was filled with a sense of exploration and discovery as I slipped past the final boulder. At the base of the dam was a large, deep pool. After watching the water carefully, I began noticing nice-sized fish cruising the depths where the sun penetrated the water, but I had no idea what they were.

I rigged my hook with a nightcrawler, knowing that few fish will refuse this bait. The smell of warm river water, rich and fishy, made me hopeful. I cast into the foamy flow, and let

Dave Greer uses a depthfinder to locate drum structure: rocky or sandy flats with few weeds.

my 'crawler drift to the depths. Immediately, I felt light, rapid tugs on the end of my rod. I let the fish take line and, counted 1-2-3 before setting the hook. The fish made one powerful run and several short ones before I could bring it into the shallows. Its thick body glowed an iridescent silvery-blue as the sun caught its side.

The fish slid easily onto the smooth slab of rock at my feet. It had a high, sloping forehead; white-lipped mouth; and a small, round tail. I had no idea what I'd caught. Then the fish croaked, making a sound like a wet hand rubbing on tight rubber. Suddenly, it occurred to me the fish looked almost exactly like the saltwater drum, or redfish, that I had caught many times before off the Texas Coast in the Gulf of Mexico, where I'd fished with my grandfather. What was it doing miles from the ocean, I wondered.

I fished the pool late into the afternoon catching many different species of fish:

Tom hoists a stringer of eating-sized drum taken on nightcrawlers. We often still-fish for drum on the banks of rivers, propping our rods in the classic English style.

smallmouth bass, channel catfish, carp, and even my first sturgeon, but the most abundant, largest, and intriguing were the strange freshwater croaking fish. I caught dozens of these, between 3 and 6 pounds.

On my way out that evening, I saw a lone angler below a bridge release a nice-sized fish back into the water. I asked him about his fishing success, and he replied, "Only a few sheepshead." The description he gave me of sheepshead matched the fish I had caught and released earlier. He said he had never heard of anyone keeping them to eat, but I figured if they tasted anything like redfish they had to be great. The next time I caught drum, I cooked them up to test my hypothesis. They were delicious.

One of the best traits of drum is they are easy to catch. The simplest method is to bait a hook with a nightcrawler, pinch on a split shot, and cast out from the bank or boat. Let the bait settle to the bottom and wait. If there

World Record: Do It for the Patch

The world all-tackle record-holder for freshwater drum is Benny Hull. Sarah Hamweh holds two fly rod records for longnose gar. And William C. Cumming is the international champion of American eel fishing.

To become a world record–holder yourself, and join the ranks of these famous anglers is a lot easier than you might think. All it takes is a little research and average angling skill.

Hard to believe? It is, unless you know a thing or two about world records and line-class categories.

Most records you read about are "all-tackle" records. That means they are for the biggest fish legally caught on a hook and any-pound-test line. But there are plenty more record categories than all-tackle. In fact, each freshwater fish species has up to 30 categories of records, many unoccupied. The vacancies are most apparent in the roughfish categories. Roughfish anglers may not get on the cover of *Sports Afield*, but they have the best chance of getting a world record.

Take freshwater drum (sheepshead), for example. According to the Freshwater Fishing Hall of Fame, one of two world fishing record-keeping organizations, the all-tackle world record for drum is 54 pounds, 8 ounces. Good luck trying to top that. But in the 15-pound-test line category, the record is only 1-pound, 9 ounces. That's a record any angler could break—if he or she knew about it.

And that's where the real skill in world record fishing comes in. The first thing a would-be roughfish record-holder must do is get a record book and locate the categories that are either vacant or are filled with relatively small fish. Fly rod tippet classes are relatively recent categories in the record books, so many fish species have no entries under the fly rod categories.

How do you get a record book and submit a world record?

1. Write to either the International Game Fish Association (3000 E. Las Olas Blvd., Fort Lauderdale, FL 33316) or the Freshwater Fishing Hall of Fame (Box 33, Hall of Fame Drive, Hayward, WI 54843). The choice is up to you, but you can't enter a record with both organizations. We recommend the Hall of Fame. If you submit a world record to the IGFA you get a little card for your achievement. The Hall of Fame sends you a certificate, a pin, a shoulder patch, and a jacket patch the size of a dinner plate. Why catch a world record if no one knows about it?

2. Find a category that looks like you might have a chance of catching a record.

3. Catch the fish.

4. Have a witness sign your world record application, which comes with your record book.

5. Have someone take two good color photos of you holding your fish.

6. Take the fish to a bait shop or butcher shop and have it weighed on a certified scale. Have the person who weighs it sign the application.

7. Have the fish species varified by a certified fisheries biologist.

8. Send the application, photos, and 50 feet of line you used to catch the fish to the record-keeping organization.

9. Wait until your record is verified and then start bragging.

Drum relate to structures just as walleyes do. On a big river, that might mean a channel marker.

you suspect holds schools of drum. Rig your line with a medium-sized hook (number 4 to 8 bait-holder), crimp on a split shot or two, 18 inches above the hook. You should use just enough weight to keep your bait gently tapping on the river bottom. Bait your hook, and cast upstream of your target structure. The current will carry the bait to the river bottom right to where you suspect the fish are.

If you are after trophy drum, try fishing with a 3- to 4-inch crayfish. Fish the big waters where trophy drum have been caught in the past. Check with your state fisheries agency for a listing of state record drum and where they were caught. If you just want to catch lots of nice eating-size fish, listen to the story told to me by Keith Sutton, a writer for the Arkansas Department of Fish and Game, and follow his advice:

"The first time I fished for drum was in the summer of 1978, when my little boy and I were fishing oxbow lakes off the White River. We had been fishing for bream, but hadn't done any good, so I thought we would stop at a little stream that came in and toss out a nightcrawler. Well, as soon as I did, a drum hit, and in the next several hours we caught one after another.

"We went back again, but this time we went out and fished the river. Once again we caught dozens of fish, averaging 2 to 3 pounds. Now we fish drum a lot and we always catch fish. It is structure fishing—we look for deep holes on the outside bends of streams, dropoffs, or anything underwater that's unusual and might hold fish.

"I almost always use nightcrawlers and have had good luck fishing all times of the day. That's one thing that I like about drum; they'll hit even in the middle of the day when nothing else is biting. Sometimes, in the hot part of the summer, I'll take my boys out and we will catch as many as 200 in a day, and rarely does a fish go less than 2 pounds."

are drum in the water, it won't be a long wait. When you feel a strike, set the hook quickly; if you let the fish run with the bait for long, your hook will become imbedded in its tough pharengeal teeth, making it difficult to remove.

When fishing lakes, look for concentrations of fish over rocky or sandy flats, free of thick aquatic vegetation. In rivers, productive fishing areas include rocky wingdams, riprapped banks, pools below dams, and eddies next to the main current. On the upper Mississippi, anglers often refer to drum hotspots as "perch holes."

Drum become more aggressive as water temperatures rise, becoming easy targets for anglers during the dog days of summer, a time when whitefish and eelpout are sulking in the depths. Wading the rivers for drum can be one of the most productive fishing methods during a hot day and a great way to cool off. Wade into position across stream from the structure

"I'd been told all my life that drum weren't good to eat, that they were real bony. But one time I said, 'I'll see for myself.' I filleted some, fried them up, and found there weren't any bones at all. I like the meat; it is firm and holds together when you cook it. We like to boil the fillets in salted water for 2 to 3 minutes and dip them in cocktail sauce."

Fly-fishing for drum is another productive technique. Drum seem to hit a fly best when the water is heating up rapidly for the first time in early summer. Fish in clear water that has high numbers of drum. Some effective fly patterns include the black Woolly Bugger and dark stonefly nymphs, in sizes 4 to 8. Use a split shot on the leader to get the fly down to the bottom. Strip the line in with a moderate, steady speed and a tight line. We have seen schools of drum chasing bait fish at the surface of a river; a fast-moving streamer would be effective in this situation.

Drum readily hit hardware, too. One spring evening on the lower Chippewa River in Wisconsin, drum, catfish, and carp were savagely striking green Mister Twister jigs just at dusk. Tom and I were casting the jigs into the foaming water below the spillway of a dam and retrieving rapidly. Almost every cast brought a strike. The mystery of what species of fish had struck added to the excitement. About half the fish we hooked were husky drum between 2 and 5 pounds.

Plugs, spinners, and spoons can also catch drum. Keep your lures near the bottom and use a slow retrieve. Bend the barbs of your hooks down, so you can release fish faster and injure fewer fish. When you get into a large concentration of drum, the action can be fast and furious—a fish a cast for as long as your arm can take it.

In some lakes, drum become so abundant that state agencies try to net them out to increase the population of other desirable fish. Drum in Lake Winnebago, Wisconsin have been netted since 1955 in a project designed to increase the population of walleye. For 10 years an average of 2.8 million drum were removed annually. Since 1985 a study has been underway to determine if this netting is helping populations of walleye and other fish. Some fisheries professionals believe removing drum from a lake like Winnebago, which has ideal drum habitat, is a waste of time and money. Ron Bruch, who is in charge of the netting project, says it is too early to tell if the removal is helping other fish populations increase in either size or number. He plans to double the

I couldn't control my joy after catching 5 drum in 15 minutes at the Ford Dam near downtown St. Paul.

netting effort and then study the game fish and look for changes.

Even with all the netting, recent population estimates show there are still about 50 to 70 million pounds of drum in Lake Winnebago, making this lake a drum angling hotspot. The fish netted from the lake are sold either fresh to local stores and restaurants or processed and sent to food shelves for distribution to low-income families.

Drum for the Table

The freshwater drum, or sheepshead, is a member of a large family of fish called the drums (*Sciaenidae*). There are 33 species of drum in the United States, of which the sheepshead is the only one to live in freshwater. The saltwater drums are among the most popular game fish along the eastern and Gulf coasts. Over 43 million pounds of black drum are caught every year off the Atlantic coast by sport anglers, and in Texas the commercial red drum (redfish) season was closed because sport anglers noticed the population and average size of their most prized saltwater game fish was dropping. Other popular species of the drum family include the speckled trout and the sand trout (also known as weakfish). In appearance, the freshwater drum looks similar to its saltwater cousins. The red drum is redder and has a longer profile. The black drum is a little darker and has a wider body. One distinct similarity is the flavor and texture of the flesh. Louisiana blackened redfish is a popular gourmet seafood dish; an almost identical dish can be prepared using freshwater drum.

Tom and I both recognized the great potential of sheepshead for the table several years ago while fishing in the Mississippi River upstream of St. Paul, near where we live. We had been fishing for trout most of the spring. Looking for some new fishing experiences and a good shore lunch, we decided to try the "Great River." We caught and kept several walleye, channel catfish, smallmouth bass, and sheepshead to eat. After filleting, the fish all looked the same—firm and white—so we decided to do a taste test. I kept the fishes' identity secret while I cooked and served them. Tom and our friend Wade both had difficulty detecting any differences in the flavor of all 4 types of fish. Drum was as good as bass, catfish, and the Minnesota state fish, walleye. We had found a fish that was abundant and easy to catch. And because of their abundance, keeping a few drum for lunch would not harm the population.

Kelly Linehan, an angler from Minneapolis, had been catching freshwater drum for years before deciding to fillet one out and fry it up. "It was fantastic," he admitted. "I had heard they taste good, but we had no idea how good. We fried the drum with a mess of crappie fillets, and to be honest, except for the size of the fillet, we couldn't tell the difference."

Freshwater drum are among the finest eating fish in the Midwest. They are easy to clean and cook, and are high in protein and low in fat. A freshwater drum fillet contains 16 to 18 percent protein and 2 to 6 percent fat, the same amount of protein and less fat than a similar-sized portion of beef. The ideal eating-size drum is between 2 and 4 pounds, large enough to clean easily, yet young enough to not have acquired any toughness or fishy flavor. The flesh is flaky, white, and firm. It can be prepared in many ways.

When you catch a fish for the table, keep the fish alive on a clip stringer, and put the fish on ice immediately when removed from water. To clean a freshwater drum, fillet it as you would a giant sunfish or crappie. Next, skin the fillet, and remove any fatty or dark tissue. Cut out the rib bones, and rinse the fillet in water briefly. (Always dry your fish fillet with a paper towel after rinsing; this wipes away bacteria that can give the fish a bad taste). The result is a clean fillet of bone-free meat, ready to be prepared in any number of ways: broiling, pan frying, poaching, or baking. Drum fillets, like those of burbot, don't hold up well in the freezer; eat them within two weeks.

RECIPES

Drum Roll

This simple sandwich is an easy and tasty way to eat drum for a shore lunch.

Roll 6 drum fillets in a mixture of ½ cup flour and ½ cup crushed crackers. Fry in ¼ inch of cooking oil over high heat for 5 minutes, turning once when light brown. Remove fish from pan, drain. Place each fillet on a sandwich roll. Top with a tomato slice and tartar sauce.

Drum Cocktail

This is a good summer dish because you can cook the fish in the morning, when it's cool, and refrigerate for later use.

Cut fish fillets into ½-inch wide strips. Drop into boiling salted water. Cook for 5 minutes. Remove from water, rinse under cold water to stop cooking, drain, and refrigerate to chill.

Serve on a bed of lettuce with your favorite cocktail sauce. (The fish can also be served hot, dipped into melted butter.)

Egyptian Gaspergou

Another tasty shore lunch idea has a touch of the Middle East.

Cut 6 drum fillets into 1-inch-wide strips. Roll ½ cup in dry felafel mix. Fry in ¼ inch of olive oil over high heat for 5 minutes. Drain. Place in pita bread with chopped tomato, cucumber, and onion. Top with Gaspergou sauce.

To make sauce, mix ¼ cup tahini, ¼ cup plain yogurt, and the juice of ½ lemon; add salt, pepper, and cayenne to taste.

Crocus Ceviche

This popular Mexican dish comes originally from Polynesia by way of Elisabeth Ortiz, a great Mexican cook. The citric acid in the limes "cooks" the fish. This is a great way to prepare many types of fish. The result is both spicy hot and refreshingly cool—a great combination.

Cut 8 drum fillets into small 1-inch squares, and arrange in a deep dish. Cover fish with juice of 6 limes. Refrigerate for 6 hours, turning once halfway through. Drain juice and reserve.

Combine with reserved lime juice 1 peeled and chopped tomato, 1 small diced onion, 2 fresh diced jalapeño peppers, ¼ cup olive oil, 1 tablespoon white wine vinegar, and, to taste, parsley, oregano, salt, and pepper. Pour over cold fish. Refrigerate until ready to serve.

Fresh Drum à la Portugaise

This is an easy dish to serve to your friends from Portugal. They will wonder where you learned it, since there are no freshwater drum in the entire European continent. Tell them that it's a secret.

Place 4 drum fillets in a heavy sauce pan. Add 1 crushed clove of garlic, 1 finely chopped onion, ½ cup chopped parsley, 1 sprig of thyme, 3 peeled, seeded, and chopped tomatoes, ½ cup dry white wine.

Bring to a boil, then reduce heat. Cover and simmer gently 10 minutes. Remove fish and keep warm on a serving dish.

Turn up heat and reduce liquid by one-third. Add 1 tablespoon unmelted butter bit by bit to the liquid, swirling the pan to mix (do not use a spoon to mix at this stage).

Pour sauce over fish, garnish with fresh parsely, and serve at once.

—RB

5

Carp

Carpe diem.
—Latin for "Seize the day."

Carpe carpium.
—Latin for "Seize the carp."

PEOPLE have long been singing the praise of carp. In China and Japan, this strong, intelligent fish has been a symbol for nobility, honor, and courage for centuries. In Europe it was a food reserved exclusively for European royalty during the Middle Ages, and today, it is still prepared meticulously by *cordon bleu* chefs in that continent's finest restaurants and hotels. In Britain, more anglers pursue carp than pursue any other species. An English "carpman" fishes from 1,000 to 2,000 hours a year, and calls it a good season to hook and land a dozen of the wary fish.

Yet here in the United States, the carp, also known as common carp, German carp, Israeli carp, German bass, buglemouth, brown bass, and hoselips, is widely ignored. And when noticed at all, it's held in disdain.

Why do most American anglers look down on a fish esteemed throughout the rest of the world? Why do they grimace at the thought of eating a fish served in fancy Parisian hotels, and roll their eyes at the suggestion they pursue a quarry prized by millions of anglers across the Atlantic?

Old World and New World Carp

The relationship between carp and American anglers began 4,000 years ago, when the Chinese first noticed the carp in its native Yellow River, which runs from west to east through central China. Each spring, carp make a spawning run up the river's tributaries, a long and arduous journey requiring the fish to leap barriers and burrow up rapids to reach their destination. The Chinese, admiring this dogged display of courage and perseverance, adopted the carp as a symbol for strength and nobility. They also began raising carp for food and ornamental displays. As is still done today, certain species of carp were held in rearing ponds outside homes and fattened for the table. Other species were bred to exaggerate colors that made them attractive pets in garden ponds.

The Japanese, heavily influenced by Chinese culture, began using the carp symbol in the 10th century. Throughout the Japanese Middle Ages, carp adorned the banners carried by samurai to symbolize the strength of this

"A carp released is a carp that can be caught again," I say to myself while releasing a beefy 8-pounder taken on a Hare's Ear nymph. Although rarely practiced today, catch-and-release might be the only way to keep this species from being fished out in popular carp waters.

Carp are native to China, where the whiskered fish are admired as a symbol of courage and nobility. Carp flags such as this one are still flown in China and Japan to bring good luck and strength to newborn children.

warrior class. Carp flags and kites that fluttered in the wind to represent fish swimming upstream were flown at boys' festivals to inspire young men to overcome obstacles and reach their goals. Parents still fly the carp flag at births to bring their children strength. In Asia, the carp remains a symbol of honor and courage on pottery, drawings, screens, and paintings.

No one knows exactly the original range of carp, other than this fish is native to Asia and the Asian watersheds of the Black, Caspian, and Aral seas. A hotly contested subject of debate among carp historians is whether the species is native to western Europe. One argument says no, because there are no records showing

carp to be in the western part of the continent before the Middle Ages. Others say that because the fish is known to be indigenous to the Black Sea, it could have traveled up the Danube as far as Germany.

Records show carp first being introduced to the ponds of Austrian nobility in 1227; however, there are also records of carp being transferred to Greece and Italy during the Roman Empire a millennium before, and the writings of European monks show that throughout the Middle Ages carp were reared in ponds at castles and monasteries. Dr. Frank M. Panek wrote in *Carp in North America* that carp might possibly be native to portions of western Europe, and are probably indigenous to the eastern part of the continent: "There is no evidence to support the common belief that [the carp] was introduced to Europe from an original range in China."

That the spread of carp throughout Europe increased during the Middle Ages is accepted by all carp experts. Nobility and clergy demanded meals of carp. The fish were held in ponds in the cellars of monasteries, where they were fattened with milk and bread until killed for the table.

Carp were brought to England in 1496 exclusively for the use of royalty. When some escaped from rearing ponds into rivers and canals, King Henry XIII offered rewards to those who could bring "carpes to the king." In 1653, Izaak Walton wrote in *The Compleat Angler* that the carp "hath [not] been long in England."

As the standard of living for the average European and Englishman improved, so did the availability of carp. Carp became a food of the bourgeoisie, and many who emigrated to the New World left Europe having developed a taste for the rich fish.

Imagine the surprise of well-to-do arrivals to America in the mid-1800s who asked for carp at restaurants and fish markets and found

Range of the common carp

the fish didn't exist here. Jews, accustomed to preparing carp for geifilte fish, were aghast. So were many Scandinavians, Belgians, Austrians, French, and Germans who served carp at weddings, Christmas, New Year's, and birthdays, and had assumed the land of milk and honey would have carp as well.

Incensed, they wrote to their new government and demanded that carp be made available. In 1876, Dr. Spencer F. Baird of the Smithsonian Institution, head of the newly formed United States Commission of Fish and Fisheries, began receiving requests from citizens for carp. By 1880, the commission was getting 2,000 letters a year.

These requests were timely; Fisheries Commissioner Baird was looking for a fish to import into the new country to replace the fast-disappearing native species. During the mid-1800s, native fish were being netted by the millions of pounds from the Illinois, Mississippi and Ohio rivers and shipped to markets in the burgeoning cities along the East Coast. At the time, fish were seen as a resource like timber and coal to be harvested and sold. The commercial depletion of fish coincided with indiscriminate logging that was turning hillsides bare, allowing rains to wash the exposed topsoil straight into the streams and rivers. This silted-in spawning gravel used by fish such as suckers and walleyes, and hid food from sight feeders such as bass and burbot.

Wetlands along river bottoms were leveed and drained, depriving northern pike and buffalo of spawning grounds. Channelization (the dredging of navigational lanes in rivers for the passage of ships) eliminated holes, dropoffs, breaks, riffles, snags and other fish-protecting structures in rivers and turned them into massive featureless canals where fish couldn't find anywhere to hide or locate small fish to eat.

If the netting and changes in the river and landscape weren't enough, towns were popping up along the rivers and dumping their

waste straight into the water. Bacteria from human and animal effluent ate up oxygen needed by many species like the greater redhorse, sauger, and drum, which began to die out.

The nation's leaders became alarmed that the rapidly expanding country would soon run out of a fisheries resource. In 1871, President Grant appointed a fish commission to oversee the country's fisheries; its first task was to find a way to shore up the flagging fish stocks. Although the commission members knew the nation's native fisheries were being ruined by human development, it would have been politi-

The man who officially brought carp to North America: Dr. Spencer F. Baird, head of the United States Commission of Fish and Fisheries. In the early 1880s, Baird was receiving 2,000 letters a year from citizens requesting carp for private ponds.

cally unwise to recommend that pollution, overfishing, wetland drainage, and logging cease. Instead, the federal government decided to find new fish species that could replace or at least supplement those dying out.

Baird wrote to Europe and received information on a variety of fish, notably the carp. He was impressed with what was being done in Europe and Asia, where the carp was a cash crop rivaling grain and livestock in sales and protein content. In his 1874 report, Baird wrote that the common carp would thrive better than most native fish because it fed on vegetable matter. While only partially correct (like trout, carp eat mostly insect larvae), such a revelation was enough to encourage more research. Two years later, Baird noted in another report further benefits of carp such as rapid growth, adaptability, harmlessness to other fishes, and good table qualities. Since sportfishing wasn't popular at the time, the commission didn't even need to mention the carp's strength, size, and sporting qualities to convince Congress to appropriate money to import carp from Germany and begin a program of raising and distributing the fish to points throughout the westward-expanding nation.

In 1877, the commission imported 345 common, mirror, and leather carp and placed them in ponds in Baltimore, where they were raised by Maryland's fish commissioner, T. B. Ferguson. The next year, some of these fish were transferred to ponds near the capitol in Washington, D.C., where soon they had produced over 6,000 carp fingerlings that were shipped to 273 applicants in 24 states. The spread of carp in North America had begun.

The U.S. government can't be credited with the first introduction of carp to the continent, however. By the time the bureaucrats finally got around to importing carp, a citizen of the Golden Bear State had been raising the species in his backyard for 5 years. Julius A. Poppe, of

By the 1920s, the Mississippi river had become one of the world's best carp fishing hotspots. This angler, beached on sand flats below the 3rd Avenue bridge in Minneapolis, holds a carp recently caught in the river.

Sonoma, California, had taken matters of fish farming into his own hands and in 1872 had gone to a commercial operation in Reinfeld, Germany to purchase 83 carp. When his ship reached California in August of that year, only 5 carp had survived. But they were hardy survivors. The handful of 6-inch fish he placed in a pond at his home had grown to 16 inches long and produced over 3,000 young by the following May.

As early as 1876, Poppe had a thriving fish farming business and was receiving more for his fish than he ever thought possible. He wrote to fish commissions around the nation, urging them to establish carp ponds to satisfy a hungry nation. "Every fish that I can possibly send to market here sells readily at one dollar per pound," Poppe claimed in a letter to the Minnesota Fish Commission in 1876. He recommended that a fish farm be established in each county to raise stock carp to sell to fish farmers, who would hold the fish in ponds or canals to fatten for market. "It would be a cheap but sumptuous food and at the same time very convenient, as they are ready to be eaten at all times of the year."

Midwestern fisheries managers didn't need to hear much more than that to be convinced that carp were the best thing to arrive from Europe since the brewery. But they had to wait several years before receiving any of the prized fish from the nation's capital. The Midwest got its first carp in 1880, when 75 were shipped from Washington D.C. to the Nevin hatchery in Madison, Wisconsin. In 1881, 163 carp fingerlings were distributed to individuals throughout the state. By this time, Baird had made Minnesota the distributing point of carp for the Northwest. Elated, Robert Sweeney, president of the Minnesota State Fish Commission, wrote to persuade Minnesota Governor Hubbard that the benefits of receiving carp would far outweigh the burden of the new responsibility: "While it would very materially

increase our labors, it enables us to secure a liberal share of these desirable fish for our own State's waters, and which we willingly accept as the compensation for our additional work and distribution."

The first fish distributed in the region only went to prominent citizens who had lobbied the federal or state fish commissions. Carp were too precious to be stocked in public waters. When Dr. S. P. Bartlett of Quincy, Illinois reported that carp were caught by hook and line in the Mississippi River as early as September 1883, he was asked if the carp had been planted in the river. He replied, "As we value carp too highly to experiment with them by putting them into the river, those taken must have escaped from live boxes or from ponds. It nevertheless demonstrates the practicability of eventually stocking our streams with this wonderful fish."

It didn't take long for others to follow Quincy's advice. Within the next 2 years, every major river in Illinois had been stocked with the newly imported fish. The city council of Ripon, Wisconsin passed an ordinance prohibiting fishing in all waters within the city limits to protect recently stocked carp.

Many state fish commissions had been started in response to the alarming disappearance of native fisheries. The carp appeared like a gift from heaven. It was good to eat, prolific, and could survive in rivers that were getting dirtier by the day. States wanted as many carp as they could get from Washington to propagate in their own ponds. The Minnesota Fish Commission report of 1883–84 read, "The increasing demand for the German carp . . . induce us to make renewed efforts to facilitate the reproduction of this generous grower and prolific fish."

Carp can live and spawn in practically all types of water, so it didn't take long for them to dominate many rivers and lakes. After only 4 years of being stocked there, carp were being

caught by commercial anglers in the Illinois, Missouri, and Mississippi rivers. Dr. Bartlett reported that in 1893 one fisherman from Illinois caught 27,000 pounds of carp in two 700-yard seine hauls. In 1894, 453,000 pounds of carp were caught in the Upper Mississippi River alone.

At first, the profusion of carp met with a receptive market. Sweeny wrote in his 1888–90 report that carp "are now to be found almost daily on the stalls of the fish dealers of St. Paul and Minneapolis and to the great satisfaction and gustatory enjoyment of many of our foreign-born citizens." The new arrivals pouring into the United States snatched up carp from fish stalls in cities like St. Louis, New York, Boston, Chicago, Kansas City, and Philadelphia, too.

For a while, the availability of carp to the huddled masses didn't lessen its appeal to the rich, who still considered the fish a delicacy. In the late 1890s, expensive hotels and restaurants in New York City were serving "Carp in Rhine Wine Sauce," a dish costing more than halibut or kingfish. But sometime around the turn of the century, carp started to lose favor with the well-to-do, who presumably began noticing on their strolls to the office that the have-nots were carrying the same species they had recently eaten at the Waldorf. America's upper class quietly switched from eating carp to fish less accessible to the poor.

"Carp are now to be found almost daily on the stalls of the fish dealers of St. Paul and Minneapolis," wrote Robert Sweeney, president of the Minnesota State Fish Commission in 1890, "and to the great satisfaction and gustatory enjoyment of many of our foreign-born citizens."

People think the goldfish is a carp, but it isn't. A goldfish is also in the minnow family, however. Both carp and goldfish have been raised domestically in Asia for thousands of years, carp primarily as food fish and the goldfish as ornamental fish. The goldfish can be distinguished from a carp by its lack of barbels. Also, goldfish have no pharyngeal teeth. The goldfish that swim wild in the United States were introduced from emptied pet bowls. They don't do too well in the wild because they are not as hardy as common carp; however, there are scattered populations throughout the United States.

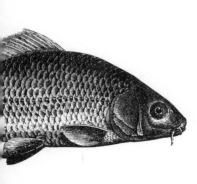

Meanwhile, many people were noticing that American-bred carp didn't taste as good as those raised in Europe. There, the raising of carp was a science, refined over thousands of years. The fish were carefully crossbred like cattle and hogs to create superior-tasting strains. In the late 1880s, the Austrian princes of Schwarzenberg, at the time the most extensive carp farmers in the world, had ponds that collectively covered 20,000 acres. The fish farmers in the United States, on the other hand, were mostly amateurs who tried to make a quick buck by dumping carp into anything that held water. Their shallow ponds filled with stagnant water produced muddy-tasting carp.

"Complaint is made sometimes that [carp] taste of mud, which is not to be wondered at, considering how little care and attention they receive to make them palatable compared to the pains taken in Europe to give them improved quality and flavor," wrote Sweeny in 1886. Seeing the connection between water quality and the eating qualities of carp and other fish species, he added, "It should be borne in mind that good water makes good fish."

Most states stopped stocking carp in the mid-1890s. A majority of the fish farmers had given up the carp trade and moved on to more lucrative ventures. Either they couldn't keep the carp alive in ponds, produced poor-tasting fish, or couldn't compete with commercial anglers, who were hauling carp in from public waters that had been stocked intentionally or accidentally. By the early 1890s, midwestern commercial anglers each year were shipping hundreds of tons of carp to eastern states. Fish farmers couldn't begin to raise a fraction of that. Fetching only 3 cents or 4 cents a pound (a far cry from Poppe's boast of a dollar a pound), carp had become so plentiful they had literally outgrown their value.

About this time, people began noticing that as carp numbers were exploding in rivers and lakes, the populations of game fish hadn't rebounded at all, and in fact had continued to deteriorate. Why, they wondered, are carp doing so well and bass and sauger so poorly?

Standing on clear-cut hillsides with a bucket of garbage in each hand, they looked down on the rivers, saw carp swirling happily in the mess humans had created, and made a correlation—albeit the wrong one—between the rise of carp and the fall of game fish. Either ignorant of or blind to the damages they themselves had wrought on the landscape, people looked past the dredged and straightened channels, drained wetlands, eroded river banks, and waters laden with human and industrial waste, saw carp roiling in the shallows, and accused them of wrecking the water.

The carp was the perfect scapegoat. It was foreign. It was thriving. And it couldn't defend itself.

The claims against carp were not without foundation. Carp do muddy waters and uproot vegetation searching for food. They have dominated some fisheries, crowding out species like bass and bluegills and increasing turbidity to the point that walleyes have a hard time seeing food. In several lakes in the Midwest, carp have been proven to uproot vegetation so much that wave action increases, causing even more turbidity. This blocks sunlight from reaching underwater plants, turning a shallow lake into a bowl of muddy water. With no food to eat, ducks move elsewhere.

Yet such instances are relatively uncommon. Carp are found in almost every fishery in the nation, and most still have plenty of good fishing. In most lakes, carp reach a balance with the other fish species. Most fisheries scientists who've studied carp agree that changes in land use have hurt game fish more than carp ever could. Carp are simply able to survive in water that is slower, warmer, and more turbid and polluted than most other fish can stand.

At the turn of the new century, however, no one understood this. People believed if they could only get rid of carp, the water would clear up and game fish would return. Where only a few years earlier they had been eagerly propagating carp, state fish commissions began trying to poison and net carp into oblivion. It didn't work. Carp are products of the environment, and as long as the water was dirty, the carp weren't budging. As George C. Becker wrote in *Fishes of Wisconsin*, "Unless we are willing to spend millions of dollars to pull out dams and restore the watersheds of our streams . . . we will have carp in abundance."

The fall in carp's glamor didn't mean people stopped eating them. The commercial catch of carp on the Upper Mississippi River averaged about 5 million pounds a year through 1950. Today, 1,000 tons of carp are harvested throughout the country, and carp is is eaten by millions of Americans. In much of Europe, carp remains a delicacy. In Austria, for example, fried carp is still the traditional main dish during the holiday season.

Why Fish for Carp?

Carp aren't just good food, they're good sport, too. Because Rob and I like to hook and fight big fish, the carp is one of our favorites. Carp grow larger than northern pike and sheepshead, they are more powerful than similar-sized redhorse and bass, and are much more accessible than walleye and sturgeon. For beginning anglers hoping to hook their first big fish or angling veterans looking to test their stalking, hooking, and landing skills, no fish satisfies as well as the carp.

Its strength is perhaps the carp's most remarkable of many admirable features. "I would say without a doubt the carp is the strongest swimmer of the warmwater species," said Duane Shodeen, a regional fisheries man-

ager with the Minnesota Department of Natural Resources. "Game fish aren't even close."

When hooked, a gar or a trout makes violent bursts. A mooneye leaps wildly from the water. What a carp does is start moving and keep going, unmindful of the person straining to hold it back. An angler hitching a ride with an 8-pound carp needs excellent rod control to keep the aquatic freight train from taking the bait, hook, and 100 yards of snapped line downstream.

If being powerful weren't enough, carp are also one of the largest fish to swim in North America's inland waters. An average carp

Weekends in the 1920s weren't spent entirely doing the Jitterbug. These fashionable anglers spent the day carp fishing before heading downtown to their favorite speakeasy.

A carp will often make a powerful run just when you think you've got it worn down. I always loosen my drag before reaching down to grab a carp in case it's got a notion to take off.

species is found in a wider variety of water. Every river that runs through a major city has lots of carp, as do ponds, natural lakes, artificial impoundments, the Great Lakes, creeks, streams, marshes, bogs, shallow lakes, and almost anything else that holds water. What's more, carp are fish of shallow water, making them easy to reach for anglers who don't have boats. Kids, seniors, and disabled anglers usually have the same chance of latching onto a rod-bending carp as a college athlete in a bass boat does.

Just because carp are easy to find doesn't make them easy to catch. Sure, at times they'll bite as eagerly as bluegills, but more often than not you have to work to get a view of that whiskered snout. We have gone out many times expressly to catch carp and returned home without a fish. Even when we found them, too often they wouldn't bite, no matter what we threw in their paths. Carp are one of the spookiest fishes that swim, scooting for cover before you even get within casting range if you're not quiet and move slowly.

The first time Rob took me carp fishing he moved like a cat, crouching to keep a low profile, while slipping from tree to tree along the shore.

"Rob," I said. "What are you —"

"Get *down*," he hissed.

I did.

After slowly working closer to the carp he'd sighted sunning in the shallows of a small lake, Rob took one cast with his rod and quickly stripped in his nymph. No luck. Before he could toss off another cast, I stood up to see what was happening, and spooked the fish into the deep water.

I learned more about carp fishing from the look Rob gave me than I would have reading a dozen books on the subject.

Another feature of the carp that makes it challenging is its sensitive mouth. Carp usually feed on the bottom, sucking in a mouthful of

caught by anglers runs 3 to 12 pounds. Many anglers admit their largest fish ever taken on hook and line wasn't a muskie, salmon, or sheepshead — but a carp.

We've hooked several over 15 pounds, and have seen some monsters — big carp of 20 and 25 pounds. The current world record for carp, taken in France in 1987, is 75 pounds. A fish of 83 pounds was netted in South Africa, and a 74-pounder was netted in Pelahatchie Lake, Mississippi.

The midwestern states' records range from 26 to 61 pounds, about the same as for muskellunge. The big difference is: Carp of that size are within a short drive for most anglers and muskies aren't. Carp of 20 and 30 pounds are accessible to every angler who holds a rod. No fish is more widespread in its range, and no ooze, water, and bottom matter and then spitting out all but the edible nymphs, crustaceans, snails, clams, insects, and leaves that make up most of their diet. When a carp takes a bait like a doughball, it holds the offering in its mouth for a few seconds, feeling and tasting to see if it's worth swallowing. Too much resistance from a weight, heavy line, or premature attempt to set the hook, and the fish drops the ball.

To catch a carp an angler must be diligent and fish with a light hand. It requires constant attention. This is no pike that pulls a bobber halfway across the lake or a bullhead that tugs and tugs and tugs at the bait until it impales itself on the hook. The carp is one of the most intelligent fish that swims.

That's why a big, round bobber works about as well for catching carp as a foghorn does for calling ducks. If the bobber's splash doesn't spook the wary fish, its resistance when the carp swims off with the bait certainly will. English anglers, who have sophisticated carp fishing techniques, use a thin quill bobber (called a "float") that moves at the very lightest touch and offers practically no resistance to a nibbling fish.

Because the carp is a light biter, it's also important to use light line. This lets you toss your bait far without having to use a big sinker, and offers little resistance to the fish when it takes your bait. A big fish like a carp caught on light line is a challenge to land. When hooked, a carp slowly moves away and then begins the surging run towards the nearest snaggy cover. A carp will wrap line around a log or lily pad just as a bass does, and when caught in rocks or riprap it will head into a crevice or hole and wrap your thin line around rocks and boulders.

Once caught, the carp is a superb food fish, with a rich-tasting meat. For anglers accustomed to the bland taste of walleye, the carp may seem too rich. But for those who ap-

preciate a wide range of seafood, the carp is a delicacy. Eaten throughout Asia, Europe, and the United States, carp continues to be one of the most popular dishes served in the world. In France, carp are bred in Sologne and then shipped live in trucks to Germany where they are used to make Hamburg carp pâté. In Alsace-Lorraine, carp are filled with cream stuffing, poached in white wine, and served with boiled potatoes and sauerkraut garnish.

British and American Carp Anglers

Although there are some carp anglers in the United States, in most waters the big, bronze fish is ignored or despised. It's a completely different story in Europe and England, however. There, the carp is third only to brown trout

In the summer of 1988, British carp angler Richard Dawson fished nonstop for 7 weeks in Michigan. He was amazed so few Americans were fishing for carp with such a profusion of superb carp water available.

Roughfish as Art

Roughfish have beautiful shapes, markings, and scale patterns that can be captured by printing the fish on paper. The art of fish printing, called *gyotaku* (ghee-o-tah'-ku) began in Japan in the mid-1700s. *Gyotaku*, which means "fish rubbing," is practised by anglers to keep exact records of their catches, and by artists who spend years refining their techniques to create the most lifelike prints possible. Gyotaku is a wonderful art to learn because even a beginner can create a fairly good-looking image.

Materials

1 fresh fish
15 pieces of large newsprint
1 tube of black water-based ink
1 one-inch-wide brush

1 tiny brush
straight pins
modeling clay.

Preparing the fish

The best fish to print are flat and have nicely defined scales. Carp and carpsuckers work great; burbot don't.

Wash the fish thoroughly with soap and warm water to remove all mucus, blood, and dirt. Pat it dry and place it flat on a table. Plug the fish's openings (anus, mouth, gill slots) with pieces of paper towel so fluids don't leak onto your print.

Spread the tail and fins out, and stick pieces of clay underneath to support them. Use pins to hold the fins in place. Let the fish dry, using a hairdryer to speed it up if you want.

Printing

Once the fins stiffen, remove the pins and slip playing-card-sized pieces of paper between each fin and the clay.

Brush ink that has been lightly mixed with water over the fish from head to tail, making sure the fins, scales, and lips are covered. Don't paint the eye.

Remove the pieces of paper from under the fins.

Now, carefully lay a piece of newsprint onto the fish. Press down firmly, rubbing the entire fish from end to end with your fingers.

Lift off the paper and voila! You've done *gyotaku*.

Paint the fish again and print more sheets. A fish can usually be printed about 7 or 8 times per side.

When the prints dry, use the small brush to paint in the eye. Leave a bit of white in the iris to make it look as if light is reflecting off the eye.

and Atlantic salmon as the fish most desired by sport anglers. In Britain, experts who catch a "twenty" (20- to 29-pound carp) or "thirty" (30- to 39-pound carp) are idolized just as professional bass anglers are here.

Izaak Walton fished for the "queen of rivers" in the early 1600s, advising anglers that the carp was one of the most difficult fish to catch: "If you will fish for a Carp, you must put on a very large measure of patience, especially to fish for a river Carp: I have known a very good fisher to angle diligently four or six hours in a day, for three of four days together, for a river Carp, and not have a bite."

Midwesterners used to seeing hundreds of carp splashing in a shallow lake will wonder that any angler ever waited so long to catch a carp. British anglers find nothing extraordinary about such waits between bites. For a die-hard English carp angler, a typical fishing trip begins weeks before the actual fishing. The water is carefully studied, "boiles" (high-protein cooked bait made with eggs) are laboriously prepared, and fishing areas are chummed for several days before the rods are even uncased. Serious carp anglers set up camp along a canal or pond with a tent, called a "bollywrap", that stretches over an umbrella that is always nearby in case of rain. Experts and novices ("noddys") alike will sit for days from dawn to dusk

staring at the line indicators on their 2 rods, waiting for a carp to take the bait.

The long waits between bites in Europe and England indicate a carp more finicky than those in our waters. Because there are many carp anglers and few carp waters, carp in Britain and Europe are caught and released so often they become warier than trout that swim in the most heavily fished fly-only waters. In the files of the British Carp Angler's Association's London office are records of individual carp that have been caught hundreds of times. In waters managed exclusively for carp swim fish that are caught 5, 10, even 30 times in a single season. Anglers even give recognizable carp individual names.

Carp caught so often are not stupid. Just the opposite. They are extremely cautious. They are captured frequently simply because of the tenacity and sophistication of the anglers who pursue them. The average carpman in England fishes between 1,000 and 2,000 hours a year. He often fishes for days at a time, around the clock, in the hope of catching a single carp. This devotion makes even our most fervent bass anglers look like weekend dilettantes.

A Briton's 10- or 11-foot rod allows light baits to be cast far, enables a quick line pickup, and gives the angler the shock absorption to resist a powerful run without breaking light line.

"Sacre bleu! Le carpe, c'grande!"
—What Monsieur Leo van der Gugten probably said when he first first caught sight of his world-record 75-pound carp on May 21, 1987, while fishing Lac de St. Cassien in France.

The classic English-style carp outfit: long rod and spinning reel loaded with light line, mounted on two rod holders. Note the plastic ring bite indicator, used on windy days.

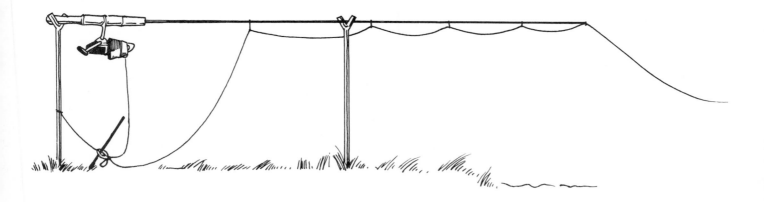

Rods are set on 2 rod rests (see illustration), one holding the end of the handle, the other about halfway down the rod. The bail is left open, and the rod is pointed slightly down from horizontal so the line flows from the spool with as little resistance as possible. The line a foot or so from the spool is connected to an alarm for night fishing or slipped into a slit in a piece of paper or plastic foam (try a piece of foam cup), and then is pulled from the spool just enough to let the indicator rest lightly on the ground. A string is tied to the indicator and attached to the rear rod support, so that when the hook is set and the line tightens the indicator doesn't fly away and litter the area.

The only trouble with this still fishing setup is that when the wind blows, so does the indicator. That's why on breezy days English anglers use a small plastic ring as an indicator. A bicycle spoke is pushed into the ground at a 45 degree angle towards the water and the ring, tied with a loose slip knot, is slipped down over the spoke. When a carp takes the bait, the ring slips off the spoke. When the angler sets the hook, the slip knot comes undone and the ring falls to the ground, out of the way.

English carp anglers use weights, but not as we do in the United States. They squeeze tiny shot the size of coarsely ground pepper grains every inch or so from the hook on up. This technique, called "ledgering," allows the weight to take the bait down but offers little resistance to a carp picking up the bait, because the weight is spread out along the line.

Not all carp angling in Britain is so refined and complicated. Many anglers fish for carp much as we do in the States. Mathusi Van Rensburg, of St. Paul, Minnesota has fished for carp many times in England with his brother and cousin, both avid English carp anglers. "We'd usually just carry a light bag and a rod and reel," he said. "One of the most effective techniques we used for carp was to simply fish bread on the surface."

The British may be the best carp anglers, but they have no monopoly on carp fishing skill. Bill Richars, of St. Louis, Missouri, has been fishing for carp since 1963, when he caught one in a pay-to-fish pond in Illinois. "It weighed 4 pounds and fought like nothing I'd ever seen before," he recalled. "I've fished for and caught only carp ever since. Caught my 5,000th carp on Labor Day, 1984."

Richars, who is 85, uses the British still fishing technique that has been slightly Americanized. At either of 2 county park ponds near his home, he sets up his folding chair and fishing rods on shore near a spot where he has consistently caught carp. Rod holders stuck in the bank hold his 3 (legal in Missouri) 6½-foot rods rods horizontal, pointing to the water. A Zebco 808 reel loaded with 20-pound-test line is mounted on each.

Richars figures he averages about 200 carp a year, averaging 6 to 7 pounds, fishing each day from exactly 10:00 a.m. until exactly 2:30 p.m. from mid-May until early October, when the water gets too cold for the carp to bite. "Once the temperature gets below 50 degrees, that's it for the carp."

Instead of a standard hook and split shot, Richars uses a rig he invented himself that is unlike anything used for carp we've ever seen. Noticing that carp sometimes have a hard time finding a bait that has settled in the mud on the bottom of the pond, Richars developed a hook–weight combination that makes the hook stand up a few inches above the bottom (see illustration).

Using a single kernel of canned corn on each hook, he casts to an area he's chummed (also legal in Missouri), and then sits back and watches his line. It usually doesn't take long: "I'll be sitting there in what I call my 'office,' gazing at the line, when a loud click on one of the Zebcos goes off. That tells me a carp has picked up the corn. Now, the way the rods are set, straight at the fish, there's nothing to hold

Kitty Welch, who with her husband owns the Café Carpe in Fort Atkinson, Wisconsin (1 hour south of Madison), says the popular folk singer Greg Brown stops by the cafe each summer to fish the carp-rich Rock River and play a gig that evening. "The first time he came here he strolled in and asked, 'Where are the fish?' I sent him out to the dam, but I don't know if he had any luck," she said. Call 414/563-9391.

back that carp going with my corn. *I* have to hook *him*, you understand. So I reach over and grab the line and pull it back hard, to set the hook. And that's when the 'hallelujah' begins!"

Once the fish is hooked, Richars lifts the rod quickly from the holder and carefully begins to work the fish towards shore. "You let the rod do the work," he explained. "He takes that first run and gives you that 1–2 that could snap the line if you don't let him run with it. He's the boss the first 3 or 4 minutes. He might go 100 feet before you can turn him."

After 10 to 15 minutes of gently working the fish toward shore, Richars reaches for his 7-foot nylon landing net and slides it into the water: "If the carp catches sight of the net he'll take off and you'll have to start all over again. That's one thing I love about that guy."

Richars releases every carp he catches "to give a buddy a chance to catch him." His affinity for the fish causes Richars to scorn anglers who use too light a line, which causes the carp to break off. "It's the conservationist in me," he says. "I visualize that poor carp, and I wonder when he'll be able to dislodge that hook and all that line in his mouth."

Another Missouri carp expert is Richars's fishing partner, "Carp Man" Dan Geigerich. A self-proclaimed carp fishing fanatic, Geigerich was the first American member of the British Carp Study Group, an exclusive club that admits only experienced, successful carp anglers, and then only after review by a committee. Geigerich was recently named secretary of the Missouri chapter of the Carp Angler's Association (CAA), a broad-based carp fishing club for novice anglers, based in London. Joining CAA chapters already established in Georgia, New Jersey, and Michigan, the Missouri chapter will be devoted to promoting an awareness of the qualities of carp fishing in the United States and importing the fishing techniques used by British and European carp anglers. "I have no doubt in my mind that the carp is go-

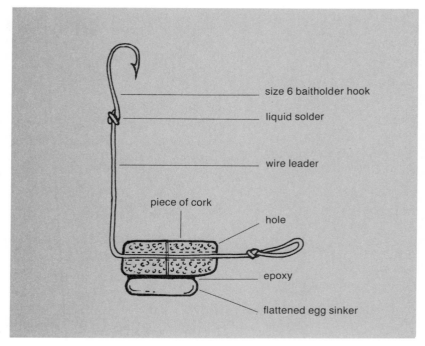

size 6 baitholder hook
liquid solder
wire leader
piece of cork
hole
epoxy
flattened egg sinker

ing to be very big in this country within 5 years," said Geigerich.

While many American carp anglers are happy to use homemade doughballs, Geigerich has extensively researched British boiled baits and has even received instructions directly from Fred Wilton, the Englishman known in his country as the father of the HNV (High Nutritive Value) bait.

"In Britain, carp baits are extremely sophisticated, the result of years of scientific study," says Geigerich. He gives the ingredients of a HP ("High Protein") bait as 4 ounces milk product protein, 1 ounce sodium caseinate, 1 ounce Aquavit (a mineral supplement for horses), 1 ounce soy flour, 2 ounces gluten (a wheat byproduct), 1 ounce of blood protein, and 5 large eggs. "To that you add flavoring, like strawberry or vanilla."

Not all Geigerich's carp baits require keys to the science lab. "Bread works real well, except that it falls apart," he remarked. "What I do is use a bagel, cut into cubes, because it has

If you fish lakes with soft bottoms, try making Bill Richars' standup carp hook rig. Epoxy a piece of cork to a flattened egg sinker. Drill a hole through the cork and thread a wire leader to which a size 6 baitholder hook has been liquid soldered. Bend the leader so the hook stands straight up, and tie your line to the other end. A piece of corn on this rig sits up about 3 inches from the bottom, in perfect view of cruising carp.

a tougher skin." Geigerich casts the cube into an open spot within a patch of floating vegetation and waits for a carp to cruise up and suck it off the surface. "It's incredible when that happens, the line just screams out."

To Geigerich, the joy of carp fishing is the mix of tranquility and heart-stopping action. "It's magical, there's a peacefulness about carp fishing as you wait for the fish to take your bait. And once you hook into a fish, there's nothing to match the fight you have on your hands."

Fishing for Carp

Carp bite at all times. However, some times are a bit better than others. Dawn and dusk seem to produce the most fish for us, and we find that carp turn off right at sundown, just when the catfish start hitting. Later on in the evening, however, the carp fishing can be fantastic. Many experienced carp anglers do best at night, often just before sunrise. Carp are spooked easily, so try to do without a bright lantern, and if you build a fire, keep in mind

that carp in the shallows can probably see the light.

If you've got a strong heart, try fishing what English anglers call the "marginal patrol"—carp cruising the shallows near a windblown shore at night, feeding on surface matter. First, an angler wads a piece of bread around the hook. Crouched behind bushes on a bank towards which a cruising carp is headed, the angler lowers the bread to the water surface, crust down, and lets it sit lightly on the surface, no line touching. With the bail open and a finger lightly on the line, the angler sits motionless, waiting silently for the carp to approach the morsel.

Those who've been there say the soft "cloop" of the carp can barely be heard as it takes the bread and slips the line from your fingers . . .

We use a 9-foot fly rod blank built with spinning guides and 6-pound-test line on an open-faced spinning reel. There's no need for any weight with this outfit; it'll send a ¼-ounce doughball as far as we need to cast. The long

Catch-and-release carp fishing could be the wave of the future. "I have no doubt in my mind that the carp is going to be very big in this country within 5 years," says "Carp Man" Dan Geigerich, secretary of the newly formed Missouri chapter of the London-based Carp Anglers' Association.

rod is sensitive, gives us good line control, and can absorb the shock of a carp's initial heart-stopping run.

Although some anglers use treble hooks (in states where it's legal), we use plain old Eagle Claw baitholders size 6 or 8. Trebles are simply too big and clumsy and you have to use a handful of dough to cover the hooks. And it's too hard to set the hook with trebles, because you have to pull through all that dough to get a barb into the fish.

On our dough balls we leave a bit of the barb peeking out. That bit of hook will often catch in case the doughball begins to pull out of the carp's mouth. Some anglers say a carp will feel even the slightest bit of protruding hook, but we figure since the fish eat clams and crayfish, the bump of a barb won't spook them too much.

Just because we use custom-built rods and light line for carp doesn't mean anyone else needs to. Carp are caught on every type of outfit, from trolling rods with bait-casting reels to Snoopy rod-n-reel units, from bamboo fly rods to bass-bustin' flippin' sticks.

If you use a bobber, go with either a tiny round one or an English quill bobber. Sometimes a bobber is good for fishing moving water because it can keep the bait from snagging on the bottom. Bobbers work better in moving water than in lakes or ponds because carp hit more aggressively when the bait is moving past them. They suck the bait in so quickly they don't have time to drop it when they feel the resistance of the bobber, giving you time to set the hook.

More has been written about doughballs than on any other feature of carp fishing, because doughballs are extremely effective and anglers love to experiment. There are so many complicated doughball recipes they would fill a thick book. Anglers throughout the United States use extensive tests at home, office, and lab to come up with secret varieties. The ingre-

dients include vanilla, anise, molasses, beer, whiskey, bourbon, strawberry Jello, cornmeal, grated cheese, cinnamon, cocoa, honey, onion, garlic, wheatgerm, cottonseed oil, corn germ, cereal, eggs, crackers, and anything else that tastes good.

Some doughball recipes are as old as sportfishing itself. Walton advises carp anglers to use "pastes," of which he said there "are almost as many sorts as there are medicines for the toothache." We have not tried his recipe recorded in *The Compleat Angler* because it's so hard on cats, but it sounds effective: "Take the flesh of a rabbit, or cat, cut small; and bean-flour, and if that may not be easily got, get other flour; and then, mix these together, and put to them either sugar, or honey, which I think better."

Doughball recipes are as unique and individual as the way you shave in the morning. Don't be content using someone else's concoction. Experiment. Add stuff no one has ever dreamed of before. To get you off on the right foot, here are three recipes guaranteed to catch carp.

I think Izaak Walton's doughball recipe is a little too hard on cats, so I go with a mixture of dough, water, and molasses.

Izaak Walton's doughball recipe called for the "flesh of a rabbit, or cat, cut small; and bean-flour, and if that may not be easily got, get other flour; and then, mix these together, and put to them either sugar, or honey, which I think better."

Rob's Carp Assassin

This is what we use.

Mix 1 part peanut butter, 1 part cornmeal, and 1 part flour. To this add ½ part molasses, ½ part whiskey, and a handful of semi-sweet chocolate chips. Mix and mold into balls the size of grapes.

1-2-3 Doughball

This is easy to remember, so you can mix it up when taking road trips. The ingredients are available in any store.

Mix 1 cup sugar, 2 cups white flour, and 3 cups cornmeal in a large bowl. Slowly add water until the mixture has the consistency of Play-doh. Flatten the glob, wrap in a cloth bag, and cook in a pot of boiling water for 20 minutes. Unwrap, put in a plastic bag, and refrigerate. Knead in additional scents like anise or bourbon after the dough cools. Mold into small balls.

Champion Doughball

Here's another simple one that works all over the country. Don't try to substitute other cereals. Carp like their Wheaties and can discern imitations.

Mix 1 cup Wheaties, 1 cup flour, 1 cup cottonseed meal, 1 cup oatmeal, and 1 cup molasses in a large bowl.

Slowly add 1 cup water and ¾ cup vanilla extract. Mold into small balls.

The number one all-around carp-getter is canned corn. It's better than doughballs, HNV baits, or nightcrawlers. Any brand of corn works, but we use Green Giant because it's canned in Minnesota and we think the fish develop a taste for homegrown food.

Corn isn't all that carp will eat, however. Anything you can find in a grocery store will work, such as gum, lunch meat, canned pet food, canned potatoes, marshmallows, meat, cheese, and vegetables. If you bring a lunch, you won't run out of bait because carp eat anything people do.

One day I was fishing with 'crawlers and couldn't catch a carp to save my life, even though they were surfacing all around me. I happened to have a few old jelly beans in my pocket. The coating had worn off, but the gel was still there. I threaded one on a hook, cast into the pool where I'd been fishing all morning, and within 5 minutes had a carp on.

Remember, no rule in carp fishing is cast in concrete. For example, even though corn is far and away the best carp bait, it doesn't *always* work. One summer, Rob and I were fishing for carp on a hot sultry day in a pool formed when the river had dropped several feet. We could see the carp splashing everywhere around us, but we had no luck with corn. Only after we switched to 'crawlers did the fish strike.

Although live bait isn't the best way to catch carp, it can be done. Rob told me a story about a giant carp he hooked on a 6-inch sucker minnow. After returning from a northern pike fishing trip, and while cleaning out his boat at the dock, Rob cast his last sucker minnow and let it soak on the bottom. "All of a sudden I looked up and my rod, which I had jammed into the end of a metal pipe, was bent double, the reel screaming," Rob told me. "As I pulled out the rod," he went on, "I tripped over a rope, which let the fish jerk the rod from my hands. The rod skidded across the dock and into the water, and I followed. Miraculously,

Having trouble with your doughball staying on the hook? Try tying a "nutter sack," a tiny nylon bag of peanut butter. Take a piece of old pantyhose and cut out a circle the size of a silver dollar. Put in half a teaspoon of peanut butter and tie it up in a sack with thread. The bag stays on the hook, but lets the smell of the peanut butter out to drive the fish crazy.

I caught the rod and clambered back onto the dock. After regaining my composure, I raised the rod tip high and started pumping the fish in. As it felt the resistance of my rod, it rose to the surface to have a look at me. What I saw was a massive carp, much, much bigger than the 28-pounder I'd caught the previous week off the same dock. My excitement turned to horror as the fish began an ever-accelerating run straight for the middle of the lake." Unfortunately, all Rob could do was tighten down the drag and watch his 8-pound-test line melt off the reel. "I'm sure that would have been my first 40-pounder."

Catching carp with bait is always a challenge, but occasionally you'll hit a spot where the fish seem to make it too easy and bite on every cast. That's a good time to try out some artificials.

Carp are omnivorous, meaning they feed on all types of plants and animals. As a result, they take a wide range of lures. We've caught carp on spinners, crankbaits, jigs, and plastic worms, and have heard of them caught on spoons. The world-record carp on 12-pound-test line, a 43-pounder, was caught on a jig.

Carp, like trout, eat mostly insect larvae. Larvae are to fish as clover is to cows. The bottoms of clean streams and rivers are literally covered in small brown, black, and gray nymphs of all sizes, from tiny choronimids as small as fleas to massive stonefly nymphs as big as your thumb. Nymphs can't escape quickly from fish like a minnow can, and they are rich in protein. No wonder carp eat them.

And no wonder carp hit nymph imitations, such as jigs. Contrary to what you might think, however, the key to catching carp with nymph imitations is not to inch them along the bottom as you do for trout, but to reel in quickly. If it's too slow, the carp will engulf the offering, immediately notice there is no taste, and reject it before you know what's happened. But with a quick retrieve, the fish will move up and take

Carp on a jig? Sure. "Carp On" Don Leeper removes a black Mister Twister from a hard-to-hold 6-pounder taken near downtown Minneapolis on a sultry July evening.

an aggressive bite at the lure or fly like a bass does.

"The first carp I caught on a fly, I was stripping in a nymph with a fast hand twist retrieve," said Rob. "I actually saw the carp follow it and suck it in."

In our estimation, no sport for carp tops fly-fishing, especially casting to sighted fish. This means sneaking up on carp in the shallows of lakes or rivers and sending a fly to fish we can actually see—and fish who can see us if we don't keep quiet and stay low. Compared by some anglers to sight-casting to bonefish in the Caribbean, this type of carp fishing demands stealth, accurate casting, and the skill to land a fish on light line.

We've had our best luck with nymph imitations, usually a big, plain nymph like a size 8 Hare's Ear, Woolly Bugger, or stonefly nymph. At times it seems to help if the fly has a bit of color like red or orange. Who knows why.

We've also caught carp on white streamers and on dries, the latter when the fish are

One for the wall—the biggest fish many anglers catch in their lifetime is a carp. Here, a 22-pounder has been mounted as a trophy to bring back memories of a hard-won battle.

"clooping," the English term for when carp cruise the surface and cloop insects, cottonwood seeds, or other items off the surface in the summer. To catch a carp on a dry is the dream of many roughfish fly rodders. I've never done it except in my sleep, but I'm sure one day I'll be there when the cottonwood hatch is on and will send a big White Wulff or Elk Hair Caddis lightly down into the path of a carp sucking cotton off the surface film.

Rob, a much better fly fisherman than I, caught his first carp on a dry years ago, and has taken several since then. "I was fishing a lake west of Minneapolis in the late '70s when I saw a carp taking cottonwood seeds off the surface," he recalled. "I hid behind some cattails and cast a number 10 Adams into the path of the cruising fish. I actually saw him suck it in. It was incredible!

Tom Keith's mulberry fly works well when carp are rising to the *Morus ruba* hatch. Tied with a chenille body, it sinks slowly just like a real mulberry.

"When I set the hook, the fish took off straight across the lake, ripping line from my reel. Finally it slowed and I was able to gain some back, but when the fish got near shore it spooked and all I could do was hold my rod high and let it run. This went on for about 15 minutes before I was able to work the carp close enough to reach down and remove the hook."

The cottonwood hatch comes off in the Midwest in middle to late summer, and it's pretty hard to miss with cotton fuzz floating every time the wind blows. Another seasonal event carp fly rodders don't want to miss is the mulberry hatch, which comes off in late June when the *Morus ruba* ripens and drops berries into lakes and streams from overhanging banks. When the berries are dropping, carp station themselves downstream from the branches and wait for the fruit. In ponds, carp cruise the shallows in the shade of trees, sucking in berry after berry.

Tom Keith, a writer for the Nebraska Game and Parks Commission, ties a mulberry fly to capitalize on the fruit feeding frenzy. He says he first got the idea when fishing with real mulberrys on a private stretch of the Blue River near DeWitt. After experimenting with spun deer hair, which proved too buoyant, Keith settled on a fly made of chenille, which floats for a while and then takes on water and sinks, just like a real mulberry. Keith ties his flies on Mustad 9671 hooks, sizes 6 to 10. He begins by tying in 2 or 3 peacock sword herls at the hook bend, as he would the tail of a regular fly. This imitates the mulberry's green stem. Next, he winds dark purple chenille so it tapers from thin near the hook bend to thick towards the hook eye. This complete, Keith palmers a black hackle feather through the body to give the fly a two-tone look, trimming the fibers to follow the contours of the fly.

To fish the mulberry pattern, begin upstream on the same side of the overhanging

mulberry plants and feed out line until the fly floats among the real berries. Another way is to cast from across stream above the bush and mend line upstream so the fly sinks slowly and naturally. It's important to set the hook the moment you see or feel a hit because the carp will reject the fly the moment it realizes the berry is fake.

Keith also ties a corn kernel fly. On a Mustad 3906B hook, size 10 or 12, he spins yellow deer hair the length of the hook shank and then trims it short into a kernel shape. To finish, he paints the top of the fly with white enamel to imitate the color of a real kernel.

"Fish the corn fly in ponds or lakes where other anglers have been using corn," Keith advises. Cast anywhere near shore where there is colored water. Allow the fly to float a few minutes, and then recast. If you think the fish

are deep, add a split shot a foot up from the corn fly, and work it along the bottom.

No matter where you live—city, suburbs, or country—there's a lake or river nearby with carp in it. The key to finding carp water is to ask around. Go to a bait shop anywhere in your state, and ask where people catch carp. When in doubt, fish below a dam on a big river. In June and July, carp are always stacked up here.

One morning in June, Rob and I were wading the backwaters below a river dam, trying to find a carp to take our nymphs. I cast to likely looking carp spots in the shallows under overhanging branches, but could hook nothing but shrubbery. Rob, on the other hand, seemed to have a carp on every time I looked.

I stopped casting and watched where he sent his fly. The water was turbid, and occa-

I'm a study of determination while competing in the Coon Rapids Carp Festival fishing contest. The winning fish, caught later by the angler to my left on frozen bread dough mixed with peanut butter, was worth a 14-foot boat, motor, and trailer.

Get the best flavor from
your carp fillets by keeping
the fish alive on a stringer
until you're ready to
head home.

the bottom, and prepared to have my shoulder pulled from its socket.

Twenty minutes later I was still casting and still waiting. Rob had caught three more carp and it was time to go. "Maybe you should have tried a different nymph," he said.

Getting blanked while carp fishing is always a possibility. Don't let anyone try to tell you they caught "carp all the time" when they were a kid. No one catches carp all the time. To catch carp as much as possible, however, you can use a few tactics we've found to be effective. The main one is movefishing, which is the opposite of stillfishing.

While stillfishing is certainly fun, and a more relaxing way to fish, it doesn't let you cover much water. We figure, Why wait for the carp to come to us when we can go to the carp? When movefishing, we move along the shore of a lake or up a river from pool to pool, looking for splashing carp or orange fins sticking out from the shallows.

We wear tennis shoes and shorts for wading the rivers in the summer and lightweight stocking foot waders and wading boots in the spring and fall. To keep versatile, we each wear a fishing vest, outfitted with a fly reel in case we see surface-feeding carp, (our custom 9-foot rods have a long cork handle with sliding reel seats that allow us to position our fly reel at the butt or spinning reel in the middle), a flashlight, pliers, one plastic box that hold flies, and another for hooks and sinkers. In one pocket we carry a carton of worms, and in the other a 35 mm film canister of dough or corn.

That's it. Nothing to carry but the rod, nothing to set down, nothing to keep going back for. This way, when we start fishing we can keep fishing until it's time to go home.

Although carp are fish of the shallows, they often go deep, especially at night and at midday. To reach those deep fish, pinch on a few split shot a foot or so above your bait. An even better technique is to pinch on one micro shot

sionally a fish would roll, but for the life of me I couldn't tell why he was casting to the spots he was casting to. Every 10 casts or so, he would hook a carp.

He could tell I was puzzled. "The bubbles," he said, as if that would tell me anything. He waited until certain I hadn't figured it out. "Look at where the bubbles are coming up from the bottom," he continued. "That's where the carp are rooting around the bottom for food."

I looked closely at the brown surface, and sure enough, tiny bubbles were rising in a dozen spots. Keying in on a bubbling area near some willows, I cast my nymph, let it sink to about 12 inches from the hook and then snap on a sliding egg sinker, ¼ ounce or so, that slides freely up and down the line. The weight brings your bait down into the hole, but when the carp takes it there will be little resistance, since only the micro shot is connected to the line.

Cast out, let the bait sink to the bottom, and keep the bail open and your finger on the line at the spool. Watch the line where it enters the water. If it moves in a direction other than the way the current flows, or if you feel on your finger a light peck, release the line for a second or two. When actively biting in warm water, carp sometimes aren't shy about smacking your bait. But ordinarily, they roll it around in their mouth a bit to see if it's worth swallowing. Next, engage the bail, and then lightly, but firmly and quickly, lift the rod tip to set the hook.

We've seen dozens of anglers hook nice carp—and then do about everything possible that's wrong until the line breaks or the hook pulls out and the fish swims away. Most anglers then get mad at their rod or reel and curse their bad luck. The problem is, luck has little to do with landing a big fish. The reason most anglers don't do it well is they catch only a few whoppers a season, hardly enough to learn any type of technique.

What most anglers do when they hook a big fish is try to muscle it in, as though they'd tied a rope to a rock and were hauling it up the bank. When you fish for big fish using line lighter in test than the fish weighs, you simply can't use this winching technique because the line is guaranteed to break. (Why fish light line? Primarily to hook more fish that are leery of thick line.)

The trick to battling a big carp on light line is to tire it out *gradually*. One time I was fishing 6-pound-test line and hooked a lunker that immediately headed downstream. All I could do was loosen the drag and go with the flow, hoping the fish didn't get so far away that my line on the water got tangled in branches and boulders. I raced down after the fish, slipping once on the rocks and dropping the rod as I slid sideways into the water. When I righted myself, the fish was still on, and had stopped in a pool.

It came to the surface, and I saw its head break the water. It was huge—at least 15 pounds. Keeping steady pressure on the fish, I reeled in slowly, tightening the drag so the spool turned easily enough for the carp to take line when it made a dash for the deep water, but not so easily that I couldn't reel line in when it was resting.

With the drag set firmly, I slowly lifted the rod up and backward, carefully pulling the fish towards me. Then I lowered the rod quickly and reeled in the slack. I repeated this at least a dozen times, until the fish was near the shore. As I reached down to grab its gill plate, I realized I had not loosened the drag. A carp that sees its captor often gets a rush of strength and makes another powerful run. My fish made a wild lunge away from my outstretched hand,

Rob visited Japan to study Asian carp fishing techniques. He caught this Japanese angler fighting a 10-pound carp on the Tama River in Tokyo. Note the reel-less rod and long-handled net.

Mirror carp—distinguished by their leatherlike skin and few large scales—are rare in the United States. This 4-pounder taken on the Cannon River in southern Minnesota made a valuable addition to my Roughfish Life List.

and raced off across the pool, while I fumbled for the drag. The line tightened like a drawn bowstring, then went slack.

Another way to play big carp is to flip off the antireverse when the fish has been hooked and play it off the reel instead of off the drag. Backreeling, as this is called, is tough to learn if you are accustomed to using a drag, but we like it for big carp, salmon, steelhead, and sheepshead because of the direct control it gives us, forcing us to concentrate entirely on the fish's motion.

When the fish runs, we backreel just fast enough to play out line that has enough tension to make the fish realize it's not home free and can't escape without a fight. The moment it stops, we reverse direction and begin reeling in, ready to switch again if the fish surges away. If all goes according to plan, there is more reeling in than reeling out, and the fish ends up at our feet.

Natural History

Carp
Cyprinus carpio
Cyprinus is the Greek word for "carp," and derives from the island of Cyprus, from where it was once thought the first carp came to Europe, and *carpio* is Latin for "carp."

Three hundred species of minnow abide in the *Cyprinidae* family. The carp is the largest. Besides its size, a carp can be distinguished from the other minnows by the 2 pairs of barbels at the corners of its mouth, 35 to 39 large scales along the lateral line, and molarlike pharyngeal teeth in its throat used to grind up snails, mollusks, and crustaceans.

Three kinds of carp swim in the United States. The most well-known is the common carp, which is bronze-colored on the top and white on the bottom, has orange dorsal and

pectoral fins, and is completely scaled. The mirror carp is brown and looks like about two-thirds of its huge scales have fallen off its smooth, leathery skin. The grass, or Amur, carp is more elongated than the other three, and has a mouth at the front of its head rather than below.

The common, mirror, and leather (a fish with no scales, completely covered in a slick, brown skin) carps are varieties of the same species and were brought to this country in 1882 in the original carp shipment to Washington, D.C. We know of no leather carp still surviving in this country. Some mirror carp are still swimming around, however. I caught one several years ago in a clean tributary of the Mississippi.

You name it, carp swim in it: Great Lakes, massive reservoirs, tiny ponds, small lakes, rivers, streams, marshes, bogs, even some tidal rivers. The ideal carp habitat is shallow, weedy, warm water with good cover and a muddy or sand bottom. Carp are mostly found in cloudy water, being shy and preferring habitat that has lots of floating debris.

Carp stick near the same types of structure that other fish do, like overhanging logs, drop-offs, eddies, stumps, and holes. In the late spring and early summer, carp congregate where streams flow into rivers or lakes before they run upstream to spawn.

We've seen carp swimming happily in clean wilderness streams and in smelly urban rivers. Although carp thrive in turbid, polluted water, the fact that they do well in the waters where humans store their garbage reflects the species' tolerance, not its preference.

One reason the carp can thrive in almost any type of water is it has keen senses of smell, hearing, and taste, allowing it to find food and escape predators in water too opaque for sight feeders to survive.

Taken from unpolluted water, the carp is one of the cleanest fish that swims.

Sometimes carp fishing is as easy as baiting a hook and reeling in a fish. But pursued with a fly rod, carp will challenge even the most experienced angler.

Its hearing is enhanced by what is called the "weberian apparatus," a unique series of small bones and ligaments that link the carp's swim bladder to the inner ear. The swim bladder of the carp works as a resonating chamber to amplify sound waves that reach the body and send them to the brain. So sensitive is the carp's hearing, it can detect a tuning fork sounded softly underwater 200 feet away. The carp can hear an angler walking along riffles far earlier than a bass or walleye can.

The sense of smell is highly developed, too. An old folk saying advises anglers to never throw back the first fish they catch because it will warn the other fish to swim away. This could be true with carp, because as with all minnows, large cells in the skin release chemicals into the water when the skin is damaged by a predator. When other carp smell this, an alarm goes off that makes them scatter.

Carp have a sense of taste like that of higher animals. The fish has specialized taste buds in its mouth, lips, barbels, snout, and throat that are linked to its brain. Carp can distinguish between salty, bitter, sweet, and sour flavors, preferring the latter two.

One thing that makes carp such a pleasurable fish to pursue is its continuous eating schedule. Carp must keep eating because they have practically no stomach. A pike can swallow a sucker and then rest while the fish is digested in its stomach and then passed into the intestine to be absorbed. For a carp, the feeding, digesting, and absorbing is all one continuous process, forcing it to constantly patrol for food.

In the spring, carp usually begin feeding when the water is about 39 degrees Fahrenheit, moving into the shallows, where the waters warm first. The warmer the water, the more active the carp, and more likely they'll take after a lure. Carp like water at 84 degrees best, but they'll still actively feed when the water is 100 degrees. Once the temperature drops below 60 degrees, they'll bite bait, but not as aggressively, and will ignore lures. In the fall, carp stop feeding when the water gets below 50 degrees. In the winter, they go deep and are rarely caught by anglers.

Anglers rarely catch small carp because the small fish feed mostly on plants. Once mature, carp primarily eat nymphs, crustaceans, and shrimp, and also rootlets, seeds, algae and plant fragments. Carp sometimes suck in game fish eggs, but it is usually done while the fish is searching for more nutritive food. Carp prefer to feed at the bottom of water less than 10 feet deep, but will eat suspended zooplankton, and in the morning and evening they often rise to the surface to feed on floating insects and seeds.

When the water reaches 41 degrees, carp begin moving upstream to spawn. Almost as strong as a salmon, a carp will burrow up strong rapids and leap small waterfalls to reach its spawning grounds, water about 2 feet deep. In lakes and reservoirs, carp seek out shallow bottomlands and marshes or flooded timber.

Spawning starts when the water hits 63 degrees and continues for several weeks. Carp spawn randomly in groups of about 2 or 3 females and up to 15 males. Females drop their

Interested in setting up a chapter of the Carp Angler's Association in your state? Send a SASE to "Carp Man" Dan Geigerich at P.O. Box 1862, St. Louis, MO 63118.

The Carp Fest, in Coon
Rapids, Minnesota, is one
of the largest fishing
festivals in the Midwest.
Visitors can play Pin-the-
Barbel-on-the-Carp, dine
on Carp Kabobs, and
picnic while watching their
bobbers dance on the
Mississippi River.

eggs over rooted vegetation and algae, and then males cover the eggs with sperm. Neither sex makes a nest or guards the eggs or young. As a result, carp have to lay a lot of eggs. A 20-pound female will drop more than 2 million at a time. When carp spawn, they splash around a lot. Not only are they having a good time, but the splashing helps mix the eggs and sperm.

Carp Cuisine

If you catch carp from clean northern lakes and rivers or from trout streams, you'll likely end up with delicious fillets. Taken from clean water, carp are actually cleaner than most other fish because they have fewer parasites than fish like walleyes and salmon.

Many people believe a carp tastes muddy because the fish feeds on the bottom. Occasionally, a carp does taste bad. This comes from industrial contaminants, human waste, and other pollutants in the water that are absorbed into the fish's blood stream and the fatty and dark areas of the meat like the blood line. If a carp comes from turbid or polluted water, it will probably have taken on some of the smell, just as a walleye or bass from the same water would. In Austria, live carp bought at the market are put in the bathtub with clean water trickling in for a day before the fish are killed. This works for any fish, and can take the muddy taste from a carp even when caught in midsummer.

For most of us, however, keeping a fish alive in the tub is impractical. The next best thing is to keep your carp alive on a stringer while you fish. String it through the lips, not the gills. If the fish is hooked deeply, cut the line rather than rip out the hook, because a fish will survive with a hook imbedded in its throat but not with a gash there.

When it's time to go home, kill the fish by knocking it on the head. Chop off the head and tail, draining out as much blood as possible. Split the belly, pull out the entrails and gills, and wash the blood from the body cavity. Put the fish on ice.

Unlike walleye and sheepshead, which can be filleted in the same time it takes to zip a jacket, carp take a few extra minutes to clean and prepare. For many connoisseurs, it is worth the trouble.

With the fish on its side, fillet it by cutting straight down just below the gill plate, as though you were going to cut its head off. Stop just before you reach halfway and turn the blade sideways, towards the tail. Run the knife parallel to the spine. Flip the fillet over, and, with the skin side down, run your knife along the bottom of the fillet to cut it from the skin. You are left with a perfect fillet. Cut out the dark vein, which runs down the side, and all the dark red meat just under where the skin was. This flesh contains the most oil and blood and is what carries any bad flavor.

The bones of a carp are a great mystery to anglers. They are hard to find when filleting, but sometimes show up inside your cheek during dinner.

Once the rib bones have been sliced off, you can remove half of the carp's other bones (see illustration) by making a deep incision the length of the outside of the fillet along the lateral line and then another one from the top of the fillet to cut a long V-channel from the fillet. This removes the 20 Y-bones and 6 straight bones above the lateral line. Below are 4 Y-bones and 13 straight bones. These can be broken up by slicing two-thirds of the way down through the fillet every quarter inch. When the fillet is fried, the hot oil seeps into the incisions and softens the bones enough to make eating a pleasure.

If your refrigerator is full and you want to have carp on hand throughout the year, you can preserve carp several ways:

Smoking. Scale the fish. Fillet, keeping the skin on. Soak all night in a salt solution that will float an egg. Rinse the fillet in fresh water. Smoke in a smoker 4–8 hours at 170–180 degrees.

Pressure cooking. This is a good way to soften the bones. Partially cook the fillet by broiling in the oven for a few minutes on each side of the fillet. Pack the fillets closely in clean jars to about 1 inch from the top. Add 1 teaspoon of salt to each quart jar. Don't add water. Cap. Pressure cook according to cooker instructions.

Pickling. This is a super appetizer that's sure to have your friends begging you for the recipe. Pickling gives carp a tangy sour taste that goes great with crackers. The fillets need not be scored, as the vinegar softens the bones. Cut the fillets into domino-sized pieces, and put in canning jars. Soak overnight in a solution of ½ vinegar and ½ water. Drain and place in a boiling solution of 3 cups vinegar and 1 cup water. Add cloves, allspice, mustard seed, salt and pepper, and lemon slices. Boil fish until done. Saving the liquid, place pieces in a sterilized jar and cover with sliced onions. Pour the boiling solution into the jars and seal.

Kids are often better carp anglers than their folks are. At the Coon Rapids Carp Fest, this boy's 7½-pounder took first place in the kids' division.

Score the fillet to break a carp's floating bones (indicated by the arrows) or fillet them out. The bones in large carp are big enough to eat around.

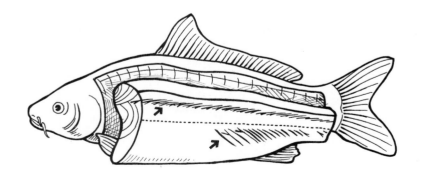

RECIPES

Carp taste great, and they are good for you, too. A 4-ounce serving of carp provides 40 to 50 percent of the protein you need in a day. Carp are also high in phosphorus, which is good for the brain. Carp are low in fat, and much of this can be filleted off. A 6-ounce serving of carp has only 213 calories.

Carp can be delicious in hundreds of ways. Your imagination is the only limitation. Europeans, who have been feasting on carp for centuries, use the fish in the finest dishes served in expensive restaurants. Many farms in France and Belgium have carp ponds where the fish is netted for dinner. In Greece, carp roe is called *taramosalata* and is prized as a delicacy. In Austria, deviled carp is a favorite dish. Poles cook carp in aspic. Hungarians serve cold carp in paprika sauce, and the Czechs have in-

C'est magnifique! We prepare a superb carp bouillabaisse for special events. This occasion? Learning I'd broken the world dogfish record in the 4-pound-test tippet category.

fluenced the Austrian dish "Carp Baked in Black Sauce."

Carp cooked *au bleu* is a delicacy served in fine Austrian restaurants in the lake region. There, live carp kept in ponds are killed and cooked immediately in boiling water seasoned with peppercorns, salt, and vinegar, and then are served with melted butter and parsley.

If you have any trepidation about eating carp for the first time, try deep-frying pieces of fillet cut to the size of dominos. Eat the golden tidbits with beer and french fries. There's no one on earth who doesn't like this.

One of the oldest recipes for carp was published over 300 years ago by Izaak Walton in *The Compleat Angler*. Prepare it and taste a bit of angling history.

"Take an carp, scour him and rub him clean with water and salt, but scale him not; then open him and put him with his blood and liver, into a small pot; then take sweet majoram, thyme and parsley, of each half-a-handful, a sprig of rosemary, and another of savory, bind them into two or three small bundles and put them to your carp, with four or five whole onions, twenty pickled oysters and three anchovies. Then pour upon your carp as much claret wine as will cover him and season your claret well with salt, cloves, mace and the rinds of oranges and lemons."

While Walton's recipe might not bring out the best in a carp (you've got to wonder about those anchovies), these 5 carp recipes—3 European, one Chinese, and one American—are renowned for their flavor.

Ponty Fuszermartassal (Deviled Carp)

Preheat oven to 350°. Heat 3 tablespoons bacon fat or lard in an 8-inch skillet over high heat until a light haze forms over it. Then reduce heat to medium, and add 3 cups finely chopped onions. Cook 8–10 minutes, or until lightly colored. Turn off the heat, and stir in 2 tablespoons sweet

Hungarian paprika. Return the skillet to medium heat and add 1 large green pepper diced and 1 cup chopped tomatoes peeled and seeded. Cover tightly and cook 5 minutes. Stir in ¼ cup dry white wine.

Scrape half the vegetable mixture into a buttered 8- by 12-inch shallow baking dish, approximately 2 inches deep. Cut 6–8 steaks 1-inch thick from a 5-pound carp cleaned and scaled. Sprinkle the carp steaks generously with salt and a few grindings of black pepper. Arrange them in one layer in the baking dish, and cover with the rest of the vegetables. Bake in the middle of the oven for 15–18 minutes, or until the fish is firm to the touch and flakes easily when prodded gently with a fork.

Arrange the fish steaks on a serving platter, cover them loosely with foil, and keep them warm in a 200° oven while you make the sauce.

With a wire whisk, beat 1 tablespoon flour into ½ cup sour cream in a small mixing bowl, then stir the mixture into the pan juices. Bring to a boil and then reduce the heat. Simmer on top of the stove, stirring constantly for 4 or 5 minutes or until sauce is thick and creamy. Cover the carp with the sauce.

Carp aux Raisins

Cut a medium-sized (5-pound) carp into 1-inch-thick steaks, and sauté with 1 chopped onion and 3 chopped shallots in ½ cup of oil in a large skillet. Sprinkle steaks with 6 tablespoons flour. Almost cover the fish with 2 cups white wine and fish stock (or water). Season with salt and a touch of cayenne. Add 2 crushed garlic cloves. Sprinkle with a few tablespoons of oil. Bring to a boil, reduce heat, cover, and simmer slowly for 20 minutes.

Drain the carp steaks and set them on a dish, reforming the shape of the carp.

Over high heat, reduce the liquid by two-thirds, remove from the heat, and beat in ¾ cup oil. Add 2 teaspoons powdered sugar, 2 tablespoons wine vinegar, ⅓ cup seeded raisins, and ⅓ cup currants and sultanas (mixed) which have been allowed to swell in lukewarm water and drained. Pour over the carp, sprinkle with chopped parsley, and serve at once.

Filets de Carpe Marinière

Fillet a medium-sized (5-pound) carp, season with salt and pepper, and poach for 10 minutes in ½ cup concentrated fish stock or water. Drain the fillets, and cover with Marinière sauce: Melt ½ cup butter over low heat. Remove from heat and let stand 5 minutes. Skim clear butter fat from top and place it in a small saucepan. Cook butter slowly over low heat until it turns light brown. Add 1 tablespoon chopped parsley and 1 teaspoon lemon juice.

Carp Dumplings

This American dish is great for winter Sundays while watching football games. The smell of cooked dumpling wafts through the house and gets your guests salivating.

First, in a 2-quart pot, make a bouillon: In ¼ cup butter, brown 1 onion, 2 stalks celery, and 1 carrot, all chopped. Add 2 pints hot water, 2 tablespoons salt, ¼ teaspoon white pepper. Boil 30–40 minutes.

Prepare the fish mixture by putting 1 pound carp fillet, 1 onion, and 2 small pieces of celery through a grinder. Mix together with 4 slices white bread, trimmed and rubbed to fine crumbs, 1 teaspoon dried parsley, 1 teaspoon salt, 1 teaspoon white pepper. Add 3 well-beaten eggs, and mix.

Drop by spoonfuls into the boiling bouillon, and cook until done (about 5 minutes). Serve with chile sauce.

Red-in-Snow Carp

In a large, heavy skillet, heat 2 tablespoons peanut oil. Add 1 chopped scallion and 4 slices chopped ginger. Add a whole 2-pound carp, scaled, 1 tablespoon sherry, ½ cup sliced bamboo shoots, and 1 cup chicken broth. Bring to a boil, cover, reduce to a light boil, and cook for 5 minutes.

Add ½ cup red-in-snow (a Chinese vegetable available from an Asian grocery) or broccoli, salt to taste, and simmer 2 or 3 minutes until done.

—TD

If you are in the Omaha area, stop in at the two Joe Tess Place restaurants for some of the finest carp in the Midwest. The restaurants feature a dinner of a ⅓-pound carp fillet with a slice of rye bread and pickles as an open-faced sandwich with fries and coleslaw. Wine is available by the glass. According to Bill Falt, manager, the fish is superb and extremely popular: "All I can say is you've got to come in and try it out."

6

Sturgeon

On the white sand of the bottom
Lay the monster, Mishe-Nahma
Lay the sturgeon, king of Fishes.
—FROM "THE SONG OF HIAWATHA,"
HENRY WADSWORTH LONGFELLOW

THE STURGEON IS MONSTROUS, but only in size, not character. Reaching weights over 300 pounds, the sturgeon is the largest freshwater fish in North America. Yet it is also one of the most placid. Although shaped like a shark and armored with massive plates, the sturgeon is harmless to all creatures but the tiny organisms it consumes through its soft, toothless mouth. Biologists who've walked among 50- and 60-pound sturgeon spawning in the shallows say the fish will simply part quietly to make way, brushing lightly against their waders. "Even the small sturgeon will lie calmly in your hand," says Dave Barsness, sturgeon specialist for the Minnesota Department of Natural Resources.

Sturgeon are so amazing, so unlike other freshwater fish in the United States, that it's hard to believe they exist. Not only do they grow larger than many humans, they live longer, too. Despite their status throughout history as one of the finest and most expensive fish on earth, they are still unknown by anglers in much of their range, and at one time in the United States were actually despised by commercial anglers.

Thought by many anglers to be a sucker, the sturgeon actually belongs to the family *Acipenseridae*, made up of fish with a long nose, under which fits a suckerlike mouth that projects out like an accordion when the fish wants to suck in food. Despite the mouth, sturgeon are no more related to suckers than they are to smallmouth bass. All sturgeon have a long body tapering to a tail that looks like a shark's, with a longer top ray than bottom. Like a piece of polished hardwood, the lake sturgeon is elegantly beautiful. Depending on the water it lives in, a lake sturgeon can be tan, buff, brown, olive, golden, red, or gray. The body is sleek and smooth, the scaleless skin stretched tight around a muscular body.

There are 25 species of sturgeon in the world, 7 of which live in North America. Two each live in the Atlantic and Pacific oceans, moving upstream into tributary rivers to spawn. Living their entire lives in freshwater are the massive lake sturgeon, the small shovelnose, and the pale-colored pallid, which is extremely rare and only occasionally gets as far north as Missouri and Iowa.

The origin of the name sturgeon is shroud-

Sturgeon caught in the late 1800s and early 1900s often weighed over 200 pounds—bigger than the men who caught them!

The name "sturgeon" comes from either German, Swedish, or Anglo-Saxon words meaning "to stir or poke around."

ed in linguistic mystery. It comes from the German word *storen*, meaning "to poke around," the Swedish word *stora*, meaning "to stir," or the Anglo-Saxon word *stiriga*, which means "a stirrer." All three reflect the sturgeon's way of feeding by gliding across the bottoms of lakes and rivers, using its sensitive barbels to locate food which it sucks up with its vacuum tube mouth.

The Fish of Kings and Commoners

Throughout the ages, the sturgeon has been one of the most highly regarded fishes in the world; at times its flesh has been reserved under threat of death for the nobility. During the height of the Roman Empire, it was served at sumptuous banquets. England's King Henry I

(1100–1135) prohibited anyone from eating sturgeon unless they were guests at his table. King Edward II, who ruled England at the beginning of the 14th century, issued this edict that declared: "The King shall have the wreck of the sea throughout the realm, whales and great sturgeons." The Lord Mayor of London and the King of England for a time divided the sturgeon that ran up the Thames: Those captured above London Bridge belonged to the mayor; those captured below went to the royal family.

Caviar, the salted roe of sturgeon, has enriched the tables of kings, czars, and other nobility since the Middle Ages. It was first served in Russia in the 13th century, but because refrigeration did not exist and transportation was slow, caviar was not found in Europe for several centuries. By 1520, Pope Julius II was dining on caviar in Rome, and in 1600, William Shakespeare used it as a metaphor to mean the choicest of items in *Hamlet* (Act II, scene 2): "'Twas caviare to the general."

When Europeans first came to the Mississippi River and the eastern Great Lakes, they had no interest in shovelnose or pallid sturgeon and quickly learned to despise the lake sturgeon. As though they'd left all knowledge of cuisine behind in Europe, where the sturgeon was served as a delicacy, the immigrants viewed the big fish as nothing but a "queer-tasting" nuisance that wrecked nets set for more desirable species.

Although the early pioneers had no use for sturgeon, the American Indians, especially the forest tribes in the northern part of this fish's range, had for thousands of years been harvesting sturgeon as a store against lean times when game was scarce. For these tribes, sturgeon were as important as bison were to the Plains Indians. The Ojibwas called the sturgeon *Nah ma*, and the Winnebago tribe referred to the huge fish as *Na hoo*. On Lake Superior, the Ojibwa people netted or speared the huge fish and then preserved them by either salting, drying, or smoking. To the Great Lakes Indians, the sturgeon was the most respected of all fish. *Na-mah* was the name given to Chief Black Hawk's great-great uncle, and there was a Sturgeon band of Ojibwa.

In the Great Lakes region, sturgeon netting was done primarily by Indian women, who waded the shallows of the big lakes in the spring and captured fish that had moved close to shore to spawn. Spearing sturgeon through the ice, a practice still followed by whites and Indians in some lakes in Wisconsin, was done by Indian men. Their technique was almost the same a thousand years ago as that used today. A decoy was crafted of wood with a tail of birch bark and a body weighted with lead. To attract a curious sturgeon, it had to be realistic and move like a fish in the water.

The hunter cut a hole in the ice and then set a small tripod of sticks over which he wrapped a blanket that covered his head and shoulders as he lay on his stomach. The blanket blocked the sun so he could see the decoy, which he lowered with one hand while waiting for a sturgeon to swim by and investigate the new fish.

"Then with spear in hand they would lie flat on their stomachs, put their head under the hood, drop the decoy into the hole and they were ready and woe to the fish that dared to come near the decoy. They caught a great many sturgeon in that way and some very large ones," recorded William Wallace Wright in 1837 of Menominee Indians fishing through the ice in what is today Wisconsin.

The trick to spearing sturgeon remains the same: Wait until after the fish checks out the intruder, and then spear it as it begins to swim away. A sturgeon approaching a decoy is wary, ready to dash for cover if it sees a false move. Once satisfied the decoy poses no threat, the sturgeon drops its guard and slowly swims away.

When sturgeon moved from Lake Superior up tributaries to spawn, the Ojibwa caught them in "sturgeon racks," traps made of branches and placed in shallow water. Another method involved corralling the fish. The Ojibwa waited for a group of sturgeon to swim up into a stream. Then they pounded pilings across the river where it narrowed upstream of the mouth. Across the pilings they lashed logs strong enough to hold a person, and between the pilings they wove basswood cords to prevent the fish from re-entering the big lake. Sturgeon "5 or 6 feet long . . . came down the river [and] the Indians, seated on the framework, caught them with hooks and killed them with clubs," recounted a white woman who as a child in the mid-1800s had seen Indians harvest sturgeon.

Captain Jonathon Carver, an Easterner who explored the Upper Mississippi River to study its natural resources, wrote in 1767 of the sturgeon he ate and saw harvested by the Indians. The fish he described were 2½ to 3 feet long and had a delicate and finely flavored flesh, better than that of trout. He said the sturgeon were taken "by watching them as they lie under the banks in a clear stream, and darting at them with a fish-spear; for they will not take a bait."

Other Europeans venturing into the wilderness we today call the Upper Midwest were amazed at how big lake sturgeon grew. Explorer Pierre Radisson wrote of fishing Lake Superior's Chequamegon Bay on the lake's south shore: "In that bay, there is a channel where we took stores of fishes, sturgeons of vast bigness." Two of the region's earliest explorers were literally struck by the size of the sturgeon. Louis Jolliet and Father Jacques Marquette were the first whites to travel down the Mississippi River. In 1673, Marquette wrote in his journal of an occasion when he and Joliet were canoeing down the river and a "monstrous fish . . . struck our canoe with

Lake sturgeon like to jump throughout spring and summer. Sometimes a fish will come completely out of the water and land with a massive splash that can stop the heart of a nearby canoeist. Biologists aren't sure why the sturgeon does this. It may be to rid its body of parasitic lampreys that occasionally attach to the sturgeon's body.

By 1917, when this photo was taken, sturgeon populations had dwindled from overfishing. Catches such as this became increasingly rare.

such violence that I thought it was a great tree." The fish might have been a paddlefish or a large catfish, but it was probably a sturgeon, which often swims close to the surface and sometimes leaps into the air.

Marquette and Jolliet sometimes netted a sturgeon and dined on its rich meat. However, the two explorers were exceptions. For some reason, before 1855 most whites in the New World would have rather eaten skunk than sturgeon. But it was the sturgeon's size that

made it most despised. Raking virgin lakes and rivers with huge nets to harvest other fish species, commercial anglers became furious when the massive sturgeon became entangled in their nets and tore them up. In retaliation, commercial anglers killed every sturgeon they caught and either dumped them back to the rivers or fed the fish to pigs. Often, huge piles of dead sturgeon were stacked on shore, then doused with kerosene and set on fire.

By the early 1850s, so many sturgeon had

been killed that people didn't know what to do with the bodies. Special barges came and took dead sturgeon away from the prime fishing waters; others were stacked on the decks of steamships and used to fire the boilers. A few entrepreneurs roamed the shores and cut open the dead sturgeon for their eggs, which, assumed to be unfit for humans, were sold as hog food. Some of the fish were boiled down, and the oil that floated to the surface was used to make paints. The few sturgeon sold as food went for about 10 cents each!

The captains who'd stoked their ships with sturgeon "logs" must have kicked themselves a few years later, when someone realized that lake sturgeon were a lot like Russian beluga sturgeon, the roe from which was made into expensive caviar. Commercial anglers switched from cursing to praising the sturgeon in 1885, when a commercial caviar-producing plant was built in Sandusky, Ohio. Five years later, another plant was built to smoke sturgeon meat.

At the end of the Civil War, the number of European immigrants rose to record highs, and the new arrivals wanted sturgeon for its meat, caviar, and the gelatin isinglass (from the Dutch word *huysenblasse*, meaning "sturgeon bladder"), which was used to clarify beer and wine, as a cement for pottery, to set jams and jellies, and as a waterproofing. Sturgeon meat, which tastes like veal, was known as "Albany beef" in New York state. Caviar produced in Sandusky was exported to Germany. Sturgeon skins were even tanned as a fine grade leather and used to make handbags, shoes, and belts. As early as 1880, millions of pounds of sturgeon were netted in the Great Lakes and sold to markets in the United States and Europe.

The lake sturgeon, which doesn't reach sexual maturity until about age 24 and breeds only every few years, had been having a hard enough time as it was surviving the ravages of fishermen who didn't want to catch them.

Once commercial anglers started seeking the fish, sturgeon numbers plummeted. In 1885, the Lake Erie harvest of sturgeon was 5 million pounds. Within only 10 years, it dropped to only one-fifth that, despite an increase in fishing pressure. Lake of the Woods, which borders Minnesota and Ontario, was described at the end of the 19th century as the greatest sturgeon water in the world. The catch there declined by 90 percent from 1893 to 1900. In 1908, Forbes and Richardson wrote in *Fishes of Illinois* that, "Lake Sturgeon have of late years been steadily decreasing and are now only rarely taken in the Mississippi on our own borders and are seldom caught in Illinois. Fishermen at Alton now see but five or six in a year that weigh over 10 pounds, whereas 15 years ago 40 or 50 large ones, weighing from 60 to 100 pounds, were taken each season."

The commercial sturgeon fishing boom was over, and fisheries biologists knew the primary cause of the sturgeon's decline. In 1930, Robert E. Coker of the U.S. Department of Commerce Bureau of Fisheries, wrote, "It is evident, therefore, that [lake sturgeons'] principal enemy and the chief cause of their decrease in numbers has been man."

While the sturgeon of North America were being killed far faster than they could reproduce, the species in Europe and Asia weren't faring much better. As commercial angling techniques became more sophisticated in the 20th century, it became easier for fishermen to find and harvest the prized fish. Sturgeon were once plentiful in several French rivers, but today the fish is rarely found except in the Garonne. In Germany, Russia, and the Balkan states, the public became alarmed at the drastic drop in sturgeon numbers and asked for strict fishing restrictions. As a result, large sturgeon are still caught there.

The original range of the lake sturgeon in North America was between the Rockies and the Appalachian mountains from central

In the 1940s, kids in Oshkosh, Fond du Lac, and other towns on Wisconsin's Lake Winnebago carried lucky sturgeon otoliths, or "ear stones" in their pockets. The marble-sized balls of calcium, taken from the heads of sturgeon, were also carried by spearers to bring them good luck during the spearing season.

The lake sturgeon is indeed monstrous, but only in size, not character. Still, this fisheries biologist is probably not as calm about holding the giant fish as he appears.

Canada down to Arkansas and Alabama. It lived in the drainage basins of the Mississippi River, the Great Lakes, and Hudson Bay, giving it one of the widest geographic ranges of any native North American fish.

Since the late 1880s, the range of lake sturgeon has shrunk, not only from overfishing, but also because dams built across rivers and tributaries have prevented the fish from reaching their spawning grounds. As human development expanded across the Midwest,

clear-cutting, wetland drainage, and other land misuse increased erosion on lands surrounding rivers and lakes. The silt that settled to the bottom of waters covered the gravel and rocks where sturgeon eggs stick and killed the tiny organisms sturgeon eat. The dredging of channels and drainage of marshes along rivers and lakes eliminated places sturgeon live and breed.

To top it off, sewage and chemicals were dumped directly into the water. Not only did this kill the mollusks and gastropods that sturgeon eat, it also degraded the water by reducing oxygen. Wisconsin has some of the best sturgeon waters in the nation, but even those continue to be damaged by dams and pollution. Many rivers are lined with paper mills that dump highly organic effluent into the water, reducing its oxygen content. In 1976, more than 50 large lake sturgeon in the lower Wisconsin River were winterkilled by a lack of oxygen. The cause? Pollution from paper mills upstream.

Another factor in the demise of sturgeon has been poaching. Untold numbers of lake sturgeon continue to be snagged with treble hooks and netted illegally because they are worth so much on the market that poachers take the risk of getting caught. Wisconsin sport anglers, serious about preserving their few remaining sturgeon fisheries, have asked their Department of Natural Resources (DNR) to slap a $2,000 fine on anyone caught illegally taking a sturgeon.

Today there is little commercial fishing for sturgeon in North America. Several hundred thousand pounds of shovelnose sturgeon are caught each year from the Mississippi, and these prized catches are sold for more per pound than any other species except catfish. The only commercial fishing for lake sturgeon is in the Canadian waters of the Great Lakes.

Although the lake sturgeon is listed as a rare species by the U.S. Committee on Rare and Endangered Wildlife Species, it can still be sport caught in some parts of the Upper Midwest. In Wisconsin, the species has been given only "special concern" status, but in most other states of its original range it is either rare, uncommon, endangered, threatened, or extirpated (meaning it no longer exists in that state or water). In the United States, sportfishing for lake sturgeon is legal only in certain waters of North Dakota, South Dakota, Minnesota, Wisconsin, and Michigan.

Wisconsin's few remaining sturgeon fisheries are closely monitored. The DNR is trying to register all sturgeon caught by hook and line to see how many are being killed each year. Length limits and extremely short seasons help keep the population near a point where it maintains itself, and on certain rivers, anglers must apply for sturgeon tags before fishing.

Minnesota has a fledgling program to reintroduce lake sturgeon into parts of its original range. Some anglers actually oppose this reintroduction, saying the money being spent to restore the region's grandest fish should go towards hatching more walleyes — in a state that has more natural walleye habitat than any in the nation. Fortunately, the Minnesota DNR realizes the ecological, intrinsic, and cultural importance of preserving and when possible re-establishing native fish species. Since 1985, over 33,000 7-inch sturgeon fingerlings have been stocked in the St. Louis River near Duluth. The fish are fry from Wisconsin, raised in Minnesota at the St. Paul fish hatchery. The Minnesota DNR hopes to re-establish a self-sustaining lake sturgeon population in the St. Louis, and in time create a protected fishery for sport anglers. In 1989, some of the original stocked fish were already 24 inches long. However, because it takes a female sturgeon over 2 decades before she can lay eggs, the program won't be able to satisfy anglers eager for immediate returns on their fishing license investment. Raising sturgeon in public water will be harder than growing bonsai trees in a goat pasture. The fish will need to be carefully protected and appreciated for their existence and historical value.

The future of the lake sturgeon is in the hands of anglers. If they demand tighter sport and commercial fishing restrictions and support reintroduction programs, our kids and grandkids could have a chance to see these massive remnants of a time when this region was pristine.

One cause of the sturgeon's decline has been dams. Rob catches, then quickly releases, a small lake sturgeon trapped below a dam on a Wisconsin river.

Natural History

Three species are native to the United States between the Rockies and the Appalachians. Only two—the lake and the shovelnose—exist in any number. The third, the pallid, is extremely rare and swims only in the lower half of the Mississippi River and its tributaries.

Lake Sturgeon
Acipenser fulvescens
Acipenser is the Latin word for "sturgeon," and *fulvescens* is Latin for "reddish yellow."

Although its scientific name describes a reddish-yellow fish, the lake sturgeon ranges in color from olive-yellow to bluish gray, depending on where it lives. Shaped like a torpedo, the lake sturgeon's cylindrical body tapers slightly from its bullet-shaped head to a narrow, slender back and thin tail. The tail looks like a shark's: longer on top than on the bot-

tom. Instead of a backbone made of vertebrae, the sturgeon has a continuous flexible rod called a notochord that is encased in cartilage. Instead of scales, the body is covered by large overlapping plates, called scutes, which on a large sturgeon can be as big as a serving dish. Over the plates is a dark thick skin that feels like a cat's tongue. The fish's head is flat, coming to a round point, with a slight upward turn at the soft snout like the toe of an old shoe.

Below the snout are four whiskers, or barbels. Underneath the head, well back from the snout, is the mouth, which can protrude out like a rubbery suction tube.

Lake sturgeon are also known as freshwater sturgeon, Great Lakes sturgeon, rock sturgeon, stone sturgeon, red sturgeon, ruddy sturgeon, common sturgeon, shell back sturgeon, bony sturgeon, smoothback, and bullnosed sturgeon.

Most lake sturgeon caught or netted today in the Great Lakes are between 20 and 55 inches long and weigh 5 to 40 pounds. Wiscon-

Range of the lake sturgeon

sin's Lake Winnebago has the largest population of big sturgeon in the United States. The average sturgeon taken there is about 50 pounds. That's nothing, however, compared to the sturgeon once caught.

In the late 1800s, an account from the *Warroad Plaindealer*, a northern Minnesota paper, read: "The largest sturgeon ever caught in Lake of the Woods—as far as anyone here knows—was brought in on the *Isabel* [a commercial fishing steamer] the first part of the week. It weighed 236 pounds, and measured about eight feet." In the April 14, 1881 issue of the *Fond du Lac Journal*, a 297-pound, 9-foot lake sturgeon was reportedly captured.

In this century, large sturgeon have also been caught, including the 2 largest on record. A specimen taken from Lake of the Woods in 1911 was reportedly 236 pounds, and a 225-pounder was found dead in Minnesota's Rush Lake in 1947. A 310-pounder stretching 8 feet and estimated to be 100 years old was taken

from Batchawana Bay on the east end of Lake Superior in 1922, and a fish of the same weight was caught from Lake Michigan in 1943.

Sturgeon in the 100-pound range are still speared in Lake Winnebago each year. In 1976, a 100-pounder was taken in Wisconsin's Lake Poygan, and in 1953, an 82-year-old fish weighing 180 pounds was speared in Lake Winnebago. That same year, a fish of 208 pounds was caught in Lake of the Woods.

The world record lake sturgeon, 92 pounds, 4 ounces, was caught in September, 1986 on 15-pound-test line by James Michael De Otis on the Kettle River in Minnesota, a tributary of the St. Croix. Minnesota has often held some of the nation's biggest sturgeon. There are so many anglers in the state that sturgeon waters, also home to other species, are filled with nightcrawlers on hooks throughout much of the year.

For 14 years, from 1968 to 1982, the Minnesota and the world sturgeon record was a

This rare albino sturgeon shows the distinguishing characteristics of the *Acipenseridae* family: bullet-shaped head, overlapping plates, and a nose like the toe of an old shoe.

162½-pound fish caught by Allen Kanaeble in the Rainy River along the Canadian border. In 1982, Kanaeble told fishing historian and author Joe Fellegy that he had actually gaffed the fish on a river that had been closed to fishing. Fellegy published the confession in his book *Classic Minnesota Fishing Stories* that year, and the Minnesota DNR reinstated a record set by Art Sanders in 1949.

The largest populations of lake sturgeon today are in Canada, in the pristine rivers draining into Hudson's Bay. The Red River, which begins on the North Dakota–Minnesota border and runs through Manitoba, has a strong population of lake sturgeon. In the United States, the lake sturgeon is still found in parts of the Mississippi River, Lake Michigan, and Lake Superior watersheds. In the Mississippi River drainage, lake sturgeon live in the Mis-

sissippi River to St. Anthony Falls in Minneapolis; the Missouri River through Missouri, Nebraska, South Dakota, North Dakota and Missouri; the Tennessee River of Alabama to southern Arkansas; and the St. Croix, Chippewa, and Wisconsin rivers and their major tributaries.

In Lake Superior, sturgeon are found in the shallow Keweenaw Bay, near the Apostle Islands, and in the St. Louis River estuary; they have been seen spawning in the Bad River of Wisconsin. In the Lake Michigan watershed, the lake sturgeon is still found in Green Bay, Lake Michigan, the Menominee River up to White Rapids Dam, the Fox River up to Lake Puckaway, the Wolf River up to Shawana, Lake Wisconsin (a part of the Wisconsin River), the Minong Flowage, the St. Croix River up to Gordon Dam, the Namekogan River be-

A World Record of Sorts

Mitch Babick, of Mercer, Wisconsin, lives and guides in the heart of northern Wisconsin's fabled muskie waters. Babick, who's been guiding for 55 years, says he's caught his fair share of good-sized sturgeon, but none as big as the world record he once landed and released—without ever catching it in the first place!

"I was guiding a group in Tank Lake when I heard this little boy on a dock screaming for help," Babick recalls. "Well, I could see he was only 7 or 8 years old, so I said to the fellows in my boat I'd better go help him out. I got on the dock and it turns out he's got some sort of big fish on and wanted me to take the rod. I had to practically pry it from his little hands, and when I did, I felt the fish and couldn't believe the size of it. I said, 'I think he's got a world record muskie here.'

"The fish took off, and there was no way the kid could have held onto that rod, so I got in the boat and we chased it a halfmile until I was finally able to raise it. I could see then it was a huge sturgeon. Then the fish swam all the way back to the dock and right into the shallows. I jumped out and pushed it up on shore, and just then the small hook the boy had been using with a minnow fell out of the sturgeon's mouth. I hurriedly put it back in the water because we didn't want to hurt it. The sturgeon just swam off.

"The thing is, a week later it died, and came floating into shore. The DNR came and picked it up and said it was 6 feet long and weighed 98 pounds. Oh, it was the same sturgeon all right. They said it died of old age. It could have been it just got too tired from that fight, because I tell you that was the biggest fish I ever fought."

low Trego Dam, and the Chippewa and Flambeau rivers. It has also been introduced into several Wisconsin lakes.

No one knows exactly how old sturgeons get. That they are long-lived, however, is without argument. Sturgeon grow older the farther north they live, because fish grow more slowly in cold water. Although not common, fish of 40 or 50 years of age are still taken from Lake Winnebago; the oldest one recorded there was 82. Several fish over a century old have been found, and a fish taken in 1953 from the Ontario side of Lake of the Woods was reported to have been 152 years old.

All these big fish are females, which always outlive the males. Of the lake sturgeon aged by biologists in one Wisconsin study, 90 percent of those 30 years and older were females. Scientists determine a sturgeon's age by cutting through the lead ray of one of the pectoral fins and counting the thin bands under a microscope; each band is a year, similar to the rings of a tree trunk.

Being so long-lived, the sturgeon is extremely slow to reach sexual maturity and spawn. Females cannot spawn until about age 20, when they are about 34 inches long and weigh approximately 30 pounds. What makes it even tougher for the species to propagate is that female sturgeon only spawn every 4 or 5 years.

Lake sturgeon spawn in May or, in northern waters, in June. They move into riffles and rapids when the water is about 50 degrees Fahrenheit, waiting until it hits 53 or so before spawning. They also spawn at the base of waterfalls and along the outside bends of rivers where there is rock or riprap and an upswelling current as the river flows against the obstructions. In the Great Lakes, sturgeon spawn in the shallows near shoals where there is strong wave action.

The spawning of lake sturgeon is one of the most fascinating sights of nature, as dramatic

as the mating rituals of prairie chickens, elk, and raptors. A group of 3 to 6 males waits in water 2 to 15 feet deep for a ripe female. The males cruise the shallow shoreline, and sometimes can be seen in large groups with their tails and snouts out of the water. When the female enters the group, several males swim next to her, facing the same direction, against the current. Then the males violently vibrate, releasing milt and causing the female to release her eggs. The eggs and milt are mixed by the current or waves, and are further blended as the males leap from the water and thrash their tails, at times so wildly the vibrations can be felt by a person standing on shore. The sound, said one biologist, is like "a ruffed grouse drumming or an old tractor starting up." The fertilized eggs, anywhere from 50,000 to 700,000 per female, stick to the gravel or rocks at the river bottom and hatch in about a week.

Lake sturgeon are fish of big water and need lots of room to roam. They prefer the shoals of large lakes and the mud on gravel-bottomed shallows of big rivers near riffles. Those taken in nets are usually in 15 to 30 feet of water, although they've been netted as deep as 140 feet. Sturgeon anglers catch the fish in water anywhere from 5 to 20 feet deep. In the winter, the fish go deeper, continuing to feed and stay active.

A fish like this 40-pounder has spawned only two or three times. Unfortunately, too many of these noble fish have been caught and killed by anglers more interested in meat than the health of the sturgeon population.

Shovelnose Sturgeon
Scaphirhynchus platorynchus
Scaphirhynchus is the Greek word for "spade snout," and *platorynchus* is Greek for "broad snout."

Also called hackleback, switchtail, sand sturgeon, flathead sturgeon, and spadehead sturgeon, the shovelnose is more common than the lake sturgeon. It is also smaller and spawns at an earlier age. Although it can tolerate muddy water better than its big cousin, the shovelnose is nevertheless harmed by pollution and siltation. The shovelnose population has declined greatly in the past 100 years. Commercial anglers fishing the Missouri and Mississippi rivers in the state of Missouri now take about 5,000 pounds of shovelnose a year in their nets, only 3 percent of what they caught in 1899.

The most distinguishing feature of the shovelnose, besides its spade-shaped snout, is its tail. While the shovelnose has a head flatter and broader than the lake sturgeon's bullet-shaped head, it can be more quickly identified by looking at the tail. The upper lobe of the tail is extremely long and whiplike, which inspired the name "switchtail." Another way to tell a shovelnose from a small lake sturgeon is to look at the eyes. A lake sturgeon has spiracles—openings above and behind the eyes. The shovelnose doesn't.

"Even the small sturgeon will lay calmly in your hand," said Minnesota DNR Sturgeon Specialist Dave Barsness. Shown here is a tiny shovelnose.

The range of the shovelnose is more southern than that of the lake sturgeon. Currently it is in the Mississippi River, the Wisconsin River up to Prairie Du Sac dam, the Minnesota River up to Granite Falls, the St. Croix up to St. Croix Falls Dam, the Chippewa River up to the Eau Claire Dam and the Red Cedar River up to the Menominee Dam. The shovelnose swims in the Missouri River in Missouri, Iowa, Nebraska, South Dakota (although it is rare in that state), North Dakota, and Montana, home of the International Game Fish Association world record, caught in 1985.

The shovelnose likes more current than the lake sturgeon does, so look for them in the deep channels of large rivers over sand and gravel or near the head of silt beds if the area is swept by a strong current. On the Mississippi River, look for shovelnose sturgeon in the tailwaters below wingdams and any other structure that creates a fast water flow. Rarely are these fish in quiet water.

The shovelnose spawns in the same way the lake sturgeon does, with lots of thrashing in the shallows and cruising near the surface. It, too, needs to migrate upstream to spawn, and like the lake sturgeon it has been hurt by the construction of dams, which block its upstream passage. Both species stop feeding while spawning, but go on an eating binge afterwards. This makes middle to late June one of the best times to catch either fish.

Not nearly as big as the lake sturgeon, the shovelnose is a modest-sized fish averaging about 20 inches long and 2 pounds. While the state record in Iowa is 12 pounds, and fish of 4 to 5 pounds are common there, in most states a shovelnose over 5 pounds is a trophy.

Fishing for Sturgeon

Before would-be sturgeon anglers rush out to try and hook one of these great creatures, they should know that sturgeon are rare and ex-

Just my luck, I catch a 4-ounce bullhead while fishing for 40-pound lake sturgeon on a tributary of the St. Croix River.

tremely tough to catch: It takes an average of 200 hours in some fisheries to catch one. Also, the fragile populations of lake sturgeon can take very little additional fishing pressure in the few areas in the United States where fishing is legal.

We believe all roughfish anglers should have a chance to see a live sturgeon in its native water at least once, and feel its sandpaperlike skin. It is so strange you can hardly believe you are holding a fish. And any roughfish angler should get to taste smoked sturgeon at least once, to share with connoisseurs throughout the world one of civilization's most valued delicacies.

But we cannot condone the killing of these fish for their meat except when it is used for rare, special occasions. We have included famous sturgeon recipes not to promote the catch and kill of this stately fish but to show that the keeping of sturgeon is a once-in-a-lifetime event, the culmination of which should be to serve the specially prepared dish at a family or national celebration.

For sturgeons to survive in the future, anglers need to understand why so few remain and what is lost when a sturgeon is killed. To take a sturgeon from a river where there are perhaps only a few hundred left and steak it out for Tuesday night supper is like using sable skins to wash a tractor.

There are three factors to key in on when fishing for sturgeon: habitat, spawning season, and food preference. For shovelnose, look for snags near fast water. Lake sturgeon are in slower water, often just off a pool or eddy. For both, one of the best locations is the fast water below dams in the spring, when fish have stacked up on their way upstream to spawn. The shovelnose will be in the current; the lake just to the side. Both bite day or night, feeding almost entirely by feel rather than sight.

Sturgeon eat nymphs (caddis fly, mayfly, chironomids, and dragonfly), crustaceans, clams, crayfish, mollusks, and sometimes fish eggs, small fish, and plants. Like other roughfish, the sturgeon has been wrongly accused of wrecking sport fisheries by eating gamefish eggs; however, scientists have found that the eggs are only a small and incidental part of the sturgeon's diet.

Sturgeon feed by swimming along the bottom, searching for food with their sensitive barbels. When they touch something that feels like food, the tubular mouth extends down over the item and sucks it in along with any gravel or other bottom matter. When it eats snails and clams, it crushes the shells in the muscular walls of its stomach.

Sturgeon can be caught with worms, nightcrawlers, snails, live fish and cut bait. All the sturgeon we've caught and seen caught were on nightcrawlers.

Once Rob and I set out specifically to catch sturgeon on the St. Croix River. The trip started auspiciously when we saw an angler on the opposite bank battle, land, and release a lake sturgeon that looked to weigh about 10 or 12 pounds. We hurried to the dam, hopeful of catching sturgeon of our own. While I tried to find my reel which I'd left back in the car, Rob

snuck up to a pool directly below the face of the dam and began fishing a nightcrawler.

Unable to fish myself, I decided to watch how it was done. At first, we only thought the pool held a few puny bluegills that continued to pester Rob's nightcrawler. But after 20 minutes or so, a long dark shadow slid out from a fastwater chute and into the shallows below the big rocks we stood on. It was a sturgeon, about 3 feet long. "This is going to be *great*," whispered Rob, lifting his 'crawler from the deep water and dropping it in front of the sturgeon.

The fish covered the 'crawler with its snout. Rob waited a few moments. "Do you think it's sucked it in?" he asked. I shrugged. "Well, here goes." He lifted the rod tip sharply, and sure enough, the sturgeon had inhaled the nightcrawler. It thrashed once and dove for deep water, almost pulling Rob's rod in with it. "Whoa! Sturgeon on!" Rob yelled, circling the pool to get below the fish. The sturgeon fought wildly, gyrating and twisting just under the surface of the water. It leaped once, twisting in midair. "This fish is out of control!" Rob yelled, trying to apply side pressure to keep the sturgeon off balance. Again and again it rose to the surface, writhing its supple body like a salamander. At last, the fish gave up and allowed me to wade in and lift it from the shallows. I pulled on the line, and the mouth extended down like a vacuum cleaner tube about 4 inches. I gingerly undid the hook and slid the fish back into the pool.

If you want to catch a sturgeon, here's what to do: Call your state fisheries office and find out where sturgeon are caught in your state. If you live somewhere that has no legal sturgeon fishing, head north. In Minnesota, there is some limited lake and shovelnose sturgeon fishing on the border waters with Ontario, Wisconsin, North and South Dakota, and on the tributaries of the St. Croix River. Wisconsin has the most sturgeon water of any state, al-

though the seasons are severely restricted and anglers need to apply for a special sturgeon tag. Fishing is open on 4 river systems: the St. Croix, Chippewa-Flambeau, Menominee, and Wisconsin. The state's premier fishery is the Lake Winnebago system. In that lake and the adjoining Fox and Wolf rivers swim about 11,5000 lake sturgeon. However, these fish are not allowed to be caught and released by anglers, only speared.

Since spearing ranks with dynamite as a way to conserve fish, we don't condone the activity, although we recognize it has a long his-tory in that and other parts of Wisconsin. However we also know that people historically baited ducks and shot deer from cars, too, but eventually those activities were seen as unethi-cal and unfair to others.

Before you head for the Badger State to try your luck, bear in mind that luck often plays a key role in sturgeon fishing. Many anglers wait *weeks* between bites. One of the best sturgeon waters in Wisconsin is the Menominee River, located along the border of Michigan. There, in the 26-mile stretch from White Rapids Dam to Grand Rapids Dam, only about 20 fish are

Rob reaches for a lake sturgeon tamed after 20 minutes of gyrating leaps and powerful runs. "It was incredible," he said. "The fish never stopped twisting."

We (Usually) Eat These Fish

"But aren't they *contaminated*?" is a question we're often asked when we tell people about catching and eating roughfish.

Our answer is always the same: Not if the water they swim in is clean. A carp caught in a clear, unpolluted stream is as safe to eat as a bass or trout from that same water. And people would no more want to eat carp from a river thick with sewage that than they would want to eat walleyes that swam there.

It's a fact that most waters in the United States are polluted in some way, and that the fish—game and rough—in those waters carry pollutants in their flesh. What's not known, however, is how dangerous the contaminants are to humans.

Some people, often those whose livelihoods depend on the sportfishing business, say the contaminants are in such small concentrations they won't hurt anyone. They claim eating a fish from a lake laced with PCBs is no worse than eating a vegetable from a local supermarket.

On the other side are environmentalists and health experts, who usually don't have a stake in fishing-related tourism. These people point to studies that show that toxins in fish *can* damage a person's nervous system and cause deformities in young and unborn children.

There is a lot of water, and many meals of fish, between the two arguments. We eat many of the fish we catch, but not indiscriminately. We've tried to learn about the water we fish in and the fish there. Using this information, we make an educated decision whether or not to eat certain species from certain waters.

To decide which fish are safe to eat, you need to answer a few questions.

1. How polluted is the water?

The primary contaminants in the lakes and rivers most anglers fish are pesticides, mercury, DDT, PCBs, raw sewage, and chemical waste. It's important to know how much of these flow into your fishing water. Cancer-causing pesticides like Dieldrin and Endrin are washed off farm fields into lakes, streams, and rivers. PCBs, used as an industrial coolant, enter water by seeping in from landfills. Mercury in car batteries and paint becomes airborne when burned in garbage, then settles to earth in contaminated rain. The insecticide DDT, now banned in the United States, is still used in countries from which it is carried in the air and ends up in this country.

Even though levels of PCBs and DDTs have dropped in many U.S. waters, scientists have been finding that these toxins are more dangerous than previously thought. Raw sewage is still being dumped into the Mississippi, Missouri, and Ohio rivers and their tributaries; runoff from pesticide- and herbicide-drenched farms has never been greater; and the use of landfills and garbage incinerators near water increases every year.

2. Does my age or sex put me at extraordinary risk?

Toxins harm some people more than others. Pregnant women, nursing mothers, potential mothers, and kids should be especially careful about eating fish from contaminated waters.

3. How fatty are the fish I eat?

Many industrial toxins attach to the fatty tissues of fish. Therefore, when you fish extremely polluted waters, don't eat fish high in fat, like salmon, buffalo, lake trout, carp, and catfish.

4. Is my fish a predator?

The higher up in the food chain, the more contaminated the fish. For example, if a minnow ate 10 pieces of algae, each containing a particle of PCB, it would contain 10 PCB particles in its body. If a whitefish ate 10 of these minnows, it would contain 100 PCB particles. When a hungry burbot or walleye eats 10 whitefish, it would end up with 1,000 PCB particles.

Fish low in the food chain are suckers, sunfish, carp, cisco, and whitefish. Fish high on the chain are gar, bowfin, salmon, lake trout, muskellunge, and flathead catfish.

5. How old are the fish I eat?

Because fish collect toxins over their lifetime, younger fish have fewer contaminants. Fortunately, small fish also taste best and are most abundant.

6. What are the healthiest ways to prepare fish?

Much of the toxins in fish are concentrated in the fat layer under the skin. Fillet and then skin your fish to remove the fat. Also, cut away any dark meat. The healthiest way to cook a fish is to let the oils drip away by grilling or broiling, or float away by poaching or boiling. Deep-frying without batter can draw off some toxin-laden fats; however, pan frying cannot.

7. How often do I eat fish?

If you only dine on fresh fish a few times a year, don't worry too much about the toxin levels. But if you eat fresh-caught fish once a week or more, you'll probably want to get a better idea of how many pollutants you're consuming with each meal.

A final note: Both roughfish and gamefish are great to eat; we do it all the time. But it would be irresponsible of us to imply we eat fish from all the waters we fish in, because we don't. We use the state fish consumption advisory as a guide, not to make the final decision to eat a fish or not. State advisories are for relatively few waters. Most of the waters anglers fish have never even been tested for toxins. Each angler should decide if the fish he or she eats is safe. Find out about the environment near your lake or river. Write to your legislator and demand a reduction in pollutants.

caught each year, at a catch rate of about one fish for every 250 hours of angling. Bring a book.

Except on the rare occasion where you keep one for a special event, let those sturgeon go. Catch-and-release takes extra care on your part because a sturgeon will suck bait well into its mouth, making it tough to get the hook out without mauling the fish. Or without mauling your hand. Dave Mueller, who raises sturgeon at his home in Mahtomedi, Minnesota, warns anglers to be careful when holding an adult shovelnose. "The scutes along the back and tail can be razor sharp," he says. "If you're not careful, they'll slice your hand wide open."

To save both your hand and the sturgeon, we recommend leaving the fish in the water and cutting the line as near the mouth as possible. The hook will rust away in no time, and the fish will be a lot healthier than if you'd tried to rip out the hook. If you want to lift the fish for a photograph, wear a pair of cotton gloves to hold the fish steady for the camera. Then ease it back into the water, head into the current, and hold the fish gently in the running water until it's got enough power and sense to swim away. If you release a fish that's still dazed, it could wash down into the rapids below and get bruised up.

The best lake sturgeon fishing in the world is in Ontario or Manitoba in the tributaries of Hudson Bay. These undammed, unpolluted rivers—like the Assiniboine in Manitoba and the Albany in Ontario—still have strong populations of huge sturgeon. It's worth a trip just to see what rivers were like in this county 200 years ago.

Feasting with Kings

Sturgeon meat is the most expensive fish you can buy. In Russia, the fish is highly esteemed and is eaten fresh or salted, and the spinal marrow is dried and used to make the legendary Russian fish pie *coulibiac*. The French braise or smoke sturgeon cut into steaks or thick slices. In some countries, the head of the sturgeon is the most prized part after the roe; after smoking, the flesh is scraped off and used in a variety of dishes. Smoked sturgeon is a delicacy throughout the world, from International Falls to Istanbul.

Recipes

Sturgeon Poached in Champagne

In a large skillet, bring 2 cups Champagne, 1 carrot, 1 onion, 3 stalks celery, 4 sprigs parsley, 4 peppercorns, 3 cloves, and 1 bay leaf to a boil. Cover and simmer 15 minutes.
Arrange sturgeon fillets or steaks in the broth.

Simmer, turning once, 10 minutes. Transfer to a shallow baking dish.
Boil the broth until reduced to ¾ cup. Strain and reserve this liquid.
In a sauce pan, melt 2 tablespoons butter, add 1½ tablespoons flour, and whisk until blended. Bring ¾ cup of milk to a boil, and add all at once to butter-flour mixture, stirring vigorously with a whisk until the sauce is thick and smooth. Add the strained poaching liquid and ½ cup grated gruyère cheese and stir.
Lightly heat 2 slightly beaten egg yolks, and mix in a bit of the warm sauce. Slowly beat this egg mixture into the remaining sauce until it is thick.
Pour sauce over the fish. Broil approximately 15 minutes in a preheated broiler until lightly brown.

Shovelnose Sturgeon Baked in Foil

Mix 1 cup mushrooms, 2 sliced onions, 1 tablespoon chopped green peppers, 2 tablespoons lemon juice, 2 tablespoons olive oil, and salt, pepper, and dill to taste.
Spread half the mixture on 4 pieces of tinfoil large enough to wrap 4 sturgeon steaks. Place fish on this mixture, top with a bay leaf and a slice of tomato. Fold foil over the fish, seal edges. Bake over hot coals for about 45 minutes.

Only one thing is caviar, and that is lightly salted sturgeon eggs, or roe. The word caviar comes from the Turkish word *khavyah*, meaning "sturgeon roe." The eggs themselves are not caviar until they have been salted. Nor can the eggs of any other species be made into caviar, although they are sometime labeled as such. Salted burbot roe, for example, is not burbot caviar. It is salted burbot roe.

The Soviet Union is the largest producer and consumer of caviar in the world. There, 5 separate sturgeon species produce different caviars, which are graded by size and color of the eggs. The most prized of all comes from the sterlet sturgeon, a species almost extinct in that country. Sterlet was the caviar of the czars and is today extremely rare even in the Soviet Union. Before World War I, only the Russian Imperial Court and other dignitaries were permitted to dine on this delicacy. It was never imported, even though it was sought by connoisseurs in Europe, England, and the United States.

Of the roe exported from Russia, the beluga (white) sturgeon's is the most expensive, especially that from beluga sturgeon caught in the Azor Sea. This caviar sells for about $50 an ounce wholesale and cannot be purchased by the public except in restaurants.

The preparation and handling of caviar is of the utmost importance, for this is what creates the delicate flavor. Most important is that each egg, or "berry" as it is called in the trade, must be whole and covered in its own fat. Crushed eggs or those only partially coated are of a lower grade than those of superior caviar.

Why is caviar so expensive? For one thing it is rare, but primarily because it tastes superb. When prepared by experts, the eggs are gooey with fat, lightly salty, and have a soft nutty taste with no hint of fishy smell.

Homemade Caviar

To make caviar you need to catch a ripe female sturgeon. We recommend you use a shovelnose, since a female lake sturgeon is too valuable to the fishery to kill. Catching a ripe female can be tough, since sturgeon stop feeding during spawning and most sturgeon waters are closed to fishing until after spawning. But if you do catch a ripe shovelnose, here's how to turn the eggs into a delicacy.

Remove the eggs from the sturgeon as soon as it is killed. Tear the globs into golfball-sized pieces.

Gently work the eggs through a screen of ¼ inch or finer by gently stirring to remove the eggs from the ovarian membrane. Let the eggs fall through the screen into a tub or bowl. Wash the eggs carefully in cold water 3 or 4 times. Drain.

Place the eggs in coldwater brine made of 1⅛ cups granular pickling salt to every quart of water for 15 to 20 minutes. There should be twice as much brine as roe.

Remove from the liquid, and drain thoroughly by allowing to drip through a strainer for about 1 hour. Keep refrigerated during this time.

Place in an airtight (this is crucial) nonmetal container and store at 26–30 degrees Fahrenheit for 1 week.

This is when the caviar is at its peak flavor. Serve at once. Store for no longer than 6 months.

The classic way to serve caviar is to heat the back of a large metal spoon and press it into a block of ice to form a depression. Using a plastic spoon (never let the eggs touch metal), scoop the caviar into the icy bowl. Garnish with lemon, and sprinkle finely chopped boiled egg, onion, or chives on top. Serve with small triangles of dry toast, crusts cut off.

—TD

7

Catfish and Bullheads

*There is a species of fish that never looks at the clothes
of the man who throws in the bait, a fish that takes
whatever is thrown to it, when once hold of the hook,
never tries to shake a friend, but submits to the
inevitable, crosses its legs and says, 'Now I lay me,' and
comes on the bank and seems to enjoy being taken. It is
a fish that is a friend of the poor, and one that will sacri-
fice itself in the interest of humanity. That is the fish that
the state should adopt as its trade mark, and cultivate
friendly relations with, and stand by. We allude to the
bullhead.*

—GEORGE W. PECK, GOVERNOR OF WISCONSIN, 1943.

TOM SAYS the bowfin is his favorite fish because it's the only species that hasn't shamed him. Of all the warm-water species, I'm partial to the channel catfish. I like how it looks, how it fights, and how it tastes. Most of all, I like fishing for channel catfish because of where the fish lives: in clear, fast-flowing streams.

There are times, lazy times, when I like to fish the warm, still backwaters, where the air is hot and moist and I paddle slowly in my float tube, casting a doughball to buffalo or a rope fly to breaking gar. But given a choice, I'd usually rather be standing in a rapids, with clear water breaking around my legs, scanning the rippling surfaces in search of a hole, break, or eddy that could hide a channel cat.

What I like is current and the dynamics of moving water. In the waters where catfish live there is more to see, to feel, to figure out. Catfishing in moving water is a fast-paced riddle I enjoy trying to solve. When I walk down the bank to a catfish stream, I take in the vista of eddies, flows, rapids, and pools—and try to think like a catfish. Putting myself in the fish's fins, I begin casting a spinner, jig, nightcrawl-er, or fly to the spots I suspect I'd be swimming were I a cat.

Catfish and I go back 20 years, to when I fished the Colorado River in Texas with my grandfather for channels and the occasional back-bending blue catfish. Early on, I liked to fish for cats because it meant I got to explore up and down the river, casting hopefully to

I've been fishing for channel cats for 20 years, usually at night, and usually with a long spinning rod, light line, and a piece of night-crawler. It's my favorite warmwater fish.

water that just had to hold a big fish. When I hooked one, I was always thrilled to see the sleek form of a channel cat, its gray-blue body lightly spotted in black, or the large and muscular blue cat, its forked tail pumping in the current.

As a catfish fan, I'm in large and enthusiastic company. Catfish are so popular in some parts of the United States that poets write songs about them, towns honor them with contests and festivals, and anglers will sit on a river bank through the night just to tangle with a "good cat." As a great eating fish, the catfish has few rivals. Demand for catfish is so great that well over 300 million pounds are raised on fish farms each year, the dressed fillets sent to supermarkets and restaurants across the South and Midwest, like "Big Cat" in Austin, Texas, which specializes in catfish entrees.

When it comes to fighting on the end of the line, catfish are as feisty as they come. Because they eagerly strike artificial lures and bait and are found in some of the most beautiful settings, they are popular as a sport fish, so popular in fact that a large portion of commercially raised cats are sent live to fee-fishing ponds.

If the catfish is so popular, what is it doing in a book about little-known roughfish? One reason is the catfish shows how attitudes by anglers towards fish can change. While the catfish has always been popular with Southerners, many anglers in Michigan, Wisconsin, and Minnesota still view it as an ugly, muddy-tasting bottom feeder not worth pursuing. A few summers ago I watched a lone angler, fishing the Mississippi River 2 miles from downtown Minneapolis, catch channel catfish on virtually every cast. Even though it was accessible to hundreds of thousands of anglers, not a single other person was fishing the spot.

The attitude in the North towards catfish is changing, however. As the numbers of popular fish like the walleye have been dropping from overfishing and pollution, midwestern anglers are beginning to look for new fish to pursue. They are quickly learning that cats fight hard and taste great. Even Minnesota—a bastion of diehard walleye anglers—has begun stocking flathead and channel catfish in popular fishing lakes.

Another reason we have included catfish in *Fishing for Buffalo* is that they are mysterious and fascinating. People have been eating, fishing for, and revering the catfish for years. Yet little is known about their habits. Many anglers who have been fishing for cats their whole lives still hold to myths and superstitions that have accompanied the species for centuries.

What Is a Catfish?

The 39 species of freshwater catfish in North America are all members of the family *Ictaluridae*, which means "fish-cat" in Latin. Those catfish living in the Midwest can be broken down into three groups, according to size. The smallest are called madtoms—like the tadpole madtom, checkered madtom, and stone cat. These tiny catfish only grow to several inches long, so they are rarely caught by sportfishing methods. However, they make good bait. Zane Grey used madtoms in the early 1900s to catch trout and bass in Pennsylvania. Madtoms are the only fish in the Midwest that have poison glands. A madtom can inject its venom through spines in its fins into a larger fish trying to eat it. Although potentially deadly to a fish, the venom is no more dangerous to humans than a mild bee sting.

The largest catfish species—the blue cat, the channel cat, and the flathead cat—are known collectively as "catfish." Smaller than catfish but larger than madtoms are the black, brown, and yellow bullheads.

Catfish and bullheads have several things in common. All have a single dorsal fin and a soft, fleshy adipose fin (see illustration). They also have a sharp spine at the leading edges of each dorsal fin and 2 pectoral fins. These spines, not the fish's whiskers or barbels as many believe, are the cause of the catfish's famous "sting." When the fish is alarmed, it raises and locks its spiked fins into an upright position. Many beginning catfish and bullhead anglers have received a painful spike in the hand which will swell and stay sore for several days. Once you learn where the spines are located, however, catfish and bullheads are as safe to hold as any fish.

Catfish spines have more uses than just ventilating human parts. Native Americans once used them as awls for leather work and as sewing needles. They would remove the spines, round the base, and file off the barbs. An ancient catfish spine that had been used by North American natives was found on the shores of Lake Huron and dated at 1,000 years B. C. Today, the spines are used as handy toothpicks following a fine meal of catfish, hushpuppies, and greens.

Another common characteristic of all catfish and bullheads, sometimes called "skin fish," is that they lack scales, causing them to feel sleek and smooth. In some cultures, people will not eat catfish because of their smooth skin. South America's Guyana has many catfish living in the local waters, but few are sold in the local markets because many Guyanese consider skin fish taboo. Their religious teachings oppose the consumption of these fish, called "children of the devil." Some myths here and in other parts of the world even blame leprosy and other skin diseases on the consumption of catfish. There is no need to worry, however, as no cases of catfish-caused skin disease have ever been verified.

All catfish have 4 pairs of barbels, or whiskers. Barbels are lined with sensitive nerve endings, similar to taste buds, that allow the catfish to taste and smell its way through the dark and muddy waters where it hunts for

food. The taste buds are located not only on the fish's whiskers; a catfish can have up to 100,000 covering its entire body. An old saying that a catfish can smell with its tail turns out to be quite true.

Catfish have a peculiar mating ritual. First an amorous male and female pair up by stroking each other with their barbels and rubbing up against each other's bodies. Next, the pair looks for a nest, such as an undercut bank, old tin can, hollow log, abandoned muskrat tunnel, or old piece of drain tile from a farmer's field. Once in the nest, they move together and wrap their tails around the other's heads, and then quiver, releasing eggs and sperm. The male guards the jellylike mass of eggs until they hatch, a behavior also displayed by the male largemouth bass. The male catfish has his job cut out for him, because many animals, including his mate, try to devour his protected charges.

In the South, folks often take advantage of this nest-guarding behavior to catch catfish by grabling, or noodling. If you want to become a noodler, first find a catfish-filled river. Then,

I took this cat with a fast-moving jig below a dam on the Mississippi River. Often, the fish will start hitting just as the sun goes down.

The noodler (left) caught this catfish by sticking his hand into its mouth and out the gill opening. With both hands interlocked, he hauled the struggling fish up onto the bank.

bank. Warning—this technique should not be attempted by small children as they could be drowned or eaten.

While the male catfish is driving predators and noodlers away, he stays on the nest and creates a continual current of water over the mass of eggs by waving his fins. Occasionally he slides a fin under the mass of eggs and gives it a vigorous shake. This keeps oxygen-rich water circulating among the eggs at all times.

When the eggs hatch, the young catfish swim around in a tight ball, protected by their father, until they separate and swim off to begin a life on their own. For some species of catfish, the earlier they leave the nest the better, because sometimes Dad will get fed up with his kids hanging around the house and try to eat them.

Catfish and Humans

That catfish are good to eat and a pleasure to catch is no new discovery. Native Americans used the catfish not only for producing tools but also as an important food source. When Hernando De Soto, the famous Spanish explorer, journeyed up the Mississippi River in the mid-1500s, he observed Indians using nets to catch catfish. The European immigrants soon began to catch catfish on their own. In 1817, Major Stephen Long of the U.S. Army Corps of Engineers reported in his journal that one morning he went down to the banks of the Mississippi River, where he was stationed, and "caught five catfish and one freshwater drum before breakfast." At Walden Pond, Henry David Thoreau took great pleasure in fishing for bullheads, also called "horned pout."

wade or swim along it during late spring, when the cats are guarding their nests, all the while groping and feeling underwater to find a nesting spot. When you discover a likely hole, slowly insert your arm. If all goes well, an angry male cat will think your arm is an invading walleye trying to eat its eggs and attack. The instant your hand is inhaled into the cat's maw, thrust it out through the fish's gills and grab it with your other hand. With hands locked, wrestle the fish from its den, and onto the

I have spent the hours of midnight fishing from a boat by moonlight . . . those experiences were very memorable and valuable to me, anchored in forty feet of water, communicating by a long flaxen line with the mysterious nocturnal fishes which had their dwelling below. I drifted in the gentle night breeze, now and then feeling a slight vibration along my line, indicative of some life prowling about its extremity of dull uncertain blundering purpose there, and slow to make up its mind. At length you slowly raise, pulling hand over hand, some horned pout squeaking and squirming to the upper air. It was very queer, especially in dark nights, when your thoughts had wandered to vast and cosmogonal themes in other spheres, to feel this faint jerk, which came to interrupt your dreams and link you to nature again.

Not all historical references to catfishing are so contemplative. In 1887, Charles H. Blakeman wrote in an article called "A Week's Sport Along the Minnesota River" about two boys he observed fishing: "Back and forth the line shot through the water, the boys having all they could do to hold on. For fully five minutes the fish fought vigorously, sometimes coming to the surface and making the water boil around him, then darting off and drawing the line so tight the boys could feel it cutting their hands. But he was at last conquered and landed. An enormous catfish, weighing at least 25 pounds."

In 1945, Robert Wolfender wrote what could be one of the first examples of the now-popular catch-and-release fishing ethic. Wolfender had been fishing Tennessee's Cumberland River, when he came upon an elderly angler. Catching sight of the 4-pound catfish Wolfender held in his hand, the old angler said, "That's a pretty small fish to what they used to be." When Robert asked how big catfish once grew, the old angler made this reply:

Back when thar war steamboats on the Cumberland River, thar was an old catfish that wars suppose' to be a whopper. He

I lift a catfish from the same waters where, 172 years earlier, Maj. Stephen Long of the U.S. Army Corps of Engineers caught his breakfast of "five catfish and one freshwater drum."

broke trot lines, and jerked cane poles right out of people's hands. There was one young buck that tried to grapple him by tyin' a rope through his gills, but that old cat carried him a mile down river before he could let loose of him. Yes sir, that fish was the grand-daddy of them all. Wal, finally my pappy forged a hook out of an old broken plowshare, then he tied it to a two-inch Manila line, and hitched a mule to the other end. Then he cut a ham in two and used half of it for bait. It took pappy two days before he hooked that old cat, but when he did it shore was a sight. Finally between pappy and the old mule they drug that old cat out of the water, and it was said the river went down an inch.

Wal, pappy just looked at that big old fish alayin' on the bank adyin', and he looked plum sad instead of glad. In a minit, without sayin' a word, he takes his pocket knife and cuts that line and he tells me to help him push that old cat back into the river. I was surprised but I know better than to talk back to my pappy, so we pushed that big old fish back into the river. Pappy set down a spell and lit his pipe. I reckon it was an hour before he spoke. When he did he said, 'Boy that was the last of the big ones, that was the grandaddy of them all.' Then he said sort of quietly, 'a man ain't got no right to kill somethin' as big and brave as that thar old catfish.' Wal frum then on fishin' just wasn't the same for me.

American Food and Game Fish, written in 1923, sang the praise of the whiskered fish, especially the largest species: "Of all the catfish the blue cat is the one most deserving of cultivation and popular favor, and which could with profit be introduced into other countries." How did the people in the "other" countries feel about catfish being introduced into their waters? The following burlesque, written for *The Punch*, an English periodical in the 1920s, sums it up.

The catfish is a hideous beast,
A bottom-feeder that doth feed on unholy
  bait.
He's no addition to your meal,
He's rather richer than the eel,
And ranker than the skate.

His face is broad, and flat, and glum:
He's like some monstrous millers thumb;
He's bearded like the pard.
Beholding him the grayling flee,
The trout take refuge in the sea,
The gudgeons go on guard.

They say the catfish climbs the trees, and
  robs the roosts
And down the breeze prolongs his
  caterwal.
Oh, leave him in his western flood, where
The Mississippi churns the mud;
Don't bring him here at all.

The reluctance of the British to welcome catfish might have stemmed from incredible stories they had heard about these fish. Even today, farmers on the Skunk River in Iowa tell tales of massive flathead catfish that crawl up from the river on hot nights to feed in the cornfields like deer.

Natural History

The different catfish and bullhead species look alike to the beginning angler. They all have whiskers, smooth skin, and spines. But each has easily identifiable traits that distinguish one from another. Use the handy Quick Cat I.D. Chart to identify the catfish you catch.

Quick Cat I.D. Chart

If the fish has:	and has:	Then it is a:
1) a forked tail	a) dark spots	channel cat
	b) no spots*	blue cat
2) a square tail	a) light bar at the base of tail	black bullhead
	b) no light bar, all dark whiskers	brown bullhead
	c) white barbels under chin	yellow bullhead
3) protruding lower jaw		flathead cat

* Large channel cats can lose their spots and look like a blue cat; if there are more than 30 rays in the fin next to the fish's anal opening, then it is a blue cat.

Channel catfish and blue catfish look similar except for the spots along the sides of the channel. Large channel cats lose their spots, however, making them indistinguishable from the blue catfish to the untrained eye.

Another way to tell the difference between different catfish and bullhead species is by size: If you catch a large cat it is probably a channel catfish, a flathead catfish, or a blue catfish.

Catfish

Channel Catfish
Ictalurus punctatus
Ictalurus means "fish-cat" in Greek and *punctatus* is Latin for "spotted."

The channel cat is a handsome fish with light blue color and dark spots scattered over the rear portion of its body. Also called the spotted cat, fiddler, blue channel, river cat, white cat, willow cat, speckled cat, fork-tailed cat, and silver cat, the channel catfish is the most popular catfish with North American anglers. It is a sleek fighting machine, and one only has to look at the fish's proportions—small bullet-shaped head, deep body, and broad forked tail—to see what make it such a powerhouse on the end of the line.

Another reason for the channel cat's popularity is its wide geographic range, including the entire Mississippi River watershed, all the Great Lakes, and the Arctic watershed in the Red River of the north, which flows into Manitoba from the Minnesota–North Dakota border. Almost every warmwater river in the Midwest has a thriving population of channel cats. Channels have also been introduced outside their native range into many waters of the West and East coasts. In the Mississippi River, channel catfish were not native to the upper portion above St. Anthony Falls until a lock and dam allowed them to swim past this historical barrier as far north on the Mississippi River at St. Cloud, Minnesota. It was probably a channel cat that Lewis and Clark wrote of in a July 24, 1804 journal entry while camped along the Missouri River: "This evening Guthrege Cought a White catfish, its eyes small & its tale much like that of a Dolfin."

Channel catfish prefer moving water, especially after the temperature begins to rise in the spring. During the bright part of the day, channels spend their time in deep riffles, pockets at the head and the tail of pools, or in the deep slots formed as water moves around boulders in the streambed. In streams, typical channel cat habitat is almost identical to that of the brown trout.

When the light is low, at night or on a

Curt Dengler lifts a mess o' flats he caught in 2 hours of fishing on a warm June evening along the Minnesota River.

clear, fish such as walleye, smallmouth bass, and northern pike were abundant. But as farmers have drained wetlands and plowed up prairies, erosion has increased to the point where over one-third of the nation's topsoil has been lost, much of it flowing into these streams, causing them to run brown. Because the channel cat is an opportunistic feeder not relying solely on site to feed, it has become one of the nation's most abundant fish.

Channel cats spawn in early summer as the water reaches 75 to 80 degrees Fahrenheit, often migrating long distances up small feeder streams, even through locks, looking for good nesting sites. The female spawns when she is 3 to 4 years old and 10 to 12 inches long. The male takes an extra year before becoming sexually mature, possibly so that he is larger than the female and can drive her from the nest before she eats all the eggs. The eggs hatch in 6 to 10 days, and the fry are guarded by the male until they leave the nest.

cloudy day, channels move into shallow, rocky flats and riffles to feed. Here, the fish are opportunistic feeders, eating minnows, insects, crayfish, mollusks, vegetable matter, or whatever else they find. Channels feed on the surface too, consuming terrestrial insects such as ants, as well as wild grapes, cottonwood seeds, American elm seeds, and other floating items.

It is in lakes and reservoirs where channels can feed on gizzard shad that they reach their largest size. In 1954, a world record 58-pound channel cat was caught in Santee-Cooper Reservoir, Georgia. Not all big channels come from reservoirs, however; in 1949, a 55-pound, 50-inch fish was caught from the James River in South Dakota.

Channel catfish are so widespread because they can tolerate warm, muddy, and slightly polluted water. Two hundred years ago, when many North American rivers flowed crystal

Flathead Catfish
Pylodictis olivariis

Pylodictis is Greek for "mud-fish," and *olivariis* is Latin for "olive-colored."

Also called the mud cat, yellow (yaller) cat, Mississippi cat, goujon, pieded (pied means "patches of two colors") cat, opelousas cat, bashaw cat, Russian cat, shovel-head cat, Hoosier, Johnny cat, Morgan cat, and flat belly cat, the flathead catfish can be well described as an olive-colored mud-fish, just as its scientific name suggests. The color can vary from olive to dark brown to a light sandy-yellow, depending on where the cat lives. The flathead's tail is square to slightly notched and its jaws are broad and powerful, the lower jaw protruding past the upper.

One of the most noticeable things about this catfish is its flat head. A Menominee Indian legend explains how this originated. The catfish tribe, at the suggestion of their chief, decided to kill and eat the moose when it came down to the water's edge to drink. The catfish began to thrust their spears into the moose, making him so angry that he trampled them with his hooves. Many of the catfish were killed. Those that escaped had their heads flattened.

Thanks to the moose, the flathead can now use its head as camouflage. The fish settles to the bottom of a lake or river, its flat head indistinguishable from the muddy surroundings. Raising its barbels, the flathead sits in wait. Soon an unsuspecting gizzard shad, one of its favorite foods, slowly swims by and touches a barbel. In an explosive instant, the huge cat head opens up, sucking in the frantic shad, which tries desperately to outswim the powerful suction current created by the opening of the massive maw. It is over in a flash. The flathead swallows and moves upstream a few feet to wait for another meal to swim by.

Young flatheads feed on insect larvae, crayfish, mollusks, worms, and almost any other living organism that can fit into their mouths. After they reach 20 inches, however, flatheads switch to an almost exclusive live fish diet. Flatheads are not scavengers, as many anglers believe. In the Mississippi River, they prefer gizzard shad, freshwater drum, carp, and even channel catfish. Flatheads have been

> *Don't talk to me o' bacon fat'*
> *Or tatters, coon or 'possum;*
> *fo' when I'se hooked a yaller cat,*
> *I'se got a meal to boss 'em.*
> — SOUTHERN FOLK SONG

found with the spines of channel catfish protruding from inside their bodies, the wounds healed and the flatheads seemingly unaffected. Flatheads love crayfish. A big cat will lie with its mouth wide open waiting for a frightened crayfish or fish looking for cover to dart inside. In a gulp it's gone, and the deadly cavern opens again.

In waters with lots of shad, drum, and carp, flatheads can grow to a tremendous size. The world record is a 5-foot, 106-pound fish caught in Oklahoma's Lake Wester in 1977. Flatheads prefer big rivers, like the Mississippi, Ohio, and Missouri and their major tributaries. They like long, slow pools interspersed with short riffles. Flatheads spend the bright days in deep pools or beneath log jams, old snags, or undercut banks. At night they slowly move into the shallows to feed.

Being such voracious feeders, flatheads can reduce the numbers of stunted panfish in a lake. The Minnesota Department of Natural

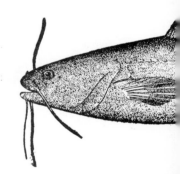

Hold a Catfish or Bullhead without Fear

Few things scare anglers more than having to take a bullhead or catfish off a hook. Having been impaled as kids, they remember the terror of trying to figure out where the sting came from, so they stand with a bullhead dangling from the line, hoping it will wiggle off the hook.

Take heart all you anglers. Holding a bullhead or catfish is easy. The trick is to put your palm on its belly and wrap your fingers around the sides. The spines are on the sides and top, so there's no way you can get poked.

Also, a bullhead or a catfish doesn't "sting" like a bee does. Nor does it jab at you with its spines. All it does is stick them up. To get jabbed, you have to impale yourself. Another thing: Big catfish (over 4 pounds) have dull spines. The ones to be careful around are the small catfish and the bullheads.

Tom Twohing and Rundi Myklebust admire their stringer of channel cats before heading home for a meal of catfish perlow. Similar to the jambalaya of Louisiana, this Georgia dish is hot, spicy and delicious.

Resources has stocked flatheads in lakes that were overpopulated with small bluegills. After a short time, the catfish had eaten most of the smaller bluegills, leaving more bluegill food for the larger panfish that anglers are after.

Blue Catfish

Ictalurus furcatus

Ictalurus means "fish cats" in Greek and *furcatus* is Latin for "forked tail."

The blue cat looks a lot like a gigantic channel cat that has lost its spots. The blue also has a higher, more humped back than the channel's, more than 30 rays in the long fin behind the anus, and a constriction in the middle of the air bladder. The blue cat is bluish-gray in color, and has a deeply forked tail and small eyes.

Also called the forked-tail cat, chuckle-head, humpback, high-fin blue, Mississippi cat, and Fulton cat, the blue catfish is third only to the lake sturgeon and the alligator gar as biggest fish in central North America. In the past 25 years, a 100-pound blue came from the Missouri River in South Dakota, a 117-pound fish was landed from the Osage River in Missouri, and in 1976 a 130-pound blue was hoisted from Fort London Reservoir in Tennessee. The verified world record is a 97-pounder that was 57 inches long, caught in the Missouri River, South Dakota in 1959. The heaviest verified weight was a monster weighing 150 pounds, taken from the Mississippi River in 1879, although Captain William Heckman wrote of a 315-pound "blue-channel" taken from the Missouri River in 1866 in *Steamboating Sixty-five Years on Missouri's Rivers.*

Blue catfish live in fast stretches of big rivers draining into the Mississippi River. Because of the extensive damming and pooling of these waters, populations of blues have declined, especially in the upper Mississippi. Blues are thought to have once inhabited the Mississippi River in Minnesota, but no confirmed records exist. Huon Newberg, a Minnesota Department of Natural Resources fisheries regional manager, says, "Its presence is questionable in Minnesota rivers today, even though each year there are unsubstantiated reports of blues being caught in the Minnesota River."

In Iowa, the blue is today found only in the lower half of the Mississippi River and in the Missouri River. In the summer of 1989, two large blues caught from the Missouri River both broke the state record. The first was a 38-pounder, the second, caught on a 10-inch minnow, weighed 40 pounds. South Dakota and Missouri still have a few stretches of the large, free-flowing river that large blues need to survive. Blues also live in lakes and reservoirs where they have been stocked or trapped when a dam was built.

Blues spawn in early summer when the water temperature reaches 70 to 75 degrees. Near southern sawmills, spawning blues will often enter hollow cyprus logs, left in the water before they are cut. After the catfish builds a nest it sometimes gets trapped, unable to turn around or back out. It is discovered only when the saw blade rips into the log.

Small blues have a diet similar to channels, but as they grow larger they begin eating fish and large carrion. Large blues like heavy, fast water. They are often found below dams in the chute of fast water coming out of turbines, where they feed on stunned gizzard shad that come washing through. Another blue cat habitat is a fast chute leading into log-filled river bend. Here, the fish will forage in the deep riffles snapping up redhorse, carp, and drum.

Bullheads

Bullheads are popular with kids and adults who like to catch a lot of good-tasting fish. In the shallow prairie lakes of southern Minnesota and northwestern Iowa, bullheads are the most commonly caught species. Each year, about 12 million bullheads are taken by anglers in Iowa alone. Bullheads are great eating, easy to catch, and abundant where other fish are scarce.

An incredibly hardy fish, a bullhead needs little more than a mud puddle to survive. In *North American Freshwater Fishing*, Mike Rosenthal tells of finding bullheads that had survived for days without water: "As a kid I dug bullheads from dry pond bottoms that looked like a huge puzzle of cracked earth. Under those conditions the fish were in the center of large lumps of dried mud. When the lump was opened it was similar to breaking an egg; each bullhead had constructed a small cell slightly larger than its body and lined with a mucus like substance from the skin of the fish. This substance apparently allowed air into the lump but did not allow the interior moisture to evaporate. When dropped into water these bullheads immediately swam away, apparently unharmed by many weeks without water."

The three species of bullheads are all members of the *Ictalurus*, or catfish, family and occupy different habitats and regions of the continent.

Black Bullhead
Ictalurus melas
Ictalurus is Greek for "fish cat," and *melas* is Greek for "black."

The black bullhead is also called yellow belly, horned pout, stinger, and river snapper. Its back is black, and its belly varies from white to bright yellow during the spawning season in the late spring. Black bullheads can be distin-

In Waterville, Minnesota, bullheads are elevated to celebrity status during the annual 4-day Bullhead Days Festival.

Jay Harriman holds the bullhead his brother Jimmy caught to win first place in the kids' division of the Waterville Bullhead Days fishing contest.

quickly becomes extremely abundant, and can become stunted at 3 inches or less. Under normal conditions the average size of the black bullhead is 6 to 10 inches. Fish of 2 pounds or more are rarely caught, although the world record is an 8-pound fish caught from Sturgis Pond, Missouri by Charles Taylor.

Black bullheads feed on almost anything they can find, such as insect larvae, worms, fish, eggs of other fish, and crustaceans. Sometimes black bullheads travel in a large school, devouring everything in its path.

Yellow Bullhead
Ictalurus natalis

Ictalurus is Greek for "fish cat," and *natalis* is Latin for "having a large buttocks," referring to the fish's long anal fin, the longest of the three bullheads in Middle America.

The yellow bullhead, also called butterball, white-whiskered bullhead, Mississippi bullhead, and paper-skin, can be distinguished from other bullheads by its white or light-colored barbels. It grows to about 2 pounds, and the world record is 4 pounds, 4 ounces caught in Mormon Lake, Arizona by Emily Williams.

Yellow bullheads need clear water and abundant aquatic vegetation to thrive. They are found in lakes from the eastern Dakotas across central Minnesota, east to New York and south to the Gulf Coast. In May or early June, yellow bullheads build nests, usually a burrow up to 2 feet deep. Creamy white, glutinous eggs are laid in batches of 300 to 700. The eggs hatch in 5 to 10 days, and the male guards the young fish until they are about 2 inches long.

guished from other bullheads by the black barbels, or whiskers, and the presence of a light band at the base of the tail fin.

Widespread in lakes and ponds across the Upper Midwest, the black bullhead ranges from southern Manitoba and Saskatchewan east to Ohio, and south to Texas. Able to withstand extremely low oxygen levels and more pollution than other bullheads, the black bullhead lives in streams and shallow lakes, often with muddy bottoms. Because each year more streams in Middle America are muddying up from erosion, the black bullhead is becoming increasingly abundant. In some shallow prairie lakes prone to winterkill, it is the only fish that can survive the winter; with no predators, it

Brown Bullhead
Ictalurus nebulosus

Ictalurus is Greek for "fish cat," and *nebulosus* is Latin for "clouded," referring to the brownish-muddy color of this species.

Also called the speckled bullhead, minister, red-cat, horned-pout, and *burbotte brune* in French Canada, the brown bullhead looks similar to the black bullhead except it has no light-colored band at the base of its tail. Unlike the yellow bullhead, all the brown's barbels are dark. Sometimes the brown and the black bullhead interbreed, making it tough for fisheries biologists—let alone anglers—to tell the hybrid from the parent species. Brown bullheads grow to an average of 8 to 14 inches; a 2-pound fish is considered large. The world record is 5 pounds, 8 ounces, caught in Veal Pond, Georgia, by Jimmy Andrews.

The brown bullhead's range extends farther north and east than those of the other two bullheads: from the Atlantic provinces of Canada, west across southern Ontario to Saskatchewan, south through the eastern Dakotas and down to Florida. Brown bullheads seek out backwaters of large rivers, oxbow lakes, sluggish rivers, and small ponds. Like other bullheads, they feed on the bottom at night on leeches, crustaceans, offal, worms, fish, and vegetation.

Brown bullheads are now popular in Europe, where they were first stocked in Germany in the early 1900s. From there they have been stocked in England, other European countries, and the Soviet Union.

Brown bullheads spawn in early summer when the water reaches 70 degrees. In some areas, they may spawn again in the fall. The male and female caress each other with their barbels, but do not clasp each other's heads with their tails as other bullheads and catfish do.

In the fall, as the water cools down, the brown bullhead burrows into the muddy bottom of the lake, turning its head down and swimming vigorously until it is under the mud. Then it places its mouth toward the surface and blows water out. This miniature geyser creates a cone of mud around the fish's mouth and a breathing passageway to the open water. The fish can remain like this for months during the winter.

Some of the finest fishing I did as a kid was in rural New Hampshire, pursuing "horned pout" in the little ponds surrounding my home. My friends and I would cut an aspen sapling for a pole, tie on a piece of monofilament, dig up a few earthworms, and spend the whole day poking around the swamps and ponds trying to collect enough fish for dinner. I would clean the fish and bring them home to my parents, who were surprisingly enthusiastic, even when the fresh fish would literally jump out of the hot frying pan onto the floor. "We all loved a meal of fresh horned pout," recalled my mom.

"Catfish"

Well, it's spring time, Carolina,
Going fishing on the river
Well I don't want no brim or crappie,
Only one thing that makes me happy:

Catfish—on my line,
Catfish—taste so fine,
Catfish—all night long,
Catfish—what I want.

Well old man bass he's pretty good,
That ain't no surprise.
But all I want is a little catfish
Just to make my nature rise.

Well, there is only one kind of fish that I choose,
The one with the moustache on his face.

*by Jim Wann and B. Simpson,
from "Pump Boys and Dinettes"*

The first thing we done was to bait one of the big hooks with a skinned rabbit and set it and catch a cat-fish that was as big as a man, being six foot two inches long, and weighed over two hundred pounds.
— From Mark Twain's *Huckleberry Finn*

How to Catch a Catfish

The traditional way to catch catfish is with bait from the river bank. Volumes have been written on trotlining, jugging, and still fishing with stink bait, dead rabbits, blood bait, and rotting chicken liver. But many cats are caught with artificials, too, and little has been said about how anglers can use lures and flies to attach a catfish to the end of their line.

Tom and I first started to think of new ways to catch catfish one summer during a Mississippi River fishing trip. As the evening light was fading, we worked our way as close as possible to the rushing water at the base of a dam where we could see hundreds of carp, sheepshead, and white bass rolling and jumping where the water gushed over a wall of rocks. Using a black Mister Twister jig, I cast to the dam and immediately caught a drum. After catching and releasing several of these, I hooked a large carp that tested the limits of my tackle as the fish streaked across the entire width of the river. The 6-pound-test line held my rod in a deep bow but did not break. By the time I had landed the carp, the light had dropped. Just the afterglow of the sunset remained and I figured it was time to return to the landing and head home.

At night, catfish move into the shallows to feed, as I explained to our friend Thusi Van Rensburg. I also suggested he'd have more luck if he faced the water while fishing.

I saw in the distance that Tom was again untangling his line from a tree, so I decided I had time for one last cast, and flipped my jig to the base of the dam. A fish grabbed the jig the moment it hit the black water and began to dart back and forth in quick, powerful runs. I was impressed by the strength and endurance of what turned out to be a 4-pound channel cat. I decided I could not leave if cats were starting to hit artificial lures, so I cast again and received another hard strike. This fish fought slower and deeper than the channel cat did. To my surprise, it was a flathead. I was amazed at how easy it was to catch these cats on a jig. I wondered, Do other anglers use artificial lures for cats, and could these fish be caught on a fly as well?

Poring over articles in fishing magazines at the public library, I discovered that a few innovative anglers around the country were using nontraditional techniques to catch cats. In Kansas reservoirs, anglers use spoons and plugs along the rocky shorelines to catch flatheads. As the weather warms in the spring, algae begins to grow on the rock riprap on the upstream side of the dams. Gizzard shad are attracted to the algae, and the bait fish attract flatheads. Flatheads don't chase down their prey; instead, they hide in the rocks and wait for the forage to come to them. When a tempting shad—or lure—comes swimming by its ambush point, a flathead bursts out and inhales the victim.

The trick to catching flatheads along riprap is to cast your lure parallel to and as close as possible to the bank. Use lures like the Lazy Ike and Flatfish that get down fast and create a commotion as they work through the water. A bright red-and-white color combination seems to be best. This is no place to use live bait, which swims into the rocks and becomes hung up. These conditions could be ideal for fly-fishing experiments. Try a diving fly, such as the Dahlberg Diver, using a sink-tip line. Al-

though I have never heard of anyone brave enough to try fly-fishing for these monster cats, it should work.

Kansas is not the only place people fish for flatheads with artificials. In the Mississippi River near Gutenberg, Iowa, anglers for years have cast and trolled large jigs for big river flatheads. Here, the key is to move your lure slowly and keep it bouncing on the bottom. Use a big jig, a half-ounce or larger, to attract the trophies. Both of these plugging and jigging techniques should work anywhere the flathead lives in relatively clear water.

Channel cats also hit artificial lures, as Tom and I have found on the Mississippi. Jigs seem

Catfish feed on insects, minnows, and crayfish living between boulders in a a rocky river bed. Jason Sundeen and Joel Dahlin took this stringer while fishing the Mississippi River during the low water of late summer.

The world record black bullhead is a monster of 8 pounds, almost as big as this stuffed one we picked up to add to our roughfish paraphernalia collection.

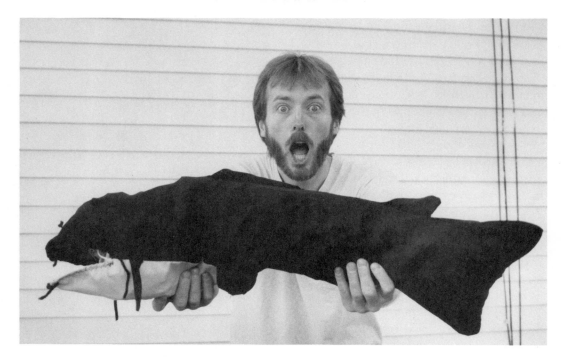

to work especially well, because you can keep them moving slowly and along the bottom where catfish feed. Some new artificial jigs are hollow and come with a tube of prepared stink bait. Squeeze the tube like toothpaste to fill the inside of the lure, which works like a bait and lure all in one neat package.

Summer is not the only time to catch channel cats. People catch them in February, even in Minnesota. The cats stack up in deep pools below dams on the Mississippi River. When it is very cold, the fish become almost dormant, but when a warm, calm day gets them feeding, anglers have been able to catch dozens of cats in a sunny location using jigging Rapalas fished slowly off the bottom.

In the early 1980s, I was fly-fishing for panfish in a warmwater lake in central Minnesota. As I walked along a dock, I saw a bullhead slowly swimming in the clear shallows, within easy casting range. I could not resist. I cast my squirrel hair nymph ahead of the fish, let it sink to the bottom, and retrieved it so it

would end up in front of the swimming fish's face. The retrieve was right on the mark, and the black bullhead turned and engulfed the fly. Fly-casting to fish you have sighted is among the pinnacles of fishing challenges. This catch was a highlight of my summer.

I also have caught bullheads on a fly when several dozen were concentrated in a creek below a dam. A streamer slowly retrieved through the school did the trick. Tom and I have also used Woolly Buggers retrieved along the bottom of pools below dams to catch channel cats. Other anglers have reported success fishing nymphs in the same manner as they do for trout. Use a floating line rigged with a 10-foot leader, a small split shot 10 to 15 inches above the nymph, and a strike indicator. Cast straight upstream or at a slight angle, over a likely-looking run. Quickly strip in the slack line as it drifts toward you. This technique allows the fly to sink deep, where the cats feed. When the strike indicator darts forward, set the hook. Large-sized flies will produce large fish. Besides Woolly Buggers, try a Hare's Ear nymph or Muddler Minnow in sizes 10 to 6.

Channels have been found to feed occasionally on surface food such as wild grapes, mulberries, and elm seeds. If you carry the mulberry fly (see the carp chapter), you will always be prepared when cats begin rising to grapes. White marabou flies fished in the surface film could also be productive when cottonwood trees are shedding their seeds. Both cats and carp will feed on this tree hatch.

For the angler looking for competition, there are plenty of catfish contests and derbies across the Midwest. The northernmost tournament in the United States is Catfish Days, in East Grand Forks, Minnesota. It is the only place in the country where anglers can win cash for catching catfish in a river flowing into the Arctic Ocean. This contest offers big money as well. The 1989 first prize was a $4,000 boat and motor, and the biggest fish won its angler a weekend in Winnipeg, Canada plus $100.

The Red River between North Dakota and Minnesota has been called the world's best catfish hole. It is also one of the most underfished rivers in the United States. These two qualities go hand in hand. Relatively light fishing pressure allows channel cats to reach huge sizes. Fishing pressure has been shown time and again to be the primary cause of reduced fish size in our sport fisheries. To try and maintain the size of the catfish in the Red River, the Minnesota Department of Natural Resources is considering imposing a special catch-and-release regulation there.

Another interesting catfish-related event is the Bullhead Days in Watertown, Minnesota. During this 4-day celebration, which began in 1964, the bullhead is king. There are fishing contests, a bullhead queen is crowned, and local bullhead crafts like bullhead wind socks and stuffed Bobby the Bullhead dolls are available for collectors. Friends and family mem-

bers who don't like to fish can watch the bullhead parade and the bullhead run, and then visit the bullhead stand, which serves fried bullhead and beer.

Gourmet Catfish Cookery

Many gourmets consider the catfish's firm, white, flaky meat among the finest for eating. To get the best quality meat possible, keep your fish fresh. This is true for all fish, but especially important for catfish, as they are usually caught in warm weather. Ensure the fish stay alive for as long as possible by keeping them in the water on a clip stringer or in a livewell. A

Tom tries the old hold-the-fish-close-to-the-camera trick to make his small bullhead look big. The key is to keep your hand out of the picture.

metal milk crate works well, too. Commercial anglers along the Mississippi used to keep their catfish alive in submerged wooden boxes until it was time to bring the fish to market. If they caught a large flathead they would have to sew its mouth shut with wire so it would not eat the other fish in the box. Keep this in mind if you catch a large flathead. If you can't keep your fish alive, clean the fish as soon as you catch them and put the dressed fish on ice in a cooler.

All catfish can be best cleaned with two pairs of pliers and a sharp knife. First, cut all the way around the head of the fish. Start at one pectoral fin, go up in front of the dorsal fin, and down to the other dorsal fin. Next, grasp the fish's upper jaw with one pair of pliers and the edge of the skin at the cut with the other pair. Peel back the skin until you have removed all of it from the fish. Small cats do not need skinning because their thin skin is edible. Make a deep cut behind the head, then grasp the fish's head and pull it down towards the belly and away from the fish. This will remove the head and entrails in one motion. To clean a large cat, nail the head to a post or tree before skinning. Finally, cut off the pectoral and dorsal fins (the ones with the spines). The fish is now ready for cooking. You can also fillet a catfish and end up with two nice bone-free pieces of meat.

RECIPES

Catfish can be cooked in a huge number of ways, from stewing to broiling, smoking, steaming, and frying. Here are some of our favorite recipes to get you started:

Catfish Perlow

A perlow is similar to the jambalaya of Louisiana but it is from the Georgia-North Carolina region.

Sauté 3 chopped onions, 3 minced cloves of garlic, and 1 cup chopped ham in 1 tablespoon oil in a pot that has a lid (leave lid off for now).

When lightly browned, add 1 chopped green pepper and 16-ounce can stewed tomatoes. Simmer 10 minutes. Add salt, pepper and thyme, to taste, and two bay leaves and a good dose of Tabasco sauce.

Add 2 cups white rice and cover with ½ inch of water. Bring to a boil, and drop in 4 small cleaned bullheads. Stir the fish in, put the lid on, reduce heat and cook 20 minutes or until the rice is done.

Southern Fried Catfish

This is how they do it in the Deep South. Fried catfish should always be served with hush puppies, grits, coleslaw, and steamed collard greens.

Soak 4 catfish fillets for 2 hours in 4 tablespoons cream and 2 teaspoons mustard. Roll in 1 cup white cornmeal mixed with salt and pepper to taste.

Heat 1 inch of oil in a hot skillet, and fry coated fillets to a light brown. Don't overcook the fish. It should be crisp on the outside and moist inside.

Iowan Pickled Bullhead

This cold fish should always be served with cold beer, corn crackers, and chilled cucumber spears. If you are not already there, close your eyes when you take a bite and imagine it's a hot summer night and you're on the farm in Iowa.

Cut up 4 medium onions and put on the bottom of a 2-quart kettle. Add a layer of 3 pounds of cleaned bullheads. Add the spices: 6 bay leaves, 1 tablespoon whole pickling spice, 2 teaspoon salt, and pepper to taste. Cover with 2 cups vinegar and 1½ cups water.

Boil slowly until fish are cooked, about 20 minutes. Chill and serve.

Chinese Poached Catfish

If you like something a little bit different and spicy, try this Asian dish. It was a big hit during the Chinese year of the "cat."

In a large, heavy skillet, heat to boiling enough water to cover 4 very fresh catfish fillets. Turn down the heat to simmer. Shred a slice of ginger the size of a 50-cent piece. Add the ginger to the water, then add the fillets. Let the fish poach for 7 minutes, then remove to a serving dish. Keep warm.

Meanwhile, heat 4 tablespoons vegetable oil in a small frying pan, and toast 3 tablespoons shredded ginger. Sprinkle 1 teaspoon salt, 2 tablespoons soy sauce, and 3 chopped green onions on the fish. Pour the very hot oil-ginger mixture over fish. Serve immediately.

Pescado Borracho (Drunken Fish)

This is a Mexican method for cooking a good sized fish, such as a 5- to 10-pound flathead. It is perfect for a party or celebration.

Preheat oven to 400°.

Rip 6 dried ancho chiles into pieces, and soak in 1 cup hot water for about 1 hour. Blend chiles to a coarse purée in an electric blender. Dust 1 cleaned whole 5-pound catfish with a mixture of flour, salt, and pepper. Brown fish in ¼ cup olive oil in a frying pan. Transfer fish to an ovenproof casserole dish and set aside.

Saute 1 chopped onion, and 2 cloves minced garlic in the remaining fish oil. Add chile puree, ¼ cup chopped parsley, 3 peeled and chopped tomatoes, ½ teaspoon cumin, ½ teaspoon oregano, and salt and pepper to taste. Cook over moderate heat 5 minutes. Add 1 cup chopped pimento-stuffed green olives, 2 tablespoons capers, and 2 cups dry red wine. Mix well.

Pour frying pan mixture over fish. Cover, and bake in oven 20–30 minutes, until fish is done.

—RB

INDIAN TEEPE - LAKE-OF-THE-WOODS-

8

Whitefish and Cisco

We can say from personal experience that a diet of whitefish alone, with no other food, can be eaten for days without ever losing its appeal.

— A Great Lakes scientist, 1836.

WHITEFISH live in beautiful, out-of-the-way places, I thought to myself, but this is ridiculous. I was standing 80 feet in the air on a narrow suspension bridge above a river in southern Ontario. Having carried a heavy pack for 6 miles, my legs were already tired. With my altophobia, they became so weak I felt I was going to fall. I wavered for a moment on the swaying bridge, wondering if I would have to turn back. Finally, the thought of fishing the pool I'd seen below gave me courage to cross.

I had been planning this trip for several years. Searching maps of Ontario's north shore of Lake Superior, I found only one major stretch of wilderness, through which ran several rivers flowing into the big lake—rivers I hoped drew fall runs of steelhead, whitefish, and salmon. I'd packed my car and headed north, looking forward to a week of fishing away from the hordes of anglers that usually crowd Superior's accessible rivers in autumn. After driving north from Duluth, I left my vehicle at the end of the road and began hiking toward the river along a spectacular trail that wove intermittently along the coves and beaches of Lake Superior before plunging deep into the forest.

After crossing the terrifyingly high bridge, I worked my way downstream to a stretch of flat bank. Below was the large eddy I'd seen from above. As usual, I decided to fish first and set up camp later, dumping my pack and uncasing my rod. Although the light was quickly fading, I could see a spot across the river where boulders in the current caused a ragged edge of water. It was here, I figured, fish migrating upstream would stop and rest. With my first cast, I dropped a number 3 Mepps spinner into the swirling edge. Before I could react, a magnificent steelhead hit the lure, jumped, and threw it into the air. I stood stunned, shaking with excitement, and thought, What a trip this is going to be!

After several more casts a bit downstream, another heavy fish struck. This one did not jump, but I could see its broad, silver sides flashing in the clear water. Using the flow to its advantage, the fish streaked downstream into the depths of the pool, where I could feel its head shake. It must be a bright steelhead, I thought to myself. After a vigorous struggle I

The Chippewa and Menominee Indians speared and netted whitefish and cisco. The fish were smoked and then traded with other bands for bison and deer meat.

139

Looking something like a sucker, whitefish are actually in the *Salmonidae* family, related to trout and salmon. For decades, the fine-fleshed whitefish was the prize of commercial anglers in the Great Lakes.

led a fish of about 7 pounds onto the smooth rock where I stood.

It was a lake whitefish. With its thick body and light silver color, the fish looked like a large Arctic grayling without the high dorsal fin. The top of its jaw overhung the bottom a bit, and it had large, bright eyes. I was happy to catch such a beautiful, powerful fish.

Whitefish are members of the *Salmonidae* family, which also includes cisco (lake herring), salmon, trout, grayling, and char. One thing all these fish have in common is that they inhabit cold water, usually less than 72 degrees. Because of this they are often called "coldwater fish." Their native range is generally in the northern half of North America

Lake whitefish, round whitefish, and the cisco are often considered roughfish by local anglers, because they are tough to catch and little is known or written about them. Well-documented facts about cisco and whitefish natural history are about as common as sympathy from a highway patrol officer. Even though these fish have a rich history in the Great Lakes commercial fisheries and are considered one of the sportiest and best-tasting fish in the northern part of the central United States, surprisingly few anglers know they even exist.

One reason lake whitefish, round whitefish, and cisco are such mysteries is they look alike and have confusing names. At a glance, you can always tell the whitefish from the cisco by looking at the mouth. The whitefish has an overbite and the cisco an underbite. Tom remembers which has which with this mnemonic device: "Whitefish" has "over" seven letters in its name and "cisco" has "under" seven letters. You can just write it on your hand, too. An angler can usually tell a round whitefish from a lake whitefish by its size: Lakes are big, usually over a pound. Rounds are rarely over 10 inches long.

Because these fish are so good to eat and a blast to catch on light tackle, it's a shame more people don't know about them. Both species were once important to early European settlers in the Great Lakes region, yet today it's rare to find anyone who knows much about them. This lack of knowledge has led to more than missed fishing opportunities for northern anglers. In the early 1970s, two species of cisco found only in the Great Lakes—the longjaw cisco and the deepwater cisco—became extinct because of pollution and overfishing.

Natural History

Lake Whitefish

Coregonus clupeaformis
Coregonus, "angle-eye" in Greek, refers to the edge of the pupil in the whitefish's eye, and *clupeaformis* is Latin for "herring shape."

Lake whitefish are one of the best-tasting freshwater fish that swims. Fresh whitefish is considered by residents along the Great Lakes a fish worth waiting in line for. The fact that whitefish at one time were almost fished out of the Great Lakes is testimony to their commercial appeal.

The lake whitefish is a large species. It averages 2 to 4 pounds, and 15 inches. Many 20-pound fish have been caught, and in 1946 a 42-pounder was taken near Isle Royale in Lake Superior.

Gizzard fish, buffalo whitefish, bowback whitefish, Ostego bass, Sault whitefish, and *grande coregone* are a few of the common names given to the lake whitefish. Whitefish have a silvery sheen to a tint of pale green to dark brown on their back, becoming lighter

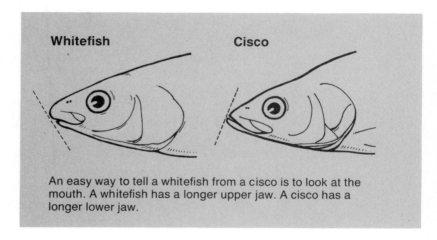

An easy way to tell a whitefish from a cisco is to look at the mouth. A whitefish has a longer upper jaw. A cisco has a longer lower jaw.

underneath. The fins range in color from clear in the Great Lakes to dark or black-tipped in inland waters, especially in Canada. The lake whitefish has an overhanging upper jaw, similar to that of the freshwater drum.

Lake whitefish are widely distributed in Canada and Alaska, living in virtually every large lake from the Bering Straits to Quebec and south to the Great Lakes, being most abundant in Lake Superior and northern Lake Michigan. They are also found in many inland

Range of the lake whitefish

lakes of northeastern Minnesota and northern Wisconsin and Michigan.

To survive, lake whitefish need lakes or rivers with a year-round supply of water cooler than 60 degrees Fahrenheit. In the Upper Midwest, the southern extreme of the fish's range, only the Great Lakes and deep infertile inland lakes have water this cold. These lakes have a layer of deep water called the hypolimneon that remains cool enough and contains enough oxygen for the whitefish to live during the hot summer.

For this deep layer to remain well oxygenated through the summer, the lake must be infertile. If a lake is too fertile, then too many plants or algae grow in the upper layer of water. When these plants die and sink into the deep water, they are attacked and eaten by bacteria, which use up oxygen and give off carbon dioxide. This reduces the oxygen in the deep water, threatening the survival of the whitefish.

In the northern part of the whitefish range, surface water remains cool enough throughout the year, and the fish do not have to descend to the depths to survive. But at the southern edge, the whitefish populations are more delicate. When lakes are developed and surrounded by cottages, nutrients from human waste leach from septic tanks through the soil and into the water. This increases the amount of algae, reducing the amount of oxygen at the bottom of the lake. Occasionally, in long hot summers, a whitefish or cisco fishkill occurs.

In the fall, after spending the summer in deep water, whitefish move into the shallows to spawn. In the United States, this migration occurs in November and December, when the water temperature has dropped to about 46 degrees. The fish look for shallow reefs covered with stone and sand in water less than 20 feet deep and spawn at night, often jumping and playing in the spawning area. The fish rise to the surface in pairs, or in trios of one female and two males. The female emits spawn on each rise, and the smaller-sized males simultaneously discharge their milt. The eggs settle to the bottom, where they receive no parental care. After the eggs hatch, the fry move into deeper water to feed on tiny free-swimming animals call zooplankton.

After a year, the young whitefish begin to feed mostly on the bottom, consuming aquatic insects such as the larvae of mayflies, caddis flies, and midges, as well as small clams, leeches, fish eggs, minnows, and crustaceans. They will, however, rise to the surface to feed if a large insect hatch is occurring.

The average whitefish grows fast, reaching 2 pounds in 3 to 4 years. A long life awaits the young fish that survive the attacks of lake trout and burbot. One of the oldest whitefish recorded was a 28-year-old taken from Great Slave Lake in Canada.

Years ago, lake whitefish were so abundant in the Great Lakes that Native Americans relied on them for their livelihood. The Cree and Ojibwa tribes fished the St. Mary's River between Lake Superior and Lake Huron, trading dried whitefish and maple syrup with other Indian bands from their permanent settlement along the shore. Using dipnets, two people fishing from a canoe could catch up to 5,000 pounds of lake whitefish in half a day's fishing. Much of the fishing was done by the women, who either dipped lake whitefish from the rapids of the St. Mary's River using a net on the end of a pole, or using gill or seine nets to trap the fish in the shallows. The nets were made by twisting the fibrous inner bark of willow trees into strands and were set in the waters of the south shore of Lake Superior, Lake Michigan's Green Bay, and other protected bays of the Great Lakes.

The Jesuit priest Father Hennepin was captured by the Dakota in the late 1600s. When he eventually escaped, he traveled up the Mississippi River through Lake Superior and wintered over on the shore of Lake Huron. "Dur-

Lake Superior, where this commercial angler works, is a whitefish angling hotspot. In the fall and spring, the sleek fish move into the shallows and readily hit lures and flies.

Always hopeful, I stand on a frozen lake near the Minnesota–Ontario border waiting for a whitefish to swim up to my lure.

ing the winter, we took whitefish in Lake Orleans [Huron] in twenty or twenty-two fathoms of water," he wrote. "They were to season the Indian corn, which was our usual fare."

In 1830, whitefish were still popular with local anglers, most of who were now of European descent. Juliette Kinzie, the wife of pioneer fur trader John Kinzie, wrote in her journal, "How bright and beautiful it [Mackinaw Island] looked as we walked aboard on the following morning. The rain had passed away, but had left all things glittering in the light of the sun as it rose up over the waters of Lake Huron, far away to the east. Before us was the lovely bay, scarcely yet tranquil after the storm, but dotted with canoes and the boats of the fishermen already getting out their nets for the trout and whitefish, those treasures of the deep."

Early settlers established fishing villages along the shores of the Great Lakes specifically to catch whitefish. The towns Whitefish Point and Whitefish Bay, on Lake Superior, were built and named in 1820. Commercial anglers used heavy linen gill nets with stones attached to the bottom and floating cedar splints at the top edge. In the 1860s, fishermen started using pound nets, which funnelled schools of whitefish into pens made of long walls of nets anchored to the lake bottom. Pound nets were extremely effective and were used widely throughout the Great Lakes. In 1885, a single area off the Apostle Islands, located on Lake Superior's south shore, was set with over 125 pound nets at one time.

Such aggressive netting quickly took its toll on the whitefish populations. In 1880, the commercial catch from Lake Michigan was 12 million pounds. It dropped to 1.5 million by 1920. Just after the turn of the century, in 1903, the cisco for the first time replaced the whitefish as the top commercial catch from the Great Lakes.

The whitefish population, severely weakened by decades of overfishing, was dealt another blow in the 1940s with the invasion of the sea lamprey. When the Welland Canal was built in 1928 to allow ships to circumvent Niagara Falls, this parasitic eel was able to sneak into the upper Great Lakes. The lamprey attaches itself to the side of large fish like lake trout and whitefish and rubs its rasplike tongue against the body to create a wound, through which it sucks out blood and fluid, eventually killing the fish. Lamprey thrived in the Great Lakes and practically wiped out their populations of lake trout and whitefish in the 1940s and '50s.

The lamprey invasion was stemmed in 1958, when the U.S. Fish and Wildlife Service began applying a compound that killed baby lamprey to the streams where the eel bred. This lampricide, called TFM (3-trifluoromethyl-4-nitrophenol), has successfully reduced the number of lamprey in the Great Lakes. With the lamprey somewhat under control, lake whitefish have been able to make a slow recovery.

Cisco
Coregonus artedi
Coregonus is Greek meaning "angle eye," and *Artedi* commemorates Peter Artedi, a Swedish naturalist considered the "father of ichthyology."

If anyone tells you he or she knows what a cisco is, be skeptical. The cisco is one of the most hard-to-identify and argued-about fish that swims in this continent. Even fisheries biologists — especially fisheries biologists — have a difficult time agreeing on what is and isn't a cisco.

One reason for the confusion is because the fish goes by many common names. In 1936, naturalist and explorer Sir John Richards wrote that the Cree Indians called cisco ottonneebees. During the same time, the fur traders began calling the fish tullibee. When Scandina-

vians who settled on the shores of the Great Lakes caught cisco, they noticed how similar the fish looked to the saltwater herring in their native country and started calling them lake herring. Other names for the cisco are blueback, bluefin, sand herring, herring-salmon, chub, and in French Canadian, *cisco de lac*.

Another area of confusion is the cisco's resemblance to 7 other closely related fish: short-nose cisco, short-jaw cisco, long-jaw cisco, bloater, kiyi, blackfin cisco, and deepwater cisco. All these species, often referred to collectively as the chubs, look similar to the cisco and can crossbreed with each other. Biologists believe that as commercial fishing in the Great Lakes reduced the populations of all these species, each began crossbreeding with others more frequently, lacking mates from their own species. Many of these fish have become extinct in parts of their native range, only to be replaced by another species. Indiscriminate stocking has also diluted the various gene pools.

Barb Shields, a Ph.D. candidate in ecology at the University of Minnesota, told me that

The cisco is a lean, muscular fish that rises eagerly to dry flies in the spring.

tullibee, lake herring, and cisco are currently synonyms for the same fish. "But this may change soon," she added.

In her research lab, she showed me several 5-gallon pails filled with preserved cisco specimens. Lifting one fish up, she pointed out its slender cigarlike shape and clear fins. Reaching into a different bucket, she showed me a much different-looking fish, with a squatter body and dark fins. The first specimen was a cisco from Lake Superior, a fish she called a Lake Superior herring. The second was from an inland lake, and she called it a tullibee. Then she lifted out another fish, that she called a dwarf tullibee, and explained that it lives in inland lakes and never grows to be much larger than one-third the size of an average Lake Superior herring, even though it has the same body shape and fin color. All the fish she showed me are today considered the same species — cisco — although Shields convinced me they are much different. Soon, she said, she may have the genetic data to prove it to fellow biologists.

Cisco are slender, sleek fish covered with silver scales. When held to a light, the scales glow with a pink or purple iridescence. Like all salmonids, the cisco has a soft, fleshy adipose fin, located just above and in front of its tail. The cisco does not grow to be as large as the lake whitefish. Adult cisco range in size between 14 and 20 inches long and weigh anywhere from 1 to 5 pounds.

The cisco leads a pelagic life, meaning it cruises for food in the open water rather than near the bottom like suckers or walleyes or in weedy cover like gar and bass. Cisco must keep feeding at all times because they never get to eat much more than hors d'oeuvres at one time. Their diet consists of zooplankton — small, free-swimming crustaceans similar to tiny shrimp. The gills of the cisco are covered with gill rakers, comblike structures that filter the small zooplankton from the water. This type of feeding is similar to a person spending an en-

tire day walking around eating popcorn one piece at at a time.

Cisco, like lake whitefish, spawn in the fall over shallow (3 to 6 feet deep) gravel and rubble reefs when the water cools to 42 degrees Fahrenheit. The male follows the female around, fertilizing the eggs as she randomly releases them over rocks. Spawning occurs at night and can last for over 2 weeks. Cisco only occasionally run up rivers to spawn.

More widespread in the Midwest than the whitefish, cisco are found in many northern inland lakes in Minnesota, Wisconsin, and Michigan. Pollution and overfishing have made the species endangered in Lakes Ontario and Erie, and the cisco is classified as rare in Lakes Michigan and Huron. In Lake Superior, however, it is making a comeback from its once dangerously low population. Cisco are still abundant in inland lakes, and are an important food source for walleye, burbot, northern pike, and lake trout. From the Midwest, their range extends north through central Canada to Hudson's Bay and the Arctic Ocean.

For years, Native North Americans and their dogs ate cisco during the winter. When European settlers arrived in the Great Lakes, they began a huge cisco commercial fishery. The fisheries supervisor at Burlington Beach on Lake Ontario wrote in 1868, "Herring frequent the bay in November and spawn in unprecedented numbers of millions." In 1918, 48 million pounds were caught from Lake Erie alone.

Round Whitefish
Prosopium cylindraceum
Prosopium is Greek for "mask," and *cylindraceum*, also Greek, means "resembling a cylinder."

The scientific name of the round whitefish refers to the large bones in the front of its eye and its cigarlike shape. Native Americans

called this fish menominee; other common names are frost fish, chivey, pilot fish, round fish, and shad waiter (because it eats shad eggs).

This small whitefish is widely distributed across Canada. In the United States, it is only in Lake Superior, northern Lake Michigan, and some of these lakes' tributaries.

The round whitefish is a small fish, averaging just 10 inches long and one pound. It has the same diet as the lake whitefish: bottom organisms such as snails, leeches, insects, crayfish, and fish. The round whitefish spawns in the fall, either running up rivers or using a shallow reef near the shore.

Long, slim, and round, like other whitefish, the round is bronze or greenish on the sides, with fins that turn orange during the spawning season, a trait the lake whitefish lacks. The mouth of the round whitefish, with its overbite, looks like the lake whitefish's.

Catching Cisco

Until casting begins not a fish can be seen, nor the slightest ripple upon the water, but no sooner have a few impaled ephemeras (mayflies) dropped upon the surface than the ciscos begin to appear. They can be seen

Several strains of Great Lakes cisco common in the 1800s are now extinct, primarily from unregulated commercial fishing.

Some of the best whitefish
and cisco fishing in the
nation is along the shores
of the Great Lakes.

coming from the depths, their pearly sides burnished by the glint and gleam of the afternoon sun. In a moment the water all about the many boats is a-ripple with eager fish, every hook has been taken, and the happy anglers are busy removing the catch and dropping it into their boats.

This passage, written by David Starr Jordan in the 1923 edition of *America Food and Game Fish*, described the fishing action on Lake Geneva, Wisconsin. Although pollution has killed off the cisco in that lake, similar sportfishing is still possible in some parts of the Midwest.

Perhaps the most famous cisco sport fishery takes place in July on the St. Mary's River, along the east end of Michigan's Upper Peninsula. Here, where the river slows after flowing through the Sault Rapids, live large mayflies called Hexagenia. Every July, these big insects rise to the surface from burrows in the soft mud of river bottoms, crawl out of their skins, and fly into the air to mate. For just a few critical moments before taking wing, the insect must

sit on the water surface waiting for its wings to dry. This is when the cisco rises up, strikes, and gulps down the newly hatched mayfly.

Armed with fly rods, armies of anglers also rise to the occasion to take advantage of the surface-feeding frenzy. At dusk, boats slowly drift down the river looking for schools of rising fish. When cisco are sighted, the anglers silently glide closer, taking care to not spook the school. Most anglers cast a size 10 to 4 dry Hexagenia imitation to the fish rising at the outside of the group to keep from scaring the fish when the fly line hits the water. When a cisco strikes, the rod is lifted quickly yet gently because both cisco and whitefish have a soft mouth that tears easily. A soft touch is necessary to land both species.

Just a few years ago, the cisco population was so strong in the St. Mary's near Line Island that daily catches of 50 to 100 fish per boat were common. Recently, however, the number of cisco has dropped. Steve Scott, a fisheries biologist with the Michigan Department of Natural Resources (DNR), thinks overfishing and the dredging of a ship channel through prime cisco habitat are to blame. In 1989, responding to the population decline, the Michigan DNR reduced the limit daily limit on cisco from 100 to 12 fish per day.

Cisco fishing is available in many other areas besides the St. Mary's. In the Boundary Waters Canoe Area Wilderness in northern Minnesota are hundreds of lakes stuffed with cisco. Shawn Perich, an outdoor writer from Grand Marais, Minnesota, fishes for cisco every spring in and around the Boundary Waters. Using a lightweight size 6 fly rod, Perich casts a yellow-bodied Adams, a dry fly, in sizes 8 or 16. He says the ciscos usually feed on the Hexagenia, for which he uses the number 8 patterns, but at times the fish are rising to smaller size 16 mayflies.

When Perich sees a school of cisco feeding on the surface, he guns his boat, then kills the motor to glide silently into the fish. "The trick is to tell from one rise in which direction the fish is headed," he said. "Then you have to be able to quickly fire off a cast to a point that will intercept the fish's course." Cisco are tough to intercept because they swim fast, requiring a quick and accurate cast. One tip is to look for the dorsal fin, which they reveal when rising. This lets you know in which direction they are heading.

Perich says the 14- to 16-inch cisco he catches are hard fighters. "After they grab your fly, they head straight for the bottom, which can be 20 to 30 feet below. There is no choice but to let them go or risk ripping the hook out."

Cisco can be caught in the spring with live mayflies, too. At night, the insects gather at street lights, where they can be collected. Use a small bait-holder hook, size 12, and a single split shot. Lower the mayfly to the bottom, where the cisco spend the bright daylight hours. Large schools can be located at this time of day using a sonar fish-finder. If the school is suspended off the bottom, a small bright jig or a tiny Swedish Pimple will often get a fish to strike.

Another good time to catch cisco is in the winter, through the ice. One popular method is to string small, colored beads along your monofilament and tie small hooks spiced with small pieces of minnow between the beads (check to see if this is legal in your state). The beads rest on the knots that hold the hooks. To find a cisco, take your sonar fish-finder out onto the ice and lower the transducer through ice holes until you spot a school. Lower the bead-hook rig, and jig it up and down until fish strike.

Catching Whitefish

Ed Migdalski, an avid whitefish angler, wrote in his book, *Angler's Guide to the Freshwater Sport Fishes of North America*, "In my estimation, the lake whitefish ranks as one of the most important sport fish of our continent." Even with such high praise from a noted angling expert, whitefish get little more than a passing glance from anglers. Many lakes in northern Minnesota are packed with lake whitefish, yet a busy day would have two anglers fishing for them. Because the whitefish spends much of the summer in deep water, thousands of walleye anglers fish all summer in lakes loaded with whitefish without even knowing the species exists below them.

When Petrus Artedi, for whom the cisco is named, was visiting his famous colleague, naturalist Carolus Linnaeus, he fell into a canal and drowned. Linnaeus, recognizing the irony of the tragedy, wrote, "Thus did the most distinguished of Ichthyologists perish in the waters having devoted half his life to the discovery of their inhabitants."

Why Fish?

Blue catfish, longnose gar, sturgeon, highfin carpsucker, greater redhorse—there is a tremendous diversity of fish living in North America, and angling is one of the best ways to learn about these fascinating aquatic animals. Not only does fishing get you outside to engage in sport and enjoy the outdoors, it also brings to your hand a living, vibrant creature, rarely seen by anyone but you and other anglers.

Some say it is cruel to needlessly annoy an animal simply for sport. What is cruel, we believe, is to pollute, channelize, fill in, and otherwise destroy the places where animals live. By fishing, you can see how nature works harmoniously, each strand of the environmental web delicately linked to the others. Such understanding helps us see how humans are linked to the earth, and what we must do to improve the lives of all living creatures that live here.

While whitefish can be caught throughout the year, one of the most exciting times is in the spring. When the water starts to warm up into the 40 degree range, after ice-out, whitefish move into river mouths flowing into a lake. This is when Tom and I put on waders and get out among the fish. We often see whitefish in the clear spring water by using a pair of polarized sunglasses to scan the flowing water. After we locate a school of fish, we cast flies or small spinners to the feeding whitefish.

To fly-fish, cast a nymph upstream of the school and let it dead-drift down along the bottom past the fish. Use a strike indicator—a tiny bright piece of yarn, foam, or cork connected to your line 3 to 6 feet up from the fly—and watch for the twitch that tells you a whitefish has been duped.

Fly rods are good choices for whitefish because they are so limber they absorb a strong run without tearing the hook from the fish's soft mouth. We use nymphs in sizes 10 to 14, gray and brown, especially with a bit of gold or silver, like a Hare's Ear, although anything that looks buggy and has soft, flowing hair will work. Other anglers use a micro jig dressed with creamy badger hair. Another way to get your fly down deep is to use a small split shot 18 inches up from the fly.

If you don't fly-fish, small spinners like Mepps size 0 or 1 and tiny ice fishing spoons work well. Tie one below a bobber so it moves just off the bottom of the stream. Again, cast upstream and let the bobber float down with the current to the sighted whitefish. The waves will give the lure an enticing action that often proves irresistible to hungry whitefish.

Bill Mitzel, an outdoor writer from Bismark, North Dakota, caught a world record whitefish in the tailrace of the Garrison Dam on the Missouri River. Mitzel was fishing for walleyes from a boat with a Lindy Rig and minnow when the massive whitefish hit. "I thought the fish was a salmon at first," he said.

"We saw it go by the boat and noticed its silver sides. It made tremendous runs, and I played it hard. Still, it took over 20 minutes to land. It wasn't until I netted it that I realized it was a whitefish. I knew that the state record was only 7 pounds and this fish would best that, so I headed straight for the scales. I was quite pleased when I found out that my 8-pound, 11-ounce fish was a new state record." Later, Mitzel learned his fish was also a world record in the 8-pound-test line category. By the way, as often happens, the hook fell out of the fish's mouth as soon as it was in the net.

One of the most exciting times to fly-fish for whitefish is when they are feeding on the surface. As the water warms in late spring and mayflies start to hatch, whitefish move out into the open waters of the lake. In the evening, they cruise just under the surface looking for the insects. Its overhanging jaw and small mouth make it hard for a whitefish to suck in a mayfly from the surface the way a cisco or trout can. Instead, it must roll over the fly to knock it underwater, and then circle and return to eat the drowned insect. Because of this habit, beginning whitefish anglers often fail to hook the fish, striking too soon and pulling the fly away before the fish has turned to take it in its mouth. You must pause a few moments after the rise. Noted fishing author A. J. McClane advises in his book *Fishing Encyclopedia* that an angler should say "*Cervagenus clupeafarmis*" after the fish pulls the fly underwater before setting the hook. The other trick, like with herring, is to determine the direction the fish is swimming so you can place your fly in its path. Whitefish are fast cruisers, moving in a straight line, rising at intervals of about 6 feet. The flies that work for herring also work for whitefish.

After the mayfly season, whitefish retreat to deeper water, usually between 30 and 50 feet. "We were drifting down the middle of a long, deep lake in the Boundary Waters, trolling

Tom jigs a Swedish Pimple near the bottom of a northern Minnesota lake stuffed with whitefish.

small spinners in about 30 feet of water," Barb Shield recalled. "All of a sudden we started catching whitefish. We stayed with that school, catching fish after fish until we had enough for a shore lunch. We rendezvoused with a friend for lunch. He had grown up in the area and was a good angler. When we arrived with our gleaming whitefish he said, 'Yuck, why did you bring those back? Look at the mouth, they're suckers. He refused to eat our catch even though we kept telling him how good they were."

There is one whitefish hotspot where all the locals know the whitefish and its superior qualities. Lake Simcoe, Ontario, is probably the most famous whitefish sport fishery in North America. The big event is the ice fishing season, when sometimes over 5,000 fish houses dot the lake.

The Lake Simcoe ice fishing method is simple: Dump cooked barley through a hole along with some salted minnows. Rig a tip-up with a "spreader," a metal wire that keeps several hooks apart at the end of the line. Bait the hooks with salted emerald shiners, and lower the rig to the bottom.

In the early 1960s, individual anglers caught up to several thousand pounds of whitefish in a season. However, things have changed in the last 15 years, said Richard Troth, a fisheries biologist in Ontario. Now, almost no young fish are caught; only older trophy-sized whitefish. The average fish taken from Simcoe is a whopping 5 to 10 pounds. Troth speculates that toxins being dumped into the whitefish spawning areas kill the eggs before they can hatch. The Ontario Ministry of Natural Resources has begun stocking

In the St. Mary's River, between Lakes Superior and Huron, two Native American women could net up to 5,000 pounds of lake whitefish in half a day's fishing.

whitefish fry into the lake to try to maintain the populations while it searches for a solution to the spawning problem.

Currently, the south shore of Lake Superior has some hot whitefish angling. Anglers do well off the piers at Marquette, Michigan and Ashland, Wisconsin. Float tubers might want to try the protected waters of Chequamegon Bay, Wisconsin in July. Here, and along the North Shore of Lake Superior, the rivers carry hatching insects out into the lake where whitefish and lake trout slurp them up. I've had my best luck on a calm evening in late June or early July. You can catch fish from shore, but a float tube helps you reach more fish and not spook them as you would from a boat. Float tubers should pay attention to the wind so they don't end up in Ontario.

Other good fishing spots for whitefish and cisco in Wisconsin are Lucerne Lake in Forest County, Tomahawk Lake in Oneida County, and Green Lake in Green County. In Michigan, try South Manistique Lake, and Whitefish Lake in Mackinaw County, Crystal Lake in Benzine County, and Higgins Lake in Roscommon County.

Round whitefish, or menominee, are a rare but interesting fish. They run up several rivers that flow into the Great Lakes in the late fall, just before freeze up. This usually happens 1 or 2 weeks before Thanksgiving. Fish for them the same way you would drift fish for steelhead, but scale down to a number 12 egg hook with a pea-sized tuft of fluorescent yarn and a small piece of earthworm. These fish are fairly small, 12 to 14 inches and less than a pound, but they fight hard and are great in the pan.

Several years ago in the late fall, I saw two older women in the pool below the first waterfall upstream from Lake Superior on Minnesota's Knife River. They were catching fish that looked like smelt and putting them in a bucket. I could see they were drifting a piece of nightcrawler on the bottom. I went down to talk, and they said they were catching menominee and fished for them every fall when the water flow was good.

For the Table

When you get home with a catch of whitefish or cisco, you are in for a treat. These fish can be cooked in many ways, and the result is always the same: delicious. When I lived in Grand Marais, on Minnesota's North Shore of Lake Superior, fall meant herring time. I would wait at the grocery store until the fresh herring was brought in from the boats. Local commercial anglers caught the herring in the big lake and surrounding inland lakes, and sold part of their catch to the town's residents. I would rush home with the fish, fillet them, sprinkle the fillets with salt and pepper, and slip them under the broiler for a few minutes. It was one of the best fish meals of the year.

The fine bones and thin skin of the herring and cisco make for easy cleaning. Simply run a sharp knife down the back of the fish to remove the thick fillets, skin, and begin cooking. The flesh of the whitefish contains high concentrations of fish oil, called Omega-3 long-chain fatty acids. These oils protect against heart disease. Eskimos, who eat lots of whitefish, have one of the lowest rates of heart disease of any people, even though they eat huge quantities of fat. Some scientists believe the fatty acids reduce the cholesterol in the blood and also thin the blood so it doesn't clot as much. To get the most heart medicine from your fish and the fewest fat calories, don't fry them.

Recipes

Deviled Grilled Cisco

This is a great way to cook herring at a beach party along the Great Lakes.

Score cleaned fresh cisco along the back and sides ½-inch deep. Sprinkle with salt and pepper, then coat with mustard. Sprinkle with white bread crumbs and oil. Grill over moderately hot coals for 6 minutes per side or until brown.

Whole Baked Whitefish

Easy and delicious, this method is perfect for a camping trip when you want to keep cooking as simple as possible.

Clean and scale whitefish, leaving the head and tail intact. Oil a piece of aluminum foil, and lay the fish on top. Season the fish with salt, pepper, and ground anise. Fill the body cavity with fresh mint, if available. Squeeze the juice of a lemon over the fish, and seal the foil well. Cook over hot coals for 30 minutes turning once, or in a 400° oven for 25 minutes.

Oven-Fried Whitefish

Worried about too much fat in your diet? Try frying your fish this way.

Preheat the oven to 525°.

Dip 4 whitefish or 6 cisco fillets in 1 cup milk with 1 tablespoon salt added. Roll in a mixture of ¾ cup fine, dry bread crumbs, ¼ cup Parmesan cheese, and ¼ teaspoon thyme. Arrange on a well-greased cookie sheet, and pour ¼ cup melted butter over the fish. Bake in the top oven rack for 10–15 minutes. Serve with fresh lemon.

Poached Whitefish

We think this is the best way to appreciate the delicate flavor of this fish.

In a large kettle, heat 2 tablespoons butter, and add ⅓ cup each of chopped onion, carrot, and celery. Sauté 5 minutes. Add 1 quart water and ½ cup dry white wine. Season with salt and pepper. Simmer 5 minutes. Lower into the kettle a 3- to 4-pound scaled and dressed whole whitefish wrapped in cheesecloth. Cover and simmer gently for 25 minutes or 8 minutes per pound. Remove the fish carefully, unwrap, and remove the skin, leaving the fish whole. Serve with Hollandaise sauce.

—RB

9

Gar

"The plates of a gar are hard. Clean one at night and you can see sparks when you start chopping."
— MIKE WALKER, LOUISIANA GAR ANGLER

FOR SOME REASON it was familiar, even though I knew it wasn't like any fish Rob and I ever caught. It looked sort of like a small northern pike that had been tied head and tail to Clydesdales pulling in opposite directions. At first, I couldn't place where I'd seen one before, but later, thinking back on the strange stick-shaped creature gasping at the water's surface, I remembered seeing something like it as a kid when our class visited the science museum. The difference was, the fish I'd seen in the river was very much alive; what I'd seen as a boy was an impression imbedded in rock that was about 100 million years old.

To call a gar (from the Old English word meaning "spear") a living fossil is no exaggeration. The gar evolved during the Cretaceous period, when dinosaurs lumbered through fern-studded swamps, sending groups of the long fish scooting for cover. The gar's armorlike scales and ability to breath air helped it outsurvive dinosaurs, woolly mammoths, and prehistoric peoples. For over 100 million years these fish have been floating lazily at the surface of stagnant pools, basking in the sunlight until the shadow of a pterodactyl or a commercial airplane passes across the water. Then, with a lazy twist, the gar takes a gulp of air and moves slowly down to the depths out of sight in the pale green water.

Compared to gar, fish like trout, drum, and mooneye are newcomers. Gar were swimming around eating froglike creatures and other now-extinct water animals before species like redhorse or walleyes had even started to work their way up the evolutionary chain.

The gar is sporty and good to eat. In addition, it's worth catching simply to hold one. In your hands, it feels like a solid tube of muscle, encased in delicately fitted armor. As the fish wiggles, you feel the interlocking plated scales bend and flex. It opens its mouth to take a breath, and you wonder if maybe it will follow you up to shore and retaliate with those needle-like teeth before you can reach the car.

At a glance, its just a fish, but as it looks up with ancient eyes, you feel a bit uneasy, like an intruder. The fish has survived ice ages, glaciers, volcanic eruptions, continental drift, and everything humans could dump into the water. "Put me down, Pal," the blank stare seems to say. "I've already been here longer than you and your kind will ever hope to survive, and I'll probably be here when any trace of your species has been brushed clean from this planet."

Native Americans along the Mississippi River often hunted gar at night, spearing fish illuminated by firelight.

Gar were one of the first fish humans caught for food. Prehistoric peoples, working across North America from Asia, used clubs and spears to capture the fish. Later, Native Americans used traps, nets, and hooks made of bone or wood. At night they cruised the shallows in canoes or dugouts, with torches ablaze on long poles overhead, and speared gar illuminated below.

The gar was especially prized in what is today the southern part of the United States. The Seminole Indians of Florida had their pick of bass, crappies, drum, and a host of sea fish, but they preferred gar meat above all others. They roasted gar whole over open fires, peeling off the shell-like skin and eating the fish like roasted corn. Early settlers in the South, where gar are most abundant, often netted and speared gar. In Louisiana, Mississippi, Alabama, and the Carolinas, gar were commonly sold in fish markets. For example, in 1880 the longnose gar was reported to be one of the principal food fishes marketed in New Bern, North Carolina. The gar's white, flaky meat has a light flavor described as a cross between fish and pork. In a 1940 issue of *Sports Afield* magazine, Jules Ashlock wrote that he had eaten "exceedingly good" fried gar fishballs.

In parts of the South gar is still sold in fish markets alongside catfish and bream fillets, and demand for gar often exceeds the supply. "I was just in Louisiana, and I saw gar selling for $2 a pound," says Keith Sutton, an angler from Arkansas. Gar meat is good steaked, smoked, or barbecued. Smoked gar is common in some areas of the South, and gar soup is a well-known dish in the Carolinas. The term "common as gar broth," is a familiar simile there.

Southern anglers are used to the sight of longnose, shortnose, spotted, or alligator gar sunning themselves at the surface and occasionally raising their beaks from the water to snatch a gulp of air. But in the North, few an-

Yee-haw! Gar on! Gar are wild fighters, often leaping clear from the water and twisting in midair before falling back with a splash.

The gar is a solid tube of muscle, covered in tight, interlocking enameled plates. So impenetrable is the armor of a big gar that it can flatten a bullet.

glers know what a gar is, where it came from, and what possible use it could have.

What on Earth Is It?

The gar is an ancient fish from the family *Lepisosteidae*, Greek for "bony scale." Restricted in range primarily to the south half of North America, the gar is a fish of warm sluggish waters. The gar is an extremely aggressive predator, similar to a northern pike in its relentless appetite, that spends much of its day chomping on minnows, small carp, and other fish. Recently hatched gar will try to devour small fish larger than themselves. This voracity won't please a minnow, but it's good news for anglers who like a fish that bites readily.

Sportfishing anglers have long despised the gar, thinking it eats bass, walleyes, and other game fish. In Louisiana even today you must slit the belly of a gar over 12 inches before throwing it back in the water. However, fisheries scientists have found that killing sport-caught gar has no impact on the gar population. What's more, gar have been proven to not affect game fish one way or the other. Gar eat primarily minnows and, since the late 1800s, carp. There are so many more of these species in a lake or river that the gar doesn't need to eat bass or walleyes. One study showed that gar are so dependent on carp that they often spawn in the same areas as these big minnows do. The newly hatched gar, which grow twice as fast, begin feeding on the newly hatched carp.

That gar are great sport is of no doubt to anglers who've ever had one on the line. Gar may be living fossils, but they are also fighting fish that will slash at a crankbait or take off with a minnow just like a bass does. Once hooked, gar will fight doggedly, refusing to near the boat or shore. Gar can be caught day or night, on spinning or fly gear, and in weather that's so hot even carp have headed to the cooler depths.

Gar have several unique features related to their long stay on earth that make them especially interesting. One is their scales, which are small, diamond-shaped enameled plates. Hard as a person's tooth, they overlap tightly along the body of the fish, creating an almost impenetrable shell. The plated skin of a gar is so tough it was used by some early pioneers in the South to cover and reinforce their wooden ploughs. As the plates can be polished to a lustrous sheen, gar skin has been used as costume jewelry and coverings for picture frames, purses, and jewelry boxes.

Gar scales look exactly like stone arrowheads and were used as such by some Indian tribes. The head of the scale is naturally serrated like the lead edges of flint arrowheads that have been chiseled to form an edge. The scale is stout at the base and fits naturally into the shaft of an arrow.

Its tough outer layer has protected the gar from predators, but another characteristic has been even more instrumental in its tenacious survival. Gars can breathe air. Like the bowfin, lungfish, and several species of catfish, the gar can take oxygen from the air through its swim bladder if the dissolved oxygen content in the water gets too low.

The gar's swim bladder, connected to its esophagus, works like a primitive lung. It is lined with a rough tissue of oxygen-absorbing cells, enabling the gar to survive in completely stagnant water by taking an occasional gulp from the surface, an action called "breaking." The gar floats along the surface and then turns partially on its side, silently belches, and takes a mouthful of air before sinking below the surface. For a short time, gar can live in water that

Range of the longnose gar

has been totally depleted of dissolved oxygen. If kept moist, it can live out of water for a day or more.

Not only can a gar breath air, it must breath air. Gars tangled in nets have drowned because the fish were unable to get to the surface for fresh air. Evidently, the need for air disappears during the winter, when the fish lie dormant in deep holes. Gar can live in water up to 100 degrees Fahrenheit, although they prefer about 90 degrees, a temperature which has either killed off almost every other freshwater species or driven them to deeper, cooler haunts.

Natural History

Five species of gar live in North America, but only 2 are found in the Great Lakes Region: the longnose and the shortnose. The others—the alligator, the spotted, and the Florida gar—are strictly southern fish.

Longnose Gar
Lepisosteus osseus
Lepisosteus is Greek for "bony scale," and *osseus* is Latin for "of bone."

Also known as northern needlenose gar, long-nose gar, garpike, garfish, common garpike, billfish, billy gar, and northern mailed fish, the longnose is the most abundant and widely distributed member of the gar family. Most anglers in the United States have at least once in their lives been surprised to see the slender beak of a longnose break the surface as the fish rolls, gulps air, and then submerges.

The snout of the longnose is its trademark and the primary way to tell it from a shortnose. The shortnose gar's mouth is only 5 times as long as it is wide, and the fish doesn't look too different from a northern pike. The thin stick-like beak of a longnose can be 20 times as long as it is wide.

Longnose are found in the Mississippi River system up into Montana on the Missouri River, through the Great Lakes (except Lake Superior, which is too cold), in the southern half of Minnesota, Wisconsin, Michigan, and North Dakota, east to the St. Lawrence River and south to Mexico. Like all gars, it likes warm water best, and is more common the farther south you go.

The longnose is a beautifully sleek fish. Its body is olive-brown on top and sides and is marked with black splotches on its anal, caudal, and dorsal fins and sometimes along the length of the body. Its body is long, thin, and cylindrical, like a snake's. The largest one ever caught was a 6-footer taken in the Trinity River, Texas that weighed 50 pounds.

Female gar lay big, bright green eggs in shallow bays and swamps that have weeds or grass, in water that is 66 to 74 degrees Fahrenheit. The female, larger than the males mating with her, leads a group of anywhere from 4 to 15 males in a circle. Some males nudge her with their snouts in the back of her body, while others are surfacing, splashing, and gulping air. The fish then congregate, point their heads to the bottom, and quiver violently, releasing sperm and eggs. The quivering group moves slowly away from the spawning area and then back again. The eggs stick to plants and bottom debris.

When the baby gar hatch they have a handsome black stripe running down each side, which they lose as they become juveniles. They use a little sucking disc at the end of the snout to attach themselves to submerged objects like logs and rocks. Soon this suction cup disappears and the tiny gar begin eating little fish. Often young gar lie motionless on the surface in groups, looking as though someone had tossed out a handful of straight sticks.

Shortnose Gar
Lepisosteus platostomus
Lepisosteus is Greek for "bony scale," and *platostomus* is Greek for "broad mouth."

Also known as broadnosed gar, stubnose gar, shortbilled gar, duckbill gar, and billy gar, the shortnose looks like a cross between a duck and a northern pike. It's smaller than the longnose, rarely reaching over 3 feet long, although it looks exactly like the alligator gar, which can get to be over 300 pounds. Like the longnose, it is spotted, but the black markings are only on the fins at the back of the body.

The shortnose gar is found in the Mississippi River drainage, from Montana down to the Gulf of Mexico, and east to the Ohio River drainage. Like other gar, it is more abundant in the South. This gar tolerates more turbidity than the longnose does, even though it, too, is a sight feeder.

Fishing for Gar

All gar species like pretty much the same type of water: warm, quiet pools with little flow and lots of weeds. Gar, which swim in groups, prefer open water like the backwaters of big lakes, reservoirs, and rivers. The bottom can be muddy or sandy, but a gar is almost always near submerged brushpiles or overhanging objects near shore. It sticks near cover primarily because that's where the minnows are. One difference between the two species is the short-nose likes the wave-washed shoals of big lakes and impoundments, and prefers some current; the longnose sticks to the calmest water it can find.

During the day, gar fin lazily near the surface of a pool. And the warmer the water, the more likely the gar will be near the top, gulping air. Unlike most fish, it's not worried about birds of prey. Since the armor of a big gar can flatten a bullet, the talons of a hawk probably don't feel like much more than a back rub. Another important thing to know about gar is they hang out in the same spots. When you locate one, it will probably be there the next day.

Evan A. Merritt, Sr. and his son Evan D. Merritt both fish gar in Panasoffkee Lake, Florida where some of the biggest longnose gar in the world are found. D. Merrritt, one of the best gar anglers in the Florida, currently holds the state record with a 41-pound, 58½-inch fish. The Merritts say the key to catching big gar is to cruise the lake at night with a spotlight and then fish the next day in areas where gar were spotted. "They'll be where you saw them the night before. The gar we catch are usually in the deeper water," said Merritt, Sr. "Not often do we find them near shore."

The gar is about as patient a fish that swims. It doesn't go ripping after its prey like a bass or a northern pike. It can't. Its tightly fitting scales are good at protecting but aren't too flexible. A bass can turn on a dime; the gar has the turning radius of a stretch limo. Therefore, instead of trying to chase down a minnow, the gar just sits and waits, and waits, and waits, until sooner or later a minnow swims close to what appears to be a stick floating in the water. In his book *History of Fishes*, J. R. Norman describes the somewhat pathetic attempt of a gar feeding: "Placing itself in a suitable position, and carefully sighting his victim, the gar

gives a sudden, convulsive, sideways jerk of its head, at the same time endeavoring to grip the prey between its jaws. Many preliminary maneuvers and tentative snaps are made before the body of the little fish is finally transfixed by the teeth. When this is accomplished the victim is gradually worked round into a convenient position, and unless it has again escaped during this process, is finally swallowed."

Understanding how a gar eats can help an angler catch and hook more fish. One of the first mistakes beginning gar-anglers make is to set the hook as soon as they feel a gar take off with the bait. More often than not, the hook pulls out because the minnow is simply resting between two thin plates of bone and the hook is probably several inches away from the gar. By waiting until the gar stops and then swallows the minnow, you can be sure the hook will be in a part of the gar where it can stick.

How do you know when the gar has swallowed your bait? Most experienced gar anglers say that after the gar has swallowed, it makes another, faster run. This is when to set the hook.

Longnose gar can reach over 40 pounds. But even gar like the one Rob holds can take a fly rod into its backing.

The alligator gar is so big and mean looking it makes a muskie look like a goldfish. It lives in the southwestern United States, going up the Mississippi only as far as St. Louis. The alligator gar looks like the shortnose except it's about 20 times bigger. The largest on record, caught in Vermilion Parish, Louisiana was 9½ feet long and weighed 302 pounds. Gar over 100 pounds are caught each year in Texas, Louisiana, Mississippi, Arkansas, and Florida. They've been known to kill swimming dogs, muskrats, and have severely wounded humans.

Mike Walker is a field biologist with the Louisiana Department of Wildlife and Fisheries, Division of Fisheries. He's been gar fishing for over 20 years, and although he specializes in alligator gar, he says the techniques he uses work just as well on longnose or shortnose gar.

Walker says there are two different ways to fish for gar, depending on the time. "The difference between night-fishing for garfish and day-fishing is the difference between night and day. When the sun goes down, we fish bait right on the bottom. But in the day, we fish near the top with a big poppin' cork" he says.

Walker uses a big shad, but says the best bait is whatever bait fish swim in the water you are fishing. He rigs his minnow the same way an angler for lake trout or northern pike rigs a smelt, by using a coat hanger as a giant needle to thread a wire leader through the fish's anus and out its mouth. The hook is tied on and pulled tight from the tail end against the face of the minnow.

"Then we just sling it out and sit in lawn chairs and wait," says Walker. "When a gar comes by, he takes the line real slow; you can barely hear the reel as it goes click . . . click . . . click . . . We let him run a ways, for as long as we can stand it. That's the hardest part. You know he's there, but you have to wait until he swallows the bait and gets the hook back into his gullet.

"When he stops and your reel stops clicking, that's when he's swallowing. But don't set the hook yet. He's going to run again, only this time a little faster. This is when you set the hook."

Walker says the power of gar is "awesome." The fish will often leap from the water when hooked and make a hard run, before allowing itself to be worked back in: "When he sees you or the boat, be ready, because he's going to go wild and you're looking at another long run."

Getting a gar into the boat can be dangerous, because the fish often thrashes about,

Gar can actually breathe air, allowing them to survive out of water for over 24 hours.

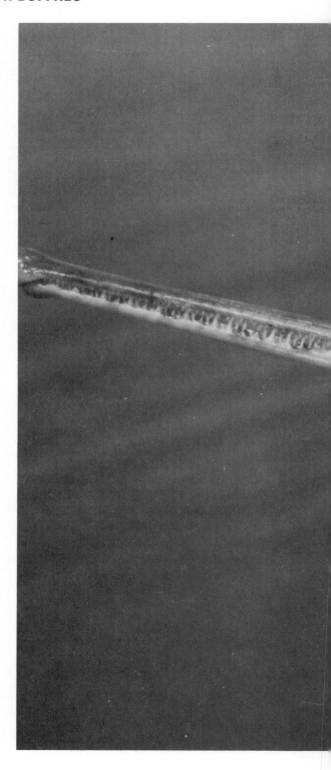

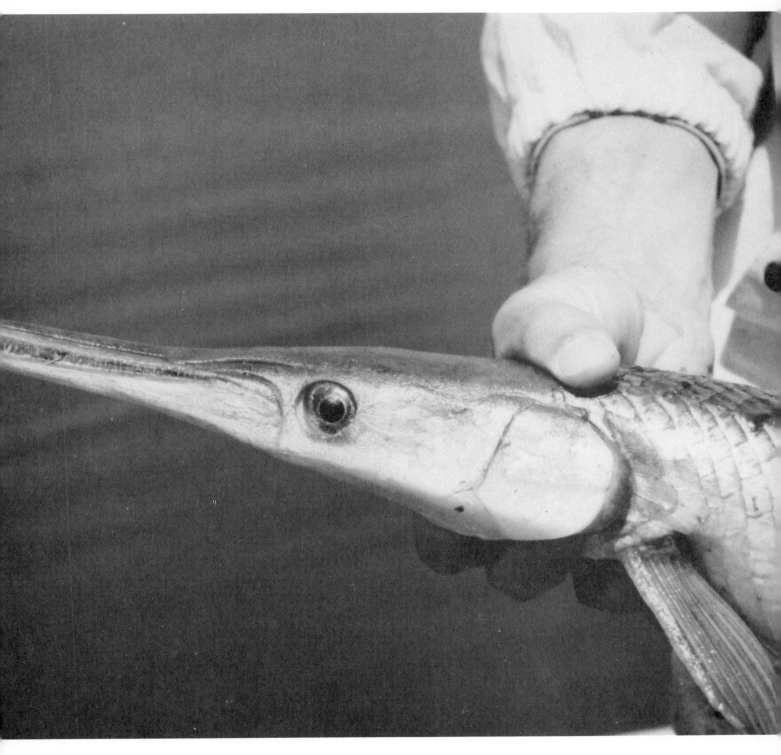

European-style Roughfishing

Europeans are the finest roughfish anglers in the world. Their techniques have been refined over hundreds of years of fishing for what they call "coarse fish," and their enthusiasm and dedication towards these species is astonishing.

A Treatyse of Fysshynge With an Angle, written by Dame Juliana Berners, and published in 1486, was the first fishing book ever written. It focused on techniques to catch British coarse fish. Since then, British and European anglers have been ever improving on the methods for catching the relatively few roughfish there, such as bream, carp, barble, tench, eel, rudd, roach, and dace.

With fewer than a dozen species to pursue (there are about 40 North American species listed in *Fishing for Buffalo*), Europeans have been able to refine their angling techniques to an exact science. Limited public access and millions of anglers have culled the dumb fish; only the wariest have survived.

Europeans fish for the same reasons we do: to enjoy nature, be with friends, and to catch fish. Like many American anglers, Europeans also fish for competition. This professional team fishing, called "match fishing," usually takes place along canals. The uniformity of canals gives each angler an equal chance at catching fish. The bank is divided into 40-foot sections, called "beats." Each team member fishes in a beat far from his teammates so there can be no communication during a match.

Before the match starts, anglers take several hours to set up. Standard equipment is a 30-foot rod, 2-pound-test line, dozens of different bobbers, and tiny hooks, sizes 20 to 28. The baits are usually different types of maggots, called "pinkies," "gozzers," "squatts," and "jokers." These are bred on decaying pigeons or chickens and are often dyed orange, bronze, or blue. Before the match starts, contestants use slingshots to fire writhing balls of maggots into the water in front of their beats, hoping to attract fish.

Matches are won by the total number and weight of the fish caught. As the fish are brought in, they are kept alive in keep nets. Sometimes the average size of the fish caught is as small as ½ ounce. A hot angler can win a match by catching a tiny fish every 2 or 3 minutes.

European match fishing is extremely popular. The World Match Fishing Championships attract teams from 23 countries and over 50,000 spectators will stand along the canal, cheering when someone from their team hauls in a ½-ouncer.

European fishing is not always so intense. Plenty of coarse anglers just want to relax by the edge of a lake or canal and catch an occasional fish. Some anglers spend their time trying to catch massive fish of individual species, usually carp. Called "specimen hunters," these anglers use "boily baits" (like our dough balls) and often know by name all the large carp that swim in the particular pond they fish. Some of the trophies have been caught dozens of times, a tribute to the careful release technique used by these skilled anglers.

brandishing its two rows of needlelike teeth. If you catch a gar and want to release it, cut the line as close to the mouth as you dare. Even if the hook is lodged back in its throat, it has a good chance of surviving, because the stomach acids will dissolve the metal in a few weeks and the wound will heal over. If you try to rip the hook out, you'll probably kill the fish and deprive another angler a chance to enjoy the sport you just had.

If you catch a big gar and want to keep it for the table or the trophy room, Walker recommends a technique for dispatching the fish that he has refined over two decades of gar fishing: "Hit him over the head with a hammer where the scales meet the head. That usually settles him down."

Bearing in mind that the gar's family name *Lepisosteidae* means "bony scale" will remind you that a gar is just a long collection of bones with some tough muscle in between. There's no place to set a hook because the mouth is just bone and sharp teeth; a regular hook out of the box usually won't be able to penetrate the beak.

Floating crankbaits work well because they have up to three treble hooks, and when a gar slashes, it often gets at least one snagged in its mouth. File each hook down until it is sticky sharp to ensure you have the best possible chance of connecting.

Two fishing methods skirt the problem of the gar's impenetrable mouth by using devices other than hooks. The first is the snare loop, which you can make yourself out of a piece of piano or framing wire. Take a 16-inch piece of wire, and, using pliers, make an eye at one end, to which you tie your line. Impale the other end through a minnow and make a loop; then bend the end of the wire into a hook and catch it below the eye and twist it. There's your snare.

When you see a gar break, toss this rig, wait until you feel it take the minnow, and then quickly set the loop, which will tighten around

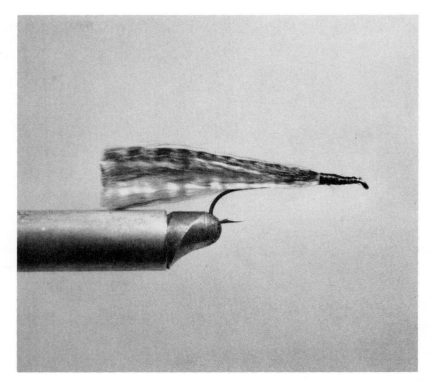

its upper beak. Besides lessening the injury to the gar, this technique is a good way to amaze your friends. You'll show up at the dock with nothing but a rod, reel, and piece of wire,. They'll think you don't know a thing about catching fish. Won't they be surprised when you return with a stringer full of gar!

An even more bizarre gar lure is a piece of gray nylon rope. Use ¼-inch rope, 3 or 4 inches long. Stick the hook in one end like you would a plastic worm, leaving the hook exposed. Use a lighter to melt the end of the hook near the eye. Unravel 3 inches off the other end. Cast to known gar spots. A gar will think it's a minnow, strike, and tangle its teeth in the frayed nylon.

Fly anglers might want to try tying the rope fly. Use a size 2 hook to which you tie on a 3-inch piece of nylon rope, tying in from the eye and working back to the bend in the hook. About 2 inches of rope will stick out; unravel

The rope fly, tied by Rob, is a piece of nylon rope tied into a number 2 hook. The unravelled strands catch in the gar's teeth.

Mike Walker cleans big gar with a hatchet and a baseball bat. We make do with a tin-snips and a fillet knife.

"Hit him over the head with a hammer where the scales meet the head. That usually settles him down."

that. Paint clear enamel on the wrapped part, and sprinkle glitter on the wet finish. Cast the fly to breaking gar.

The gar's habit of breaking makes it easy to locate: You don't need a fish locator or even much experience to find one. "Most of the time I fish gar in the summer when they are breaking," observed Keith Sutton. "We fish the oxbow lakes, where gar are often so plentiful you can catch them anytime of the year except in the dead of winter. Usually we find them at the mouths of feeder streams, where they are feeding on minnows drawn to the running water."

Sutton prefers live bait for gar. Because the longnose he catches run 10 to 15 pounds, he uses a 1/0 or 2/0 treble hook (baited treble hooks are legal in Arkansas, but not in some states). "I find the biggest problem with gar is getting a good hook set. You need to sharpen your hooks until they are pin-sharp."

When he locates breaking gar, Sutton hooks a 3- to 6-inch shiner minnow through the lips and clips on a big bobber about 6 inches from the fish. "I'll cast the rig upstream and let the bobber float the shiner down into the school of gar. Gar seldom make a hard hit. Usually the bobber will slowly go underwater

as the fish takes off slowly with the minnow in its mouth."

Sutton agrees that waiting for the gar to swallow the bait is one of the hardest parts of gar fishing, but it is essential to get a good hook set. "Waiting until they stop to swallow has really improved my catch rate," he says. "When you set the hook, the water's going to explode. The gar will jump out of the water and thrash and carry on. A fish 10 pounds or so will give the most exciting fight you'll ever have. Nothing I hook can top the gar."

Sutton said that one of his best days gar fishing came when he was fishing with some friends completely uninterested in gar fishing—until they saw him start hooking fish: "We were fishing off a houseboat about 50 yards from the bank near a creek that was drawing shad. I could see the gar breaking, so I put on a big minnow and cast out. At first my friends said they'd just watch. Well, they started seeing me catch gar and pretty soon they all had a pole in their hands and were fishing. In two days we hooked about 100 fish, but to be honest we only landed 6 or 8. They are powerful fighters, and even though we use 12- to 15-pound test, we still lose a lot of fish."

Gar for the Table

Walker cleans alligator gar with a hatchet and a baseball bat. Longnose and shortnose gar, however, can be cleaned easily with a tin snips. Cut around the circumference of the fish at the gills with the snips and then snip down the lateral line on both sides. Peel the skin away as you would husk roast corn and reveal two long strips of prime fillets, like the tenderloin on a cow, that slice out easily.

"We eat gar several ways," says Walker. "We bread the fillets and fry them up. Or we make gar patties. To do this, you boil the fillets and then grind the meat with green onions and garlic. Then boil and mash some potatoes and mix that in with the ground gar meat. Flatten a handful into patties and fry. These taste real good, and you can pack the patties between sheets of waxed paper and freeze them. That way you've got gar patties anytime you want."

In parts of the South, notably Louisiana, Mississippi, Florida, and South Carolina, gar is commonly eaten and is sold in markets. "I know people who think it's the best tasting-fish that swims," says Merritt, Sr.

Recipes

Bayou Bill's Barbecued Gar

One of the best ways to eat gar is after it has been cooked in a fire pit.

Dig out a 12- by 12-foot pit and fill it with logs, which are burned and reduced to a hot ash. Stretch woven fence wire over the pit. Lay whole dressed gar on top. Douse gar occasionally with barbecue sauce, applied with mops.

Macaroni and Gar Salad

This is a great way to use gar left over from the fire pit.

Mix 2 cups cold, cooked gar with 2 cups cooked macaroni. Add chopped carrots, celery, red onions, and cabbage. Toss this mixture with ¾ cup mayonnaise, 2 tablespoons chopped parsley, 2 tablespoons fresh dill, and salt and pepper to taste. Chill, and serve on a bed of cold lettuce.

Gar-on-the-Cob

Place whole undressed gar over hot coals, roasting 5–10 minutes per side. Remove from coals and peel off the skin using a tin snips. Hold gar by head and tail and eat like roasted corn.

—TD

"I felt as though there was nothing left on earth I would want to achieve after that honor," said Tom of his certified bowfin world record.

10

Others

*Down in the Louisiana backcountry they will tell you
that a cooked bowfin will 'uncook himself' if left
overnight. And that if buried with the proper ritual
under a sympathetic moon, a bowfin will invariably
convert himself into a live snake!*
—HAVILAH BABCOCK, *Sports Afield*, 1944

Just as writers of game fishing books lump species like carp, drum, and suckers together and stick them toward the back of the volume, we've had to gather the less-common roughfish and put them ignobly in the "Others" chapter.

But just because bowfin, American eel, goldeye, and mooneye are near the back of this book doesn't mean they aren't as fascinating to catch and read about as the roughfish superstars. They are here because we've only caught a few and can't tell too many fishing stories, or because so little is known about them they couldn't stand as chapters on their own.

We hope both situations change soon. Tom is intensely jealous that I've caught an American eel and he hasn't. He says he'll never be happy until he takes one from the Mississippi River. And I'm just as determined to replace him as the bowfin world record-holder in the 4-pound-test tippet fly rod category.

And as for the lack of information on these and other little-known roughfish, we hope fisheries biologists and anglers across the na-

tion take this chapter as a challenge to study and write more about these interesting fish.

Bowfin
Amia calva
Amia, is Greek for an ancient type of fish, and *calva* is Latin for "bald," referring to the fish's smooth scales.

The bowfin's a fish legends are made of. It looks more like a serpent than a fish, lives in swamps and bayous, eats anything that swims, and can breathe air and survive out of water for weeks. If those features can't be made into folklore, nothing can.

Although bowfin are a little-known fish in northern states, they have a long and rich history in the South. Early French explorers of the lower Mississippi River called the bowfin *poisson de marais* (fish of the swamp) or *poisson-castor* (beaver fish). Another common name, shoepike, comes from the French name *choupique*, which translates into "cabbage-pike." One of the earliest records of the bowfin comes from Le Page Du Pratz, in his *Historie di La*

Range of the bowfin

The bowfin, "if buried with the proper ritual under a sympathetic moon... will invariably convert himself into a live snake," wrote Havilah Babcock in 1944.

Louisiane 1758, in which he wrote "*Le Tchoupic est un très-beau poisson*" ("The bowfin is a very fine fish").

Besides shoepike, the bowfin carries several evocative common names such as dogfish, mudfish, cottonfish, speckled cat, spottail, German bass, buglemouth, lawyer, scaled ling, grinnel, blackfish, cypress trout, and John A. Grindle.

The bowfin is a primitive species, closely resembling prehistoric fish that lived over 100 million years ago. It is the last survivor of a large family of fish now found only in fossils. Some of the bowfin's most primitive features have allowed it to survive since the time of dinosaurs. Unlike any fish but gar, the bowfin can use its air bladder as a lung when oxygen levels drop in the water where it lives. This adaptation has allowed the bowfin to survive in some remarkable situations. James Gowanloch, in his book *Fishes and Fishing in Louisiana*, wrote, "They have actually been plowed up alive in the lowland fields of Louisiana, weeks after flood waters have fallen and the land has become dry enough for cultivation to

begin." In Canada, a bowfin was dug up from the earth where it was living in a chamber 4 inches below the surface, one-quarter mile from the nearest river! In another incident, a pond that had been stocked with bowfin was drained and remained dry for 21 days. When the pond was filled again and stocked with goldfish, 24 bowfin were found living in it, having survived for 3 weeks in the caked mud of the pond basin.

Because of its ability to breath air, bowfin can live in water where no other fish except gar can survive, places like swamps, weedy bays, and warm backwaters of rivers. The range of the bowfin extends from Florida and the southern Appalachian Mountains, north throughout the entire Mississippi watershed and into the Great Lakes.

It's a fact that bowfin are weird-looking. A long cylindrical body, scaleless or "naked" head, and long dorsal fin that extends two-thirds the length of its body make the fish look like a thick snake. Two barbels, short and tubelike, are located near the bowfin's nostrils. Bowfin are olive-green on back and pale yellow on the belly. The adult males have an ocellus—a black spot haloed in bright green at the base of the tail. Instead of attacking the vital head or body, attackers will often strike this spot, which looks like a big eye. Bowfin average 4 to 5 pounds and 20 inches long. The world record is a 21½-pounder taken in South Carolina.

In spring, as bowfin prepare to spawn, their lower fins and bellies become a bright, almost fluorescent green or aqua. The males build bowl-shaped nests in the shallows, usually near some type of cover, and line them with cut sticks and vegetation. Males defend the territory around the nest, biting at the fins of other males who come too close. After a female is attracted to the nest, she lies on the bottom and the male circles about her, sometimes nipping her sides and snout. Then both fish violently shake their fins and release eggs and sperm.

The male guards the eggs and, by moving his fins, keeps a steady flow of water moving over them. Once the eggs hatch, the young attach themselves to the bottom with a sticky organ on the tip of the nose. After a week or so, the young bowfin form a tight swimming ball and follow the male around.

Bowfin live mostly on a diet of live fish and crawdads; they also eat insects, frogs, and crustaceans. Biologists once found the leg bone of a bird in a bowfin stomach, but could not tell if it was from a wild bird or a fried chicken drumstick. Because they eat game fish and are not popular yet with anglers, bowfin have been blamed for the decline of sport fishing in many lakes. Many states have hopefully tried to net or poison bowfin from lakes to improve game fish populations. The fears that bowfin seriously threaten bass or walleye population has little scientific foundation. Many of the finest sport fish lakes in the Upper Midwest have healthy populations of bowfin. Possibly bowfin keep the lakes' population of panfish and sport fish from becoming overabundant and stunted.

Bowfin are aggressive predators. In *Fishes of Wisconsin*, George Becker writes of being attacked by a bowfin while standing on a bank. The fish rushed at him, coming out of the water and up the bank almost a foot. When he placed a pole in the water, the fish attacked it, biting the end.

This aggression makes bowfin great sport for anglers. In the spring of 1988, Tom and I were exploring the marshy Gull River in central Minnesota, casting to spawning bluegills. Ahead of me, I saw Tom crouch and stare intently into the water. Turning, he whispered, "Rob, it's a big cabbage-pike." Even though I knew he only had his light 5-weight fly rod rigged with a size 12 Hare's Ear nymph, I said, "Go for it! It might be a world record on your 2-pound-test tippet." After several casts, the

Try to "lip" a bowfin as you would a bass and you'll end up with only half a thumb. Better to use a pliers.

fish snapped up the fly and plowed towards the river channel, leaving behind huge swirls of mud. Between several long runs, the bowfin gyrated wildly, frothing the water surface. Soon the fish was on shore, and we admired its bright green fins. Usually we release our bowfins, but in this case, Tom was sure it was a world record in the fly rod category, so we rushed into town to find a certified scale. Two weeks later, after submitting his application to the Freshwater Fishing Hall of Fame in Hayward, Wisconsin, Tom received a letter congratulating him on his new certified world record. "It was almost too much," he told me. "I feel as though there is nothing left on earth I will want to achieve after that honor." Tom received a certificate, pin, and a patch the size of a dinner plate, which he now wears on the back of his fly-fishing vest.

An Arkansas angler keeps two bowfin for the table. Dishes like creamed bowfin on toast are popular in many parts of the South.

stand on. Here, approach the fish in a float tube, or belly boat, to avoid spooking them.

Although anglers release most bowfin, in the interest of maintaining a balanced fish population, people occasionally keep some for the table. In the 1930s, a state forester wrote in *Fishes and Fishing in Louisiana*, "The choupique is considered an essential food in the backwoods and hinterlands. These folks usually catch large amounts of choupique, behead them, clean them and split them up the back to the tail and then sun dry them and pack them away in dry salt, similar to the dry codfish. They are used for various dishes such as fishballs, jambalaya, and gumbo." Another good way to cook bowfin, according to the book, is to "skin the fish from the tail to the head. The fish is then cleaned, the backbone removed and the bowfin is then divided into halves which are then cut into pieces and fried in deep fat, like doughnuts."

Many other methods besides fly-fishing can be used to catch bowfin. Almost any plug, either topwater or deepdiving, will work. Bowfin usually feed by sucking in their prey the same way largemouth bass do, so any techniques for bass catch bowfin. Live minnows fished on a bobber or the bottom work particularly well.

Bowfin are one of the hardest fighters that ever took a hook. Keith Sutton, in an issue of *Arkansas Game and Fish*, wrote, "Hooked near the surface [bowfin] can put on a dazzling show of aerobatics unrivaled by the sportiest freshwater game fish." Spring is one of the best seasons to catch bowfin because they're in the shallows and you can cast to sighted fish. If you can wade the shore, like Tom did for his world record, you're lucky. Most of the time bowfin are in areas where the bottom is too soft to

RECIPES

Smoking is the best way to get the most flavor from a bowfin, and these recipes from Louisiana turn smoked bowfin into tasty main dishes.

Smoked Bowfin

After cleaning, make a long cut from the inside down the back just deep enough to make the fish lie flat. Place fish, scales down, in a tub of brine made of 1 pound salt added to a gallon of water. Cover the fish and leave in the brine overnight.

Place in hardwood fuel smoker at high heat for 5 hours. Then cool it down and smoke 15 hours.

Panned Bowfin

Place the opened and spread-out fish in a pan. Dot with butter, and add a little milk. Place in 350° oven for 15 minutes until thoroughly cooked.

Served with muffins, this makes a delicious breakfast dish.

Creamed Bowfin on Toast

Melt 4 tablespoons butter in a saucepan. Add two tablespoons flour. Slowly stir in 2 cups of milk and cook until thick. Add 1 cup smoked bowfin, broken into small pieces.

Serve hot on toast. This soothing meal is good for kids with stomachaches.

Smoked Bowfin Patties

Take 2 cups ground fish, 2 cups cracker crumbs, 1 egg, and ½ cup milk. Beat egg, add remaining ingredients and form into patties. Fry in oil until golden brown.

Serve patties with potatoes or rice, or in a hamburger bun with lettuce, onion, tomato , and a splash of Tabasco sauce.

American Eel

Anquilla rostrata

Anquilla is Greek for "eel" and *rostrata* is Latin for "long-nosed."

We won't pretend the American eel, also known as silver eel, elver, and Atlantic eel, isn't the strangest fish to swim in fresh water. Hold a carp in one hand and an eel in the other and it's hard to believe they're related in any way. But they are. Contrary to myths that have them growing from rocks and hair, eels are regular fish like sunnies, gar, and mooneye. It's not surprising people have been confused about eels throughout the ages. The eel has one of the strangest and most mysterious life cycles of any North American fish.

Eels are migratory, a fact that was known over 2,000 years ago. However, it wasn't until about 80 years ago that the mysterious life cycle of the eel was partially explained. The ancient Greeks thought European eels, similar to American eels, were the children of Neptune. The Roman scholar Pliny the Elder believed baby eels were produced when the adults rubbed against rocks. Throughout history, others have theorized that eels arose spontaneously from snakeskins, grass dew, and horse hairs that fell into water. Until the beginning of

the 20th century, all that was known was that each fall, large adult eels moved out of ponds and sloughs where they lived and into rivers leading into the ocean, and that each spring the same streams would fill with small dark eels, called elvers.

Early scientists knew that adult eels moved down rivers and into the ocean to spawn, but where, how, and when they spawned re-

Because their origins are so mysterious, eels have been a source of myths for centuries. It was once believed they arose spontaneously from horse hairs that fell in the water.

This eel was caught by a Lithuanian angler in the Soviet Union. Eel are considered a delicacy throughout Europe.

spent 5 to 10 years living in ponds and headwater streams, start descending to the sea. At this time, they average 20 to 35 inches long and weigh 2 to 4 pounds. The eels travel together, sometimes massed together in balls. This is when most eels are caught for the table.

When the females reach the saltwater estuaries at the river mouths they are met by the smaller males, which live their adult life there. The eels then move out to the deep sea, traveling for 2 to 3 months until they reach spawning grounds somewhere south of the Bermuda Triangle.

Today, much mystery still surrounds this stage of the eel's life cycle, but biologists do know a few facts. Spawning takes place sometime between late winter and early summer, with the adult females producing between 5 and 30 million eggs each. Scientists believe the eels die after spawning because no adults have ever been found migrating upstream from the sea. European eels travel great distances to spawn in the same area as American eels do.

After the eggs hatch, they grow into a larva eel called leptocephale. This is rare, since the juveniles of most fish species resemble the adults. At one time, the leptocephale were considered a different kind of fish unrelated to the eel. The leptocephale, also called "glass eels," are so transparent that when placed on a printed page the type can be read clearly through them. They are cigar shaped, but flat like a leaf.

The glass eels drift with the warm Gulf Stream current until they reach the Atlantic Ocean and Gulf of Mexico shorelines, about one year after hatching. At this time they change into elvers, resembling the adult eel, but are smaller and lighter colored.

In the spring, when the elvers are 2 to 3 inches long, they enter freshwater streams and turn black. Traveling at night in the shallows near the bank the elvers migrate upstream, overcoming numerous obstacles. When they

mained a mystery. "We know then, that the old eels vanish from our ken into the sea," said Dr. Johann Schmidt in his book *Breeding Places of the Eel*, (1922). In 1904, Schmidt began his research on this basic question of eel biology and eighteen years later published his discoveries. This is what he found:

Eels are catadromous, meaning they spawn in the ocean and spend their adult life in fresh water. This behavior is the opposite of salmon, which spawn in fresh water and grow in the sea. In the fall, adult female eels, which have reach a difficult rapid they will crawl out of the water onto land to pass it. To get around a dam, elvers will crawl up its face or move through the locks. Once in the headwaters, elvers have been known to travel through flooded or even dewed fields, and pass through tunnels, aqueducts, and underground streams to reach the lakes and ponds where they spend their adult life. In Italy, a marked eel traveled 31 miles underground to reach a pond! This is how eels can reach ponds that have no apparent access to the sea.

Eels can live a long time. One 88-year-old eel was kept in captivity from 1863, when it was 3, until 1948. They can also grow quite large. One specimen was 48 inches long and weighed 16 pounds; another was over 5 feet long.

Eels feed mostly at night on living prey. In one study, the stomachs of 300 eels from New Brunswick, were found to contain mostly larval insects, including mayfly, dragonfly, and midge nymphs. In addition, some minnows, crayfish, snails, and earthworms were eaten. Eels also consume sea lamprey larvae when available.

During the day, eels lie buried in the mud. When the sun drops, they emerge, sometimes crawling out of the water into damp fields in search of worms and frogs. One eel escaped from an aquarium and was found alive more than 24 hours later. On warm wet August evenings, when eels are feeding voraciously and are excited, they can be heard making chirping or sucking noises. The noise is produced by eels releasing air through a duct from their air bladder.

Eels live a simple life of burying themselves in mud, eating insects and minnows, and crawling around farm fields until they are ready to spawn. Usually, as winter weather cools the waters, eels bury themselves in the mud and lie dormant until spring. In the fall, mature eels change from a yellowish or dark

A youthful eel resides in a tiny tidal pool;
He was lithe as gutta-percha, and as pliable
From his actions and contractions he appeared to
* be a fool,*
But his virtue was completely undeniable.

—CARRYL

green color to a metallic sheen and head to the sea. It is at this time that they get the name silver eel and make the best eating. Leaving their home water, sometimes crawling over land, the female eels begin their long migration to the tropical seas.

American eels live in watersheds in eastern North America that flow into the Atlantic Ocean. This includes the entire Mississippi River watershed, the streams of the Gulf of Mexico coast, the Atlantic Seaboard, and the Great Lakes drainage all the way to the coastal streams of Labrador. It is amazing that eels, born near Bermuda, are still able to reach inland waters of Minnesota and Wisconsin by passing over or around 24 dams on the Mississippi River. However, few make it so far north because the dams are a major obstacle. Although declining in abundance throughout most of the Middle America, eels appear to be recolonizing in some new areas. On September 9, 1980, Dave Wandersee caught a 38-inch American eel on the Crow River in Minnesota. It was the first eel recorded above St. Anthony Falls in Minneapolis, the historical barrier that once blocked upstream migration. Eels have also been found recently living in Lakes Superior, Michigan, and Huron. The opening of the Welland Canal in 1922 allowed eels to bypass Niagara Falls, which once stopped their migration. When eels first appeared in the Great Lakes, many people had no idea what they were. As recently as 1974, a Wisconsin news-paper headline read, "Fisherman Nets Strange Creature." It was an American eel.

Sport anglers catch eels several ways. One that takes a strong stomach is called bobbing. A long thick thread is attached to a needle and pushed lengthwise through several dozen nightcrawlers to form a long, dripping, squirming chain. The whole mess is coiled into a loose clump and lowered by a line onto the bottom of a stream where migrating eels are passing. After 15 to 20 minutes, the "bob" is brought quickly but smoothly to the surface, in the hope that eels have begun to swallow the nightcrawlers and their teeth are entangled in the thick cotton thread. Anglers quickly hoist the writhing mass of eels, thread, and night-crawlers into the boat, where they hold it over an open gunny sack into which the eels drop.

I used a more conventional technique to catch my first and only eel. When I was young, I lived in New Hampshire, which, being close to the Atlantic Ocean, had a good population of eels. One afternoon, my fishing partner, Brian, and I were fishing for brook trout from a bridge over the Exeter River. Our technique was to cast a hook baited with a worm into the deep pool below. Here we would let our bait sit, until a trout bit. After one cast, late in the day, I felt a gentle nibble. Thinking it was probably a creek chub, I carelessly set the hook. It was no creek chub.

At first, I thought I had hooked the bottom. Then the dead weight started to throb. There were no runs or leaps, just a constant and vig-orous resistance. Slowly I worked the unseen shaking and throbbing fish to the bridge. Brian was guessing it was a large brown trout or bull-head. What emerged from the water was a long, snake-shaped fish about 3 feet long. Brian was excited. He had eaten eel often and thought they were great. I let him have it be-cause I'd never seen one and had no idea what to do with it.

Because eels sometimes actually leave the water and crawl up on land, they are the only fish (except walking catfish) that can be caught by casting *away* from the water. This type of fishing is unnerving for many anglers who are not used to fishing with their backs facing a lake or river. We find water known to hold eels and then wait until a warm, humid evening be-fore trying this technique. Eels feed on night-crawlers and worms in the low-lying areas, so we key in on these spots, casting to places on land where an eel might hold.

One time I was fishing for eels with Tom in northern Iowa at a swampy pond that drained into the Des Moines River. Having no luck casting into the pond, we turned around and began casting in the opposite direction. We fished for about 15 minutes, and concluded the eels weren't biting that night. As always when land fishing for eels, we were optimistic that the next time we tried this technique we'd have better luck.

Casting towards land or towards water, an-glers only occasionally catch eels. This is espe-cially true in inland waters where pollution and dams have hindered the migrations of elvers. When eels are caught, it is usually by accident, and most surprised anglers don't know if they have caught a fish, a snake, or a new form of life. If you do catch an eel, don't be afraid. Rather, consider yourself lucky to be one of the few in your state who have ever seen one.

For thousands of years, people have been using eels for food and other purposes. Eel oil has been used as medicine and lubricants. Eel skins make a supple leather once used for lining buggy whips, book binders, and fine sus-penders. Today, they are still made into belts, wallets, and purses.

In 1857, Theodatus Gaulick, in *A Treatise on the Artificial Propagation of Certain Kinds of Fish* ventured the opinion that "this most singular fish is discerned by most persons who have eaten it, as one of the best for the table."

In fact, eels are so popular in Europe that up to 500,000 pounds of live American eels have been imported in one year. In 1984, live eel elvers sent to Japan from the United States were selling for $400 to $500 dollars a *pound*! Demand for eels in Europe exceeds supply because pollution and damming have wiped out many native eel habitats there years ago. Historically, European canals were filled with eels and barge men carried 3-tined spears to impale the fish as they moved along the canal. Many eels now eaten in Europe come from commercial catches in Canada, where over 1 million pounds are harvested each year.

Eels make fantastic eating. They have a sweet, meaty flavor, and are good smoked, jellied, pickled, grilled, fried, baked, and in soups. The elvers are boiled and then pressed into delicious eel cakes. In Spain, these small eels are an expensive treat in the spring. A large pot of oil is heated until very hot, then 10 cloves of garlic are added, followed by a red chili pepper. When the garlic begins to turn brown, a pound of fresh elvers is added to the oil. The browned delicacies are fished out of the oil and eaten individually like fondue.

Germans enjoy eels in dill sauce. In England, eels are traditionally prepared as the dish jellied eel. In Italy they are fried in olive oil, then cured in vinegar. The Japanese consider smoked eels a delicacy. In New England, the traditional way to prepare eel is in a stifle, a casserole of layered eel, potatoes, onions, and salt pork. The Pennsylvania Dutch make eel into a soup.

RECIPES

To skin an eel, cut a ring around the head with a knife. Nail the head to a board or get someone to hold it with a pair of pliers while you pull the skin down and away from the head. The skin should turn inside out and peel off like turning a glove inside out.

New England Eel Jelly

Clean and skin 6 eels. Cut each into 3 pieces. To 1 quart water add 1 pint vinegar, 2 sliced onions, salt and pepper, ½ teaspoon allspice, ¼ teaspoon cloves, and 4 bay leaves. Bring the mixture to a boil, add fish and cook 10 minutes. Remove the fish and place in a mold. Strain liquid and save. To the liquid, add 2 tablespoons gelatin dissolved in ¼ cup water. Cook 15 minutes, pour over fish, and chill.

Unmold the jellied eel onto a bed of lettuce, and serve.

Eel Italiano

Italians prepare the traditional Christmas Eve meal of eel by cutting 2 eels into 3 pieces each and frying in hot oil just until stiff. Remove the eel from the pan.

In ½ inch oil, sauté ¼ cup chopped onion, 1 chopped shallot and ½ cup diced mushrooms 10 minutes. Return the eel to the pan. To this, add ½ cup white wine and 1 cup tomato sauce. Simmer the whole thing with the lid on 25 minutes.

Serve the dish sprinkled with fresh parsley, tarragon, and chervil.

Eel Orly

Here is a simple and delicious way to cook your eel.

Fillet a skinned eel as you would a very skinny walleye. Season fillets with salt and pepper, dip in beaten eggs, then in bread crumbs. Fry for 5 minutes.

Serve on top of a little hot tomato sauce and garnish with fried parsley sprigs.

Goldeye

Hiodon alsoides

Hiodon is Greek, referring to structures at the base of the gills that have teeth on them, and *alsoides*, also Greek, means "shadlike."

This beautiful fish, also called Winnipeg goldeye, yellow herring, toothed herring, shad mooneye, La Queche, and weepickeesis, has a blue to blue-green back, silver sides, and a white belly. The large silver scales are irides-

Range of the goldeye

cent gold, pink, and blue. One of the most striking features of this fish is its large eye lit with a bright yellow iris.

Goldeye are fish of the North. They live in the watersheds of the Mississippi, Ohio, and Missouri rivers. In Canada, goldeye swim in the Red and McKenzie rivers, which flow into the Arctic Ocean.

Adult goldeye average between 12 and 15 inches long. In Canada, a big goldeye would be 16 inches and 1½ pounds; farther south in the Mississippi drainage, the fish reach 3 pounds, and 20 inches.

The goldeye lives in the slow, muddy waters of lakes, the backwaters of large rivers, and the swamps and marshes connected to rivers. In the spring, goldeye move towards shallow, firm-bottomed areas to spawn. Humans have never seen the spawning act because it occurs in muddy water. After spawning, goldeye begin feeding indiscriminately on any animal they can fit in their mouths, preferably surface insects.

Both mooneye and goldeye have a dorsal fin located far back on the body, directly above the anus. The sure way to tell the two species apart is to compare the locations of the leading edge of the dorsal fin. If the dorsal fin lines up in front of the anus, the fish is a mooneye. If it lines up behind the anus, it is a goldeye.

One of the most popular ways to catch goldeye is with an insect such as a grasshopper on a small hook, fished 12 inches below a bobber. In the evening, goldeyes can rise to insects on the surface. This is the time I get out a fly rod and rig it with just about any floating pattern, since goldeye aren't selective feeders.

One of the most famous fish dishes eaten in Canada, listed on the Canadian Pacific Railway's menu, is Winnipeg Smoked Goldeye. The special smoking process that changes the flesh of this fish from ordinary to extraordinary was discovered by Robert Firth in 1886. Firth, a butcher who migrated to Winnipeg from Hull, England, smoked goldeye and was able to sell them for 25 cents apiece. Previously, goldeye were sold as dogfood at less than one cent per pound. One day he overcooked some of the fish he was smoking and found the taste was even better than before. The recipe was improved further when he began freezing the goldeye to remove moisture and soaking them in a sugar-salt solution before smoking.

Winnipeg Smoked Goldeye

First freeze the goldeye for several weeks. This removes excess moisture. Then defrost the fish in brine solution, with enough salt and sugar to float an egg.
Dip the fish in a red vegetable dye called aniline. Hot smoke 5–7 hours over oak wood.

Goldeye and mooneye, cousins, are among the wildest roughfish you'll ever see erupt from the water. These members of a family of fish found only in central North America are beautifully bright. When hooked, they leap into the air, their iridescent scales glimmering in the sunlight. It's no wonder Tom calls them "freshwater tarpon." Both species provide great fly

I admire the iridescent silver sides of a freshwater tarpon, also known as mooneye. The fish was hooked on a small jig from the St. Croix River.

Mooneye are a fascinating fish because they look so unlike other species that swim in fresh water. When hooked, they cut back and forth in the current like a crazed sunfish, often flying out of the water.

rod sport because of their habit of feeding on insects at the water surface. Hooking one of these silver leapers on a 4-weight fly rod in a fast river will make you question all the hoopla about trout.

Mooneye
Hiodon tergisus
Tergisus, the Greek meaning "polished," refers to the mooneye's bright silver color.

Mooneye are similar to goldeye in many respects except they prefer clear, unsilted water. This has led to their decline in the silted rivers of Nebraska and South Dakota, where they are now classified as endangered. Mooneye also like swift waters instead of the slow waters preferred by goldeye. Mooneye live in the Mississippi River and Lake Michigan watersheds, as well as the Red River of the North and Lakes Erie and Ontario. They are a fish of big water, preferring large rivers and open lakes.

Besides the different position of its dorsal fin, the mooneye is a brighter silver than the goldeye and the iris of its eye is silver instead of yellow. As with the goldeye, one of the most striking features of this fish is its large eye. Other common names for the mooneye are toothed herring, river whitefish, *laquaiche* (French), notched-finned hiodon, cisco, and freshwater tarpon.

The mooneye deserves its nickname "freshwater tarpon." Its large silver scales and tendency to jump when hooked remind me of the big jumpers of the Florida flats. Mooneye feed near or on the surface, and I have often seen them rising on warm evenings. During late summer, mooneye feed heavily on grasshoppers blown into the water. They also consume small minnows, crayfish, elm seeds, and other available foods.

I stumbled into a mooneye mecca on a trip to the St. Croix River in Wisconsin to catch white bass. In a large eddy near shore I saw several fish surfacing, so I cast a deer hair popper into the rising school. My fly was sucked in with a splashy rise. At first, I thought I had hooked a white bass, but when the fish started

Tom and I flyfish the evening hatch for mooneye on a midwestern river.

repeatedly leaping into the air, I knew it was something else. As I brought it closer, I noticed the incredibly bright, gleaming sides of the fish, and its huge eye looking right back at me. That afternoon I caught several more mooneye, continuing to enjoy the good sport and bright sides of these fish.

Tom could very well be the mooneye world record-holder if he were not such an ardent catch-and-release angler. One evening, he and I went to the Mississippi. When we reached the spot where we launch our canoe, I realized I had left my rod at work. While I went back for my rod, Tom waited by the river and cast a number 2 Mepps spinner to pass the time. When I returned, he told me he had caught the largest mooneye of his life. "The tarpon must have gone 3 pounds!" he told me excitedly. "It was incredible, exploding from the water like a geyser, then cutting up and downstream, back and forth, until I could ease it up onto the sand." It wasn't until the next day that we discovered in our record books that the world record mooneye is only 1 pound, 15 ounces. "Oh

well," Tom said, "what would I have done with another patch?"

In 1923, David Starr Jordan, described in *American Food and Game Fish*, the angling qualities of mooneye. "It is a beautiful, attractive fish, reaching 8 to 12 inches. They are eager biters and take indiscriminately the feathered lures, small spoons, grasshoppers, grubs, and other natural bait . . . . They rise freely to the artificial fly in the early spring months, but seem to disregard it as warm weather approaches, at which time they favor the grasshoppers, above all other lures. Anglers in Canada prize highly the sport of casting for them. In these waters this fish is said to leap, when hooked, repeatedly in the air."

I have never eaten a mooneye, preferring to release these fish to jump another day. If you decide to try one for the table, it has been reported that they are good if prepared the same way as goldeye.

—RB

11

Recent Exotics

"This could be the beginning of the end of Lake Erie's fabulous walleye fishing."
—DAVE KELCH, OHIO STATE UNIVERSITY SEA GRANT PROGRAM, COMMENTING ON THE INVASION OF THE ZEBRA MUSSEL.

T HIS FISH is so *bizarre*. Where do you think it came from?"

All anglers occasionally catch a fish that looks unlike anything they've seen before. Their first inclination is to believe the fish is some kind of exotic that was stocked by the state fisheries agency or dumped into the water from someone's aquarium.

But most of the time, the strange-looking fish you catch isn't foreign at all; it is native to the waters you fish. You've never seen it before because you either don't know how to catch it or have never seen anyone else catch one. In the Mississippi River alone, swim anywhere from 150 to 200 species of fish, almost all of which are native, or indigenous, to that river. Yet most anglers see only a dozen or so in their lifetime.

There are some exceptions, however. These are the real exotics, species that today swim in waters we fish; but didn't 150, 50, or even 20 years ago. Some exotics, like the pink salmon, the ruffe, and the white perch in the Great Lakes, were introduced by accident. Others, like the carp, the brown trout, and the rainbow trout, were part of deliberate state and federal programs to stock new species in waters where they didn't previously exist.

Sometimes, this manipulation of nature doesn't too drastically affect the environment where the new species is placed, like with steelhead in the Great Lakes. Other times, the introductions get out of control, as carp did in the late 19th century. When done without considerable planning and care, a new species can either ruin the new habitat or start showing up in waters the planners never intended them to swim in. No new species can be stocked without it doing something to the aquatic environment. Sometimes the effects are minor, sometimes major, but there are always some consequences to be weighed against the value of adding a new fish to a lake or river.

Fish species are usually introduced in waters humans have already fouled up in some way. These introductions are often done to satisfy anglers who have demands for recreation that can't be met without some sort of environmental meddling. Stocking is often seen as a quick fix to a problem created by water quality that has been wrecked by pollution from cities and siltation from eroding farm fields.

Imported like fine porcelain from Germany in the 1880s carp, were reserved for America's most prominent citizens. Within 20 years, the exotics were swimming freely in most rivers and lakes across the country.

The brown trout is another exotic. First imported from Germany in 1884, today it is found across the continent, usually thriving in streams made too warm for native brook trout by deforestation.

In North America, hundreds of exotic species of fish, plants, and animals now live and reproduce successfully. Many have drastically affected the populations of plants and animals that grow here naturally. Some changes are judged as good and others are judged as bad, depending on how human interests are affected.

The German brown trout introduction is seen by most people as a success. First stocked in New York's Long Island in 1884, the brown trout was imported to take the place of the native brook trout that had disappeared from streams destroyed by logging. Browns could reproduce and thrive in waters warmed from sunlight that streamed in across the barren hillsides, while the native trout simply died out or moved upstream to colder waters. Today, many trout anglers who catch browns are unaware the fish are not native to the United States, and that they are probably fishing waters that were once cold enough to sustain brook trout. The carp, introduced to this continent 10 years before the brown trout, is seen by most anglers as an exotic introduction failure. Carp, which have become widespread in the past century, are despised because many anglers blame them for the declining number of game fish in many waters.

Although fish introductions in the past have often been disastrous, they are still being done throughout the country. Chinook salmon are today stocked in the Great Lakes, putting the native lake trout and rare lake-run brook trout at risk; grass carp are being stocked in ponds where they are accidentally flooded into major riverways; and some states are importing from Europe the zander and seeforelen, giant relatives of walleyes and brown trout, in an attempt to placate anglers who demand more and bigger fish.

Non-native, or exotic, fish harm or benefit other species by disrupting the food chain. All life in a lake or stream begins with the sun, which causes microscopic plants and water weeds to grow. These plants are called primary producers, because they are the first link in the food chain. Aquatic animals that eat these plants are called the primary consumers. Converting the plant food into animal material, they are the second step in the food chain. Primary consumers range in size from microscopic zooplankton—shrimplike animals that strain algae from the water with their legs—to 100-pound grass carp, which can eat entire cattail stalks. Species such as sunfish and cisco that eat the tiny animals like nymphs and zooplankton are called secondary consumers. At the top of the food chain are top-level consumers like the burbot that eat the sunfish and cisco. A circle is formed in the food chain when the burbot dies and is eaten by bacteria and fungus, releasing the nutrients that were locked up in the predator to be used again by plants.

When a new fish is inserted into this finely tuned ecological mechanism, something gets thrown out of whack. Stock walleyes in a lake, and the bass have less food to eat. Accidentally dump the European ruffe in a lake, and soon the native perch disappear. Xenophobia, the fear of foreigners, is unhealthy to a modern, globally linked human society. But it's essential for the health of natural communities. Foreign species simply don't belong in new territory, because they upset the delicate webs of life that have been woven over time.

Exotics don't always have to come from another continent. The rainbow trout originally swam only in streams of the Pacific Northwest. Today it lives across North America, including the Great Lakes, which now boast some of the best rainbow trout fishing in the world. Pacific salmon, like the chinook and the coho, are Great Lakes exotics. Other examples of exotics imported from within this continent are the smallmouth bass, which is native to the Mississippi River and its tributaries but has been stocked in northern Minnesota lakes, and the rainbow smelt, which didn't reach Lakes Superior and Michigan from its native streams along the East Coast until it was planted in Michigan to provide a forage base for game fish.

Fish move from one body of water to another naturally or by way of human activities. A waterfall will block the migration of fish into the upstream portion of a river. Over a long period of time, however, the barrier can erode down to a rapids, through which fish can swim upstream and colonize new waters. When fish reach a new home naturally, it happens slowly, often over thousands of years, giving the entire ecosystem a chance to adapt to the new arrival. The construction of canals and the stocking of fish, however, accelerates the process of new species introduction far faster than nature can adjust. As a result, many watery environments have changed radically.

For eons, Niagara Falls stopped fish moving up the St. Lawrence River from entering the Great Lakes. The Welland Canal was built to allow ships to circumvent the massive barrier. What no one planned on was that fish would use the canal, too. Almost at once, white perch, American eel, alewife, and other fish began to colonize the upper Great Lakes.

None was as disastrous as the sea lamprey. This parasitic native to the Atlantic Ocean attaches itself with a suction cup mouth to another fish and uses its rasplike tongue to rub a hole in the flesh, from which it sucks blood and body fluids. To the lamprey, the Great Lakes were an endless smorgasbord of juicy fish. The lake trout population, already reduced by aggressive commercial fishing, was almost wiped out by the parasite. Not only did this create a great loss to sport and commercial anglers, it also completely upset the food chain. Other newcomers, alewives and smelt, overproduced in the new water with no predators to eat them. When these fish ran out of food, they died off by the millions. In the 1940s, beaches were often covered with dead smelt and alewives, and bulldozers had to be brought in to clear them away.

Another way fish are accidentally introduced is when foreign ships dump their ballast water. Empty ships coming from freshwater ports in Europe often fill their holds with up to 6 million gallons of water to keep stable in the open ocean. When in ports like Duluth or Detroit, they dump the water—and any organisms they took in that survived the voyage

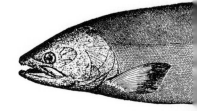

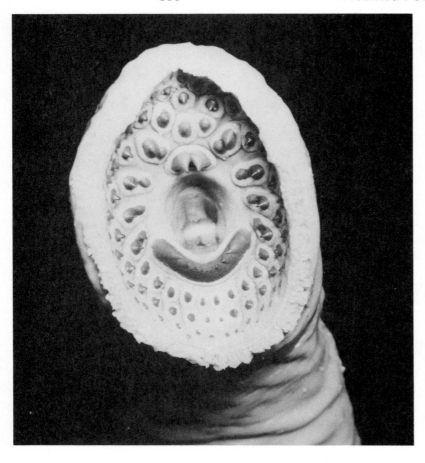

The sea lamprey, which first bypassed Niagara Falls in the 1920s with the construction of the Welland Canal, chewed into Great Lakes whitefish and lake trout populations in the 1940s and '50s.

across the sea—to make room for cargo. It's like having a foreign lake dumped into one of ours.

This is probably how the European zebra mussel, a shellfish, reached the Great Lakes. First recorded in Lake Erie in 1987, within a year zebra mussels had colonized a large portion of the shallow-water reefs in the western part of the lake with beds of up to 30,000 mussels per square meter of lake bottom. Mussels feed by straining algae and zooplankton from the water. If billions of mussels cover the lake bottom as predicted by some scientists, they could remove most of the zooplankton eaten by bait fish. And as the minnow population drops, so will the number of walleyes. Charter-boat captains are already saying the water over

traditional fall walleye feeding reefs is clearer than they've ever seen it, and that fishing success has dropped off in these areas.

One deterrent to the seemingly inevitable spread of the zebra mussel throughout the Great Lakes is the freshwater drum. Equipped with pharyngeal molars that can crush a mussel's hard shell, drum may be the only species that can keep this exotic at bay.

Too often, exotic fish introductions have been the result of carelessness or a desire to compensate for environmental damage such as pollution. We believe it's time for more anglers to recognize the potential danger of species introductions and ask their state fisheries managers how new fish could damage native species. We can be grateful for the exotics like brown trout and steelhead that have been accepted by sport anglers. And we can learn to appreciate and understand those that anglers don't like but are here to stay, such as carp and pink salmon. As for those fish that have yet to be introduced, we think they should stay where they are.

Three exotics—pink salmon, grass carp, and ruffe—are relatively new to middle America. We've included them in *Fishing for Buffalo* because they are all considered roughfish. Two have potential to be recognized as sport, and the third, the ruffe, shows how an accidental introduction could be destroying a major fishery.

Pink Salmon
Oncorhynchus gorbuscha
Oncorhynchus is Greek for "hook-snout," and *gorbuscha* is Old Russian for "pink salmon."

Anyone who fishes the shores of the Great Lakes in the fall has seen them, finning quietly off the mouths of streams, or charging up shallow rapids to reach spawning gravel. They're pink salmon, of 2 or 3 pounds, and today they are found everywhere in the Great Lakes from Duluth to the St. Lawrence.

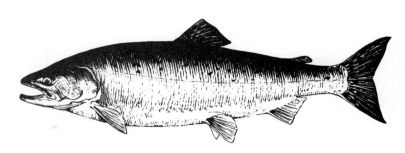

These relatively small fish, also called humpies and hump-backed salmon, are pretty much ignored by salmon anglers looking for 20- and 30-pound chinooks. But pinks deserve some notice. They are a delicious sport fish when caught before they begin spawning. Taken on light tackle, they fight like miniature chinooks, charging from a stream out in to the open water. They also show what can happen when people carelessly dump fish into a lake.

The native range of the pink salmon is in the rivers flowing into the North Pacific and Arctic oceans, extending from northern California along the Canadian coast to northern Alaska. A small native population of pinks lives in the McKenzie River, which flows into the Arctic Ocean from Canada. Pinks are the smallest of Pacific salmon. Adults in the Great Lakes average 1½ to 3 pounds, rarely reaching over 5 pounds.

Pinks got into the Great Lakes by accident. In 1956, the Canadian government stocked pinks in rivers flowing into Hudson's Bay, hoping to establish a population of these fish that natives could use for food. The young fish were flown north by plane from a hatchery in Thunder Bay, Ontario. After the last planeload of pinks was stocked, about 21,000 remained in the hatchery. Not knowing what to do with the leftover fish, hatchery workers flushed them down the drain. The drain pipe flowed into a stream that was a tributary to Lake Superior; following their migratory instinct, this is where the pinks headed.

At the time, no one worried because it was thought that the young pinks could not survive entirely in fresh water. In 1959, anglers on Minnesota's North Shore of Lake Superior were surprised to catch several pink salmon as the fish made spawning runs into tributary streams. Within 10 years, pinks had spawned in most streams leading into Lake Superior and had been found living in Lakes Huron and Michigan. By 1979, they were reproducing in

Lakes Erie and Ontario, and over the past decade have became so numerous that charter-boat captains in Lake Huron call them a nuisance for hitting lures trolled for the trophy-sized chinooks.

The explosion of pinks has several explanations. Pink salmon live only 2 or 3 years, so they reproduce at an early age and can do so in conditions where other salmon and trout can't. In the fall, all 5 species of Pacific salmon living either in the ocean or the Great Lakes swim upstream to spawn. The female builds a nest called a redd by scooping out a shallow dish in a bed of pea-sized gravel. After she lays some eggs in the nest, a male moves in to fertilize them. Then, the female moves upstream, where she digs another redd, covering with gravel the eggs in the downstream redd. After spawning, all adult Pacific salmon die.

The next spring, after the eggs have hatched, the baby pink salmon, or fry, quickly move out of the rivers and into the lake. This gives pinks an advantage over other Great Lakes salmonids like steelhead and chinook. The fry of these larger species stay in the rivers for a year before moving to the lake. During a hot summer when the river levels drop and warm, many of the tiny steelhead and chinook die, while the young pinks are thriving in the cool lake.

After only 2 years of living in the lake, the adult pinks return to the rivers where they were born to spawn and start the cycle over again. The spawning run usually begins in early to

The pink salmon, accidentally dumped down a drain in an Ontario hatchery, now spawns in most tributaries of Lakes Superior, Michigan, and Huron.

Pink salmon are often the first visitors to Lake Superior tributaries in the fall. When still silver, the flesh of this salmon is superb. At all times it is a scrappy fighter on light tackle.

pinks another spawning advantage over other species when the fall river flow is too low and warm for fish to enter.

Young pinks feed on zooplankton during their first year, moving on to insects and small minnows as they grow. Adult pinks schooling off river mouths in late summer feed on terrestrial insects and rainbow smelt.

Sometimes, it's hard to tell pinks from young chinooks or cohos; however, unlike the other two, pinks have black mouth and gums, 13 to 17 rays in their anal fin, and large dark spots on their tail and back. While in the lake, the pink takes on a bright silver coat, but when it enters a river to spawn it changes. The spots on its tail and back begin to darken, the once-bright sides become a mottled olive-green, and the male develops a hooked jaw called a kype and a large hump on its back. This inspired the common name humpback salmon. Once pinks enter the stream, their flesh becomes too pale and soft to eat fresh, although it is still tasty when smoked.

No matter what stage of deterioration they are in, pinks are a great game fish when caught on light tackle. In the summer, when they are in the open lake, they are caught in the upper 50 feet of the lake on small silver or chartreuse plugs and spoons trolled behind a boat.

mid-September around Labor Day, when pinks begin to gather off river mouths and wait for the first cool weather of the fall to move into the rivers. Occasionally, adults spend 3 years in Lake Superior before spawning, because the cold water has fewer nutrients and retards their growth. Since most pinks live only 2 years, the fall spawning run used to be only on odd-numbered years. But growing numbers of 3-year-old fish have created pink salmon runs in even-numbered years, too.

Pinks don't always spawn in rivers. I have seen them building nests in the beach gravel where a stream entered Lake Superior, and some anglers have seen them spawn as far as 15 feet offshore in the open lake. This gives the

If you don't have a boat, you can catch pinks in late August when they move close to shore before making their spawning run. Several years ago, while fishing along Lake Superior, I came across a large school of pinks a few yards off the beach near a river mouth. From a cliff above the river, I looked down into the clear waters of Lake Superior. The darker river water streaking out into the lake was warm from the hot August sun, and as I looked closely, I noticed a large school of silvery-green fish holding tight against the flow of the river but not entering it. I realized they were pinks waiting for a cooling rain before running up the river.

Down at the beach, I rigged my 7-weight fly rod with floating line and a 10-foot leader tapered to a 4-pound tippet, and selected a number 10 streamer with a hot-orange body and a black bucktail wing. I had never heard of anyone fly-fishing for pinks in the Great Lakes, but I couldn't see why it wouldn't work.

I waded into position, being careful to move slowly and not spook the fish. My first cast landed where I thought the edge of the school was. A quick retrieve brought no results. After several casts, I had calmed down enough to let the fly sink deep. My slow, steady retrieve was rewarded with a hard strike. Raising my rod sharply, I found myself hooked to a bright silver torpedo streaking for the lake. That run, and several that followed, took me deep into my backing. Eventually, I pumped the little powerhouse into the shallows.

I landed several more fish on my fly rod before the school spooked and moved out into deeper water. The fish, averaging 2 pounds and 17 inches, put up an incredible fight for their size. When I could no longer reach them with my fly rod, I began casting a number 1 Mepps spinner with my spinning rod spooled with 4-pound-test line. I caught a few more bright pinks this way and kept them for dinner that I cooked on the beach. The flesh of the fish was bright pink and when grilled over the fire. it tasted fantastic.

Even though spawning pinks usually have pale, inedible flesh, they are still a blast to catch. I sight-cast to these fish using a 4-weight fly rod, floating line, and a 12-foot leader. When I spot a school in the shallow gravel flats of a stream, I use the same upstream nymphing technique that works for trout and channel cats. But instead of a nymph imitation, I use a tiny orange yarn fly that imitates a single pink salmon egg. To make this fly, snell a small egg hook, size 12, to the end of the tippet. Under

What's a Watershed?

Throughout *Fishing for Buffalo* we often refer to "watersheds" when we talk about where fish live and what affects the water they swim in. A watershed is an area of land that water flows over and through to fill a lake or form a stream. Boundaries between these areas are called divides.

Watersheds can be tiny or huge. If a low spot in your yard fills with water following a rain, then that part of the yard that drains water into the puddle is its watershed. The high line of land between your neighbor's puddle and yours is the divide. The Mississippi River's watershed, by contrast, is huge, covering the entire central part of North America from the Rocky Mountains east to the Appalachians and from the Canadian prairies south to the Gulf of Mexico. All the land that drains rainfall into the Mississippi River's tributaries is included in its watershed.

Since fish living in one watershed can rarely swim over a divide into another watershed, the divides form the boundaries of a fish's range. Only occasionally, where the divide is low and swampy, can a fish move across a divide and into a new watershed.

The water quality of a river is directly affected by what happens in the surrounding watershed. Generally, the cleaner the watershed, the cleaner and healthier the river and the fish that live there. If you are interested in what affects the sturgeon, suckers, and drum in your favorite roughfish river, look beyond the water and into the land surrounding it.

I'm in humpy heaven as a pink salmon surges downstream with my fly on a tributary to Lake Superior. An hour later, Tom and I broiled two red fillets over an open fire for shore lunch.

the snell loop place a half-strand of orange or chartreuse yarn. Pull the snell tight, and trim the yarn with a scissors until it's the size and shape of a small garden pea.

To fish this fly, pinch onto the tippet 1 or 2 BB-sized splitshot 12 to 18 inches above the fly. Six feet up from that, pinch on a foam or cork strike indicator to the fly line. Cast several yards upstream of the closest fish, all the while keeping a low profile so you don't spook the school. Strip in the slack line so it never gets below you and watch the fish with one eye and the strike indicator with the other. This takes practice. If the fish's mouth opens or the indicator darts upstream, set the hook.

Spinners also work well for river fishing. As with all spinner fishing for salmonids, keep the retrieve slow so that the blades barely turn. Wash your spinner with unscented soap, and sharpen the hooks every dozen casts or so.

In 1988, Tom and I were fishing for steelhead on Wisconsin's Brule River when a bright 3-pound pink salmon slammed my number 2 Mepps spinner. For several minutes, I thought the trophy-sized pink was a steelhead—it was so silver and fought so hard. I still don't know why that pink was so bright; it was several miles from Lake Superior and should have been olive-green and about dead. But when I met Tom later that day, we filleted it and the meat was as red as a steelhead's. We sprinkled the fillets with salt, pepper, and lemon juice and broiled them for 3 minutes on each side. Tom still says it was the best salmon he's had in his life.

Grass Carp
Ctenopharyngodon idella
Ctenopharyngodon is Greek for "comblike throat teeth," and *idella* is Greek for "distinct."

To catch a grass carp, eat a banana. When you're finished, put the peel on the hook and cast into the lake. A clump of coontail weed will work fine, too.

Obviously, the grass, or white Amur, carp is no ordinary fish. Unlike most sport fish, which eat either nymphs or minnows, the grass carp is a voracious but strict vegetarian that eats aquatic plants and other organic material. Also, it is an exotic, brought to the United States from Asia to control the spread of water plants in southern lakes. In addition, the grass carp grows faster and larger than almost any fish that swims in North America; in its native water it reaches weights up to 100 pounds, and a 60-pounder was caught in Arkansas.

A recent arrival to this country, the grass carp could turn out to be an extremely popular sport fish in a few years. Besides being big and good tasting, it fights hard, leaping from the water like a largemouth bass on steroids. The grass carp could also become a big problem. Many environmentalists point out the possibility that this big plant-eater could begin chowing down on valuable aquatic vegetation needed by other fish and wildlife.

The native range of the grass carp is the Pacific slope of Asia from the Amur River near the Chinese–Siberia border south to Thailand. These chubby, torpedo-shaped fish look somewhat like common carp but have no barbels and the mouth is in front of the head rather than underneath. The body of the grass carp is dark olive on top, turning to brownish-yellow on the sides, with a white belly. It has large, darkly outlined scales that make an attractive pattern.

The first grass carp were imported to the United States from Asia in 1963 to control water weeds clogging ponds. The initial 70 fish were stocked in ponds in Stuttgart, Arkansas, where they produced more fish that were stocked in other research ponds and in many private and public lakes that were thick with aquatic vegetation.

The grass carp did what they were imported to do: eat massive amounts of aquatic algae and weeds. Young grass carp eat insects and

Recycling Your Roughfish

Anglers worried about toxins in their roughfish or those who aren't interested in killing the fish they catch will want to practice catch-and-release fishing. Catch-and-release is when an angler lets a fish swim away after it has been caught. It was first practiced by trout anglers who realized that trout streams can't produce as many big fish as they could catch unless fish were returned to the water. Catch-and-release has since been accepted by most muskellunge anglers, tournament bass anglers, and roughfish anglers who want to make sure there are plenty of fish to catch in the future.

The idea behind catch-and-release is that every fish returned to the water is one that can be caught again. With the growing number of anglers, their increasingly effective fishing equipment, and a limited number of lakes, catch-and-release is the only way to increase the size of fish in lakes.

It's easy for an angler to understand why he or she should practice catch-and-release. It's harder to know how to do it. For one thing, not every fish can be released. When a hooked fish—a freshwater drum, for example—fights against a line it uses up oxygen and produces lactic acid in its muscles. This stress can cause the exhausted fish to die even after it has been released, which is why you should avoid playing a fish for too long. The sooner a hooked fish is brought to the boat, unhooked and allowed to swim away, the better its chances of surviving.

Also, a fish that is hooked deeply in the throat or stomach has a greater chance of dying than one hooked in the mouth. Fish caught with artificial lures are far more likely to survive than are fish caught with bait. Why? Fish swallow bait and get the accompanying hooks caught deep in their throat or stomach. Fish caught on lures are usually hooked in the front of the mouth, where there is little tissue to be damaged. If a fish bleeds from the throat or gills as a result of being hooked, it will probably die.

What you need:
Needlenose pliers
Hook remover
Wire cutters
Extra hooks

What to Remember:
1. Roughfish are fragile. They are covered with a mucus that protects the skin from infections. Try to handle fish as little as possible so the mucus is not scraped off.
2. Don't let fish thrash in the boat. Large fish such as carp, gar, buffalo, and sturgeon can easily damage their internal organs. Don't lift large fish from the water. Release them while they are next to the boat.
3. Never hold a fish by the eyes. That's a sure way to blind or kill a fish. Hold it just behind the gill covers.
4. Bring your fish in as quickly as possible. The sooner a fish is reeled in and released, the better are its chances of surviving.

5. Don't release fish kept on stringers or in livewells without aerators. Fish dragged along a boat or kept in a tank of warm water rarely survive. If you plan to release a fish, do it right away.

6. Use barbless hooks. They help you release a fish easier and quicker. File or bend down the barbs on the hooks you're now using. If the fish swallows the hook, cut the line. The hook will soon rust away and the fish has a better chance of surviving than if you try to rip the hook out or dig around the throat with a hook remover.

7. Salt helps fish lie in livewells. Salt reduces stress and stimulates mucus secretion. Any type of uniodized salt works well if added to the livewell at a rate of 0.5% (0.7 ounces of salt/gal. of water).

8. *Keep small roughfish for eating. Release the big ones for other anglers to catch.*

zooplankton, but as they get larger they begin grazing on the tips of floating and underwater plants. The larger the fish grows, the less particular it gets about the plants it will eat. Doretta Malone, who raises grass carp in Arkansas, said she has seen a carp pull an entire cattail stalk up from the roots and carry it to the middle of the lake to polish it off. Five or 6 grass carp stocked in a weed-choked pond will eat their weight in vegetation each day.

As people were hauling grass carp around to clean up lakes, few were thinking about what would happen if some escaped into a river and began to spread. Then it happened. In 1966, grass carp were accidentally released from several experimental ponds in Lonoke, Arkansas into a tributary of the Mississippi River. In 1970, grass carp escaped through an outlet in a lake and entered another river. By 1972, the species had shown up in 40 states, the fastest any fish has ever spread in North America.

The grass carp has its drawbacks and advantages. Many states, fearing the grass carp will invade and eat aquatic plants used by fish as cover and ducks as food, have banned the stocking of the species. They point to the common carp as an example of what could happen should the grass carp spread into waters where it's not wanted.

Proponents of the grass carp argue that fundamental biological differences between the two species prevent the grass carp from ever invading watersheds as its cousin did. Grass carp need large rivers to spawn successfully; common carp can spawn almost anywhere. Grass carp eggs are laid in the spring and they need continuous river flow to keep them moving and off the river bottom. If the eggs settle to the bottom, they are usually smothered by silt and suffocate. Even when laid in moving water, grass carp eggs won't survive unless the water is rising and is at a specific temperature. What's more, the cold weather in northern regions delays grass carp from reaching sexual maturity. Grass carp in Moscow, which has a climate similar to that in Minneapolis, Minnesota, take over 10 years to mature.

Some environmentalists, while acknowledging the breeding limitations of the grass carp, are still troubled by its possible spread into new waters. It's a fact that grass carp are currently spawning successfully in the Mississippi River. Barry Pierce, an aquatic biologist, warned in *Grass Carp Status in the United States*, "Even with limited spawning, successful reproduction in the United States is cause for alarm if the fish has the capacity to dominate the fish populations of natural aquatic ecosystems."

Shaped like a bullet, the amur (grass) carp is a powerful swimmer that can leap clear of the water. Banana peels make great bait for this vegetarian, which, it is said, can leap up from lakes to pull apples off trees.

Nuisance weeds in ponds and lakes can be removed by three common ways: herbicides, mechanical weed mowers, and grass carp. Herbicides are often a waste of time and money because the nutrients in the plants they kill remain in the water, creating massive algae blooms soon after the chemical application. Mechanical mowers work well, but they kill many game fish seeking refuge in the weeds. Grass carp are a more environmentally sound way to control weeds, because they eat the plants at a rate that releases nutrients back to the lake slowly.

Vaughn Paragamian, a fisheries biologist with the Iowa Department of Natural Resources, said he thinks grass carp are the best way to keep weeds in check: "We knew grass carp were coming, so we decided to start learning about the fish and stocking them where it was appropriate." Approximately 60 percent of the anglers in Iowa fish from shore. In ponds once too choked with weeds to allow bank fishing, grass carp have opened up miles of shoreline to angling. Since the species can't reproduce in ponds, Paragamian says he sees no reason to stop using grass carp to control weeds.

The Arkansas Game and Fish Commission reported in the late 1980s that grass carp can control weeds better than any other agent without harming the native fish population. However, some states are not convinced grass carp won't end up grazing in lakes that don't need plants removed. Some states only allow a new, sterile, genetically altered grass carp to be stocked in their waters. These fish can't reproduce, which should keep the grass carp population in check.

Grass carp could be the lesser of two evils. There's no denying that lakes choked with weeds often need to be cleaned out. Adding chemical herbicides isn't the answer, and mowers chew up fish as they mow down the weeds. If stocked only a few at a time in lakes not susceptible to flooding, sterile grass carp could be the way to go.

Grass carp are superb food fish. The meat is white and mild. The fish has large, easy-to-find bones like those in a buffalo, and can be filleted, steaked, or cooked whole.

On the end of a fishing line, the grass carp is an exceptional fighter. One trait that catches the attention of any angler is its ability to leap. Paragamian says that once, while raising the lid of a cage holding grass carp, a fish jumped out of the water past his head. Grass carp are said to actually jump up to grab leaves and even apples off trees.

In southern states where grass carp are caught for sport, anglers wrap the tender tips of coontail water weed around a hook, then slowly stalk along the shoreline until they spot grass carp grazing on surface plants. They cast the coontail glob at the fish, and wait for it to suck the bait in. Malone says she knows people who have good luck catching grass carp with banana peels, too. The floating doughball also has taken its share of hungry grass carp.

Floating Doughballs

Mix 1 part peanut butter (warm it in the microwave first for easier mixing) with 1 part Rice Crispies and 1 part crushed cornflakes.
Place a grape-sized glob of this mixture and a green party marshmallow on a 2-inch-square of white, sheer pantyhose. Stretch it tightly over the doughball and tie up the ends with green thread to make a ball. Roll the ball in green food coloring.

To use this sturdy bait, thread a baitholder hook through the pantyhose material and cast the ball into waters where grass carp feed. The marshmallow and Rice Crispies will keep the dough ball floating on the surface.

Although the grass carp seems like one exotic that can actually improve the environment, we hesitate giving it the roughfish angler's thumbs up. Maybe we're naive, but we think that instead of importing exotics to control the weeds in lakes, people should be solving the problem of why the weeds are there in the first place: runoff from overfertilized farms and yards dumping too many nutrients into the water.

Whether grass carp are a biological fad or become standard fare in the waters of middle America remains to be seen. One thing's for sure, however. If they ever get to Minnesota, Tom and I will be casting banana peels and coontail in anticipation of a strike and the sight of a furious 40-pound plant-eater exploding from the water.

Ruffe
Gymnocephalus cernua

One of the Great Lakes' most recent invaders is the ruffe. This fish, like the zebra mussel, reached Lake Superior in the ballast water of a ship from Europe that was dumped into the harbor at Duluth. In 1987, 33 ruffe were found in Minnesota's St. Louis River estuary. By the next summer, several thousand were caught in the same waters; the next year the number doubled. Ruffe have been found at the mouth of Wisconsin's Brule River, 30 miles to the east of Duluth, indicating the fish is spreading rapidly.

The ruffe is a relative to the native yellow perch. Although smaller, it is much more aggressive than the perch and competes with its cousin for food. Ruffe accidentally introduced into Scotland's Loch Lommond replaced the native perch there in less than 4 years. In Russian lakes where ruffe have invaded, whitefish populations have been reduced by one-half. Ruffe reproduce extremely fast. In its first year, a female can produce between 100,000 and 150,000 eggs. To make matters worse, ruffe can spawn twice a year.

Although the ruffe is a fine-tasting fish, it is too small to interest sport or commercial anglers. Jim Selgaby, a fisheries biologist with the

The ruffe is quickly filling up the western end of Lake Superior and spreading east. It arrived in the ballast of a ship from Europe.

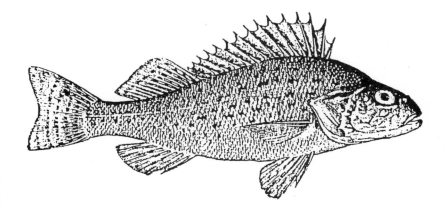

U.S. Fish and Wildlife Service, is studying the exotic ruffe and its effect on Great Lakes fish. "There is a grave danger that the ruffe will spread throughout North America," he cautioned. "It's an adaptable fish that could do substantial damage to the Great Lakes ecosystem. Once the ruffe is established, you can't get rid of it; all you can do is keep it from dominating the fish community."

The sea lamprey, another disastrous exotic mentioned earlier, was controlled at a cost of millions of dollars and years of research. The lamprey population is kept in check only by continuous applications of a lamprey-killing toxin to the streams where they breed.

Today, researchers are working to understand the life cycle of the ruffe, to see if there is a way to stop its spread. Several steps have been taken. It is now illegal to take minnows for bait in ruffe-infested waters; if you catch a ruffe, you must return it to the water (this prevents anglers from transporting ruffe from one river to another); and the catch limit on large game fish has been reduced in some waters to increase the number of fish eating the ruffe. In addition, the U.S. Coast Guard is considering a law that would require all ships bound for freshwater ports in the United States to exchange their ballast water at sea. This would replace the foreign fresh water with mid-ocean saltwater and reduce the chance that foreign species could reach our lakes.

Like the passenger pigeon, many fish native to North America have disappeared. Overfishing, exotic species introduction, pollution, and habitat destruction have worked against indigenous species like the harelip sucker and the shortjaw cisco. One argument against exotic introduction is the risk of losing native fish species. Each species has a unique genetic code that has evolved over hundreds of thousands of years. To lose any of these unique animals through carelessness is like burning a Renoir painting.

Several beautiful strains of cutthroat trout in the western United States are on the verge of extinction after introduced rainbow trout bred with the cutthroats and diluted the native gene pool. In many streams throughout the country, the brown trout has taken over many miles of native brook trout water. The lake trout populations in northern Minnesota lakes have declined in part because smallmouth bass, imported from southern Minnesota, eat all their food.

What's so great about native species? Three things. First, all animals, including humans, have an intrinsic value. Most forms of life on this planet have existed for thousands or millions of years, and no one species has the right to knowingly cause another to disappear.

Second, each species fills a niche in the different ecosystems, the webs of life that include humans. Because each animal is dependent in some way on all the others, there is no way to predict what could happen to the rest of the ecological team if one member is destroyed.

Third, many species have some medicinal value. Over 80 percent of the drugs used in medicine come from plants, and certain fish oils reduce the risk of heart disease. If the blue sucker becomes extinct, we lose more than the opportunity to catch it and add it to our Roughfish Life List; we eliminate a unique piece of life from our waters, and the possibility it could help humans and other creatures.

What this has to do with roughfish is simple: All species—whether they have lips or not—deserve the best we can do to keep them healthy. In an ecological sense, no creature is better than another. That anglers rush out to begin catching drum is not as important as that they begin to understand what drum are and that drum have just as much right to swim in a lake as walleye do.

For fish to survive in the future, it is up to anglers to take more responsibility and initia-

The key to good fishing isn't importing or stocking more fish. It's keeping the waters of native fish clean and clear. Wisconsin's Namekagon River, pictured here, is a healthy stream supporting strong populations of trout, smallmouth bass, and redhorse. Included in the National Wild and Scenic River program, it will be preserved as a beautiful fishing stream into the future.

tive to protect the aquatic environment. Anglers determine what state and federal fisheries agencies do. For example, Trout Unlimited, a private conservation and angling organization, has led trout management away from stocking genetically similar hatchery trout, which can eliminate native trout strains, towards protecting trout habitat and preserving wild trout strains.

One of the most important steps to protect all species of fish is to preserve habitat—the places where the fish live and breed. Suckers and smallmouth bass can't survive in a prairie stream that is turned into a ditch to drain water from a corn field. Sturgeon and walleye die when a heavy rain causes raw sewage from a city's sewer system to overflow into a river.

The way fisheries in your state are managed reflects the ignorance or knowledge of anglers there. If much of your license dollar pays to raise fish in a hatchery, it means something is wrong with the aquatic environment where fish should reproduce naturally. Instead of asking fisheries managers to stock fish in a lake, ask them why fish aren't spawning there. Have too many wetlands been drained? Are housing developments ringing lakes with over-fertilized lawns? Are cattle wading through trout streams?

Most fisheries biologists are closet ecologists, forced to stock fish by a system fueled by angler demands. Many of these state and federal officials understand the importance of managing the land and the water to create clean, natural conditions that favor native fish. But as public employees, they can only do what the public asks them to do.

It's time anglers began asking for fisheries management that is environmentally sound and focuses on the entire ecosystem, not just a particular game fish. Over the long run, the results will be cleaner water, healthier species, and more fish—game and rough—on the end of your line.

—RB

References

Becker, George C. *Fishes of Wisconsin*. University of Wisconsin Press, 1983.

Bueno, Bill, editor. *The American Fisherman's Guide*. Prentice-Hall, Inc., 1952.

Carlander, Harriet Bell. *History of Fish and Fishing in the Upper Mississippi River*. Upper Mississippi River Conservation Committee, 1954.

Churchill, Edward P., and Over, William H. *Fishes of South Dakota*. South Dakota Dept. of Game and Fish, 1938.

Cooper, Edwin L., editor. *Carp in North America*. American Fisheries Society, 1987.

Eddy, Samuel, and Surber, Thaddeus. *Northern Fishes*, Charles T. Branford Company, 1960.

Forbes, Stephen A., and Richardson, Robert E. *The Fishes of Illinois*. State of Illinois, Dept. of Registration and Education, 1920.

Gowanloch, James. *Fish and Fishing in Louisiana*. Louisiana Dept. of Coservation, 1965.

Iowa Dept. of Natural Resources. *Iowa Fish and Fishing*. Iowa Dept. of Natural Resources, 1987.

Jordan, David Starr, and Everman, Barton Warren. *American Food and Game Fish*. Dover Publications Inc., 1969.

Migdalski, Edward C. *Angler's Guide to the Freshwater Sportfishes*. Ronald Press Company, 1962.

Norman, J. R. *A History of Fishes*. A. A. Wyn, Inc., 1949.

Pflieger, William L. *The Fishes of Missouri*. Missouri Dept. of Conservation, 1975.

Phillips, Gary; Schmid, William D.; and Underhill, James C. *Fishes of the Minnesota Region*. University of Minnesota Press, 1982.

Pierce, Milton P. *Carp and Carp Culture, Minnesota State Fish Commission*. Johnson, Smith & Harrison, 1883.

Scott, W. B., and Crossman, E. J. *Freshwater Fishes of Canada*. Fisheries Research Board of Canada, 1973.

Roughfish Life List

Use this handy life list to keep track of the species you catch.

BURBOT

Burbot   Date _____ Place caught _____

Comments _____

_____

_____

SUCKER

Bigmouth buffalo   Date _____ Place caught _____

Comments _____

_____

_____

Smallmouth buffalo   Date _____ Place caught _____

Comments _____

_____

_____

Black buffalo   Date _____ Place caught _____

Comments _____

_____

_____

Highfin carpsucker   Date _____ Place caught _____

    Comments _____

    _____

    _____

River carpsucker   Date _____ Place caught _____

    Comments _____

    _____

    _____

Quillback carpsucker   Date _____ Place caught _____

    Comments _____

    _____

    _____

Blue sucker   Date _____ Place caught _____

    Comments _____

    _____

    _____

Spotted sucker   Date _____ Place caught _____

    Comments _____

    _____

    _____

Northern hog sucker   Date _____ Place caught _____

    Comments _____

    _____

    _____

White sucker   Date _____   Place caught _____

    Comments _____

_____

_____

Longnose sucker   Date _____   Place caught _____

    Comments _____

_____

_____

Shorthead redhorse   Date _____   Place caught _____

    Comments _____

_____

_____

Silver redhorse   Date _____   Place caught _____

    Comments _____

_____

_____

River redhorse   Date _____   Place caught _____

    Comments _____

_____

_____

Golden redhorse   Date _____   Place caught _____

    Comments _____

_____

_____

Greater redhorse Date _____ Place caught _____

Comments _____

_____

_____

Black redhorse Date _____ Place caught _____

Comments _____

_____

_____

DRUM

Freshwater drum Date _____ Place caught _____

Comments _____

_____

_____

CARP

Common carp Date _____ Place caught _____

Comments _____

_____

_____

Grass carp Date _____ Place caught _____

Comments _____

_____

_____

Mirror Carp　　　　　　　Date _____ Place caught _____

　　Comments _____

　　_____

　　_____

STURGEON

Lake sturgeon　　　　　　Date _____ Place caught _____

　　Comments _____

　　_____

　　_____

Shovelnose sturgeon　　　Date _____ Place caught _____

　　Comments _____

　　_____

　　_____

CATFISH

Channel catfish　　　　　　Date _____ Place caught _____

　　Comments _____

　　_____

　　_____

Blue catfish　　　　　　　Date _____ Place caught _____

　　Comments _____

　　_____

　　_____

Flathead catfish   Date _____   Place caught _____

       Comments _____

       _____

       _____

Black Bullhead   Date _____   Place caught _____

       Comments _____

       _____

       _____

Brown Bullhead   Date _____   Place caught _____

       Comments _____

       _____

       _____

Yellow Bullhead   Date _____   Place caught _____

       Comments _____

       _____

       _____

WHITEFISH

Round whitefish   Date _____   Place caught _____

       Comments _____

       _____

       _____

Lake whitefish Date _____ Place caught _____

Comments _____

_____

_____

Cisco Date _____ Place caught _____

Comments _____

_____

_____

GAR

Longnose gar Date _____ Place caught _____

Comments _____

_____

_____

Shortnose gar Date _____ Place caught _____

Comments _____

_____

_____

BOWFIN

Bowfin Date _____ Place caught _____

Comments _____

_____

_____

EEL

American eel   Date _____ Place caught _____

        Comments _____

_____

_____

MOONEYE

Mooneye   Date _____ Place caught _____

        Comments _____

_____

_____

Goldeye   Date _____ Place caught _____

        Comments _____

_____

_____